HARD TO NIRVANA

A SOLO BICYCLE JOURNEY THROUGH TIBET AND ALONG THE HIMALAYAS

MATTHEW CULL

LIFE'S PASSION PUBLISHING

Hard Road To Nirvana

A Solo Bicycle Journey through Tibet and along the Himalayas

Text by Matthew Cull
Photographs by Matthew Cull

Copyright © 2013 by Matthew Cull

All rights reserved. No part of this publication may be reproduced or transmitted in any form or by any means, electronic or mechanical, including photocopying recording or any other storage or retrieval system without the written permission of the publisher.

First Edition: July 2013

ISBN-13: 978-1482713800
ISBN-10: 1482713802

Life's Passion Publishing
P.O. Box 929
Aspen, Colorado, 81612
USA
www.matthewjkcull.com

A voluminous thank you to Laurie and Mona
who helped so ably with editing and suggestions

Also from Life's Passion Publishing and Matthew Cull:

Solo Bicycle Journeys Across Six Continents:
The Lure of the Next Bend

The six set

International Celebration of Culture series of hardcover fine art photography books:

Women, An International Celebration of Culture and Gender
Men, An International Celebration of Culture and Gender
Kids, An International Celebration of Culture and Children
Parent and Child, An International Celebration of Culture and Family
Faith, An International Celebration of Culture and Belief
Marketplace, An International Celebration of Culture and Commerce

Contents

The Journey In	1
Eastern Tibet	9
Lhasa	45
Central Tibet	81
Nepal	115
India	143
The Journey Out	205

1

The Journey In

I loaded the panniers onto my bicycle in the dark and walked the bicycle down the grass slopes to the road and set off by feeble headlamp into town. I had idled away the afternoon before sitting on the grass, hidden from the road by a rough mud wall, doing my best not to be spotted. I had camped with a wild sense of anticipation of the early morning's stealth ride. The road wound into the town. It was eerily quiet, dark and deserted, not a streetlight to help. As I rode slowly along the lines of homes, I roused every dog behind the high walls and gates of the homes which inadvertently set up a succession of barking animals that punctured the darkness and followed my progress. So much for stealth.

I came to a T-intersection with the Sichuan-Tibet road, highway 318. At least this was my assumption, for there were visible signs. Before I could realize what was going on I slid under the half raised checkpoint gate. The police were asleep, clearly used to the barking dogs.

A little further on I stopped and shined my light at one of the white concrete kilometer marker posts on the side of the road to confirm I was on the right road and going in the right direction. The sounds of the dogs receded into the rear distance. With the brief bliss of pavement I began the next climb, a mere 11 kilometers (7 miles) to the next pass, Lao La. This would be a quickie by comparison to the monsters I had been climbing so far on the journey. After the anticipation and excitement of running the Markham checkpoint at night, I began to relax and settle into the riding.

Barely had I come out into the open fields after leaving the town when I could see that I was approaching the form of a walled compound with a few buildings inside. There was more barking, which gained in intensity as I approached. My cycling speed matched the increase as I anticipated the worst case scenario. As I drew up alongside the gate to the compound I could see the reflection of my headlamp in the eyes of two huge black dogs rushing towards me within the compound. For a brief moment I tried to ease my anxiety with the thought that they were locked in behind the iron gate. My pace and heart beat began to pick up and I could soon feel and hear the dogs charging up behind me on the road, only their eyes visible, their violent energy attacking me.

Fueled by panic I accelerated even more, my frantic energy unconcerned with the fact that I was going uphill at an elevation of 4,000 meters (13,200 feet). My heart raced, my lungs heaved, my legs pedaled furiously and my voiced yelled at the ferocity closing in. The dogs caught me. I could feel the push of the dog as it hit and latched on the rear panniers. Another two dogs, judging by the number of eyes around me, joined in the chase.

I was hopelessly out-gunned, surrounded on three sides by vicious animals, at night, weeks away from help, in a foreign land, doing something that was, by the rules of the national authorities, totally illegal. I pushed harder.

I had only one thing going in my favor, the mechanical advantage of one of the world's most efficient machines, even with its hundred pound baggage load. The eyes began to disappear, the dogs let go of my panniers, and the barking receded into the distance.

A couple of kilometers later, sure that I was safe, I began to relax. I was breathing desperately. The burning sensation in my lungs would last the rest of the day and into the next. I stopped above the last of the homes and fields.

Light was spreading out over the sky. I took off my headlamp, pants and tights, leaving my shorts. I continued to the top of the pass on what had become a dusty gravel road. The hills and valleys lay below me, cast in the warm welcoming glow of the morning light. It was beautiful.

****

Tibet has held an almost mystical attraction for those who love mountains, high plains, vast spaces and culture that is strong and tough yet pious, devoted, spiritual, and lives in harmony with its spartan unforgiving landscape. The Tibetan people have developed a complex society and a deep spirituality sitting on top of the world in a rarified air. Happily isolated, deeply convicted, they lead simple lives with a complex religion that seems only appropriate for such an elevated location. Yet they have jousted position with various Chinese empires for centuries, caught in power struggles between far away empires of which they know nothing of, intruders have invaded their land to find enlightenment, explore its vast terrain, climb its mountain summits, protect its frontiers, and pillage their resources.

And I was one. I, too, felt that yearning to explore Tibet and to feel the spirit of these people. I had been serenading Tibet for years, getting close but never quite able to take the plunge into the land itself. At one time or another I had visited Sikkim and Nepal to the south, Ladakh and Kashgar to the west. In 2002 I had skimmed the far northeastern corner of Tibet, through the region of Amdo, cycling up onto the plateau, only to drop back into "mainland" China a week later. So close but yet so far.

But to go to Tibet I didn't want the confines of the rules imposed by the current occupying government. I did not agree with their presence in Tibet, nor could I condone their abysmal treatment of the Tibetans, treatment that involved torture, killing, and the destruction of temples, homes, sacred sites, and their very culture. I couldn't possibly experience Tibet in a tin can of a vehicle, squeezed tight with a bunch of strangers, following the agenda of the guide, ripping by the very things I had come half a world to explore. The Chinese government wanted their tourists contained and controlled, just as they treated their citizens, escorted by a guide, driven by a driver, following preordained routes at high speeds seeing only what they deemed appropriate.

My freedom to explore at will had been unleashed long ago. In 1984 I had mounted a large over-loaded bicycle on the coast of Oregon, on the west side of the United States, and begun a journey that would take me 18 years and through 52 countries on six continents. The bicycle had become an instant hit. It was the ultimate travel tool. It allowed me to travel, explore, move through a landscape and a people at a sedate speed that provided the time to see and experience, unhindered by glass, metal, speed, or apparent affluence. I had felt the weather against my skin. I had seen, and returned the waves, thumbs up, and warm smiles of folks along the road, I had been able to stop anywhere to soak up scenes and vistas. I had met people who had respected my effort and felt unintimidated by a lone white guy on a bike.

I had followed rivers, fjords, coasts and mountain ranges. I had traversed plains, forests, tundra grasslands, and deserts, and crossed more mountain passes than I can remember. I had visited the holy sites and temples, and experienced the festivals and rituals of Christians, Buddhists, Hindus, Muslims, and those who believed in nats.

But it rarely came easy. Cycling involved effort, and plenty of it. There was exposure to the elements, to traffic, to crappy roads, to gravity. Trials and difficulties came almost as thick and fast as joys and thrills. This, though, had always just been a part of the experience. A foreign land did contain bad weather, it had lousy roads and voluminous traffic, and long dull uninteresting sections, but all those invariably came to an end. The crappiness was always replaced by breathtaking scenes, wonderful folks and grand experiences. What made or broke the experience was solely my attitude. The only thing making this a grand adventure or a miserable failure was me. I could go on and make this a magnificent journey or wallow in negativity. I had always chosen the former and my cycle journeys across large chinks of planet became the best thing I had done with my life. Six long journeys, six continents, later, I still couldn't put the bicycle aside.

Bicycle travel was a roller coaster of a ride. It was so much more than sitting back and watching the world go by. So much more involved than travel as entertainment which was how organized tours seemed to me. I was continually drawn by the the lure of the next bend in the road or trail. Bends that held continual surprises, another grand vista, a wonderful interaction with a friendly local, another crushing disappointment of an endless climb or destroyed road ahead. Each day was full of unexplored next bends, the road wandered at will, each day bringing a diorama of new, different and exciting. Each day held the unknowns of place, people, and emotional explorations.

My journeys became my life's passion. I lived through periods of work and stability conjuring the next journey ahead, envisioning freedom and the sights, experiences, and sensory explorations to come. My journeys contributed to my drive to live and succeed, and in turn defined who I was and how I was to think. I gained a different perspective on life and how I wanted to live my own. I came to value simplicity, experience and humanity over money, goods and career advancement. The best times of my life happened with everything I needed loaded on a bicycle. Why did I need anything else? I cycled by folks who were happy with very little. Why did society need anything else?

It was just no contest then. In spite of the Chinese government rules that foreign tourists should be in groups with permits and guides, I would simply have to do this on my own. I could walk in, ride a horse in, or cycle in. I would go by bicycle, as was my habit, and go permit free.

I set the map on the table and considered my options. Getting into Tibet offered four simple routes. North, south, east, west. It just so happened that the most scenic was also the hardest physically, and possibly legally. Eastern Tibet was a deeply indented landscape of deep gorges and snow capped ranges. The road on the map made simple straight work of massive climbs, bone-shaking roads and a land that was off-limits to foreigners without the required guides, permits and groups. And especially off-limits to lone guys on bikes.

A recurring theme of my journeys had been the successive introduction of ever increasing challenges. With each journey I introduced new variables, new obstacles, different challenges. With each passing journey I gained the skill set to handle these challenges so that for the next journey I was more prepared, and more confident. Its a logical progression for anyone growing and progressing in just about anything, like life.

This continued upping of the ante made the journeys just what they were supposed to be: adventures. And adventures, by their very definition, involved challenges, unknowns, and variables, the nature of which are never quite known until they sit staring one in the face. These adventures involved fears and nerves, queezy stomachs and doubts. They also involved reward and accomplishment and satisfaction and the attainment of confidence and self worth. You just can't have one without the other. Adventure is not about complacency or comfort.

There had previously been culture, language, topography, roads, isolation, non-western countries and the complete lack of help. On my last journey, through China, the concept hit home that it was me, alone, and 1.3 million people who talked, thought, and did things quite differently to me. And there hadn't been many signs to point the way.

In Tibet it would be all of the above. Plus doing it all illegally.

I felt a certain kinship with Alexandra David-Neel, a strong and capable French woman, who in 1924, snuck across the closed border with her young companion, disguised as Tibetan pilgrims. She made it to Lhasa and spent two months there. Both she and I couldn't help ourselves but steal into Tibet under the cover of physical and metaphorical darkness to a land that had fascinated us for years and held an irresistible attraction.

I knew also that other attractions laid nearby. Running along the south of Tibet was the Himalaya, forming a topographic and cultural boundary separating the thin cool dry Buddhist air of Tibet from the thick hot crowded Hindu plains of India to the south. It would be a logical extension of a Tibetan journey to cross the Himalaya into Nepal and continue along the range west, to continue the topographic link, to join regions of similar belief and culture, to complete the path of a Buddhist mountain journey through the middle of Asia.

It was appropriate perhaps that I would travel through the Tibetan Buddhist lands via the means that gave the greatest enjoyment and satisfaction to me and required the most effort. A central tenement of Buddhism is the leading of a life that ultimately gathers enough merit to attain nirvana, a profound peace of mind associated with the liberation from the cycle of death and rebirth. In Tibetan Buddhism merit was often attained by devotees taking pilgrimages to Lhasa, the capital, and to important temples and holy sites within the Tibetan lands. The more difficult the journey, by walking, or prostrating the entire way, the greater the merit. I would be a in a sublime high altitude landscape of mountains and plateaus, by its very nature a land of the gods, taking a hard won pilgrimage, in search of my own nirvana. I had no doubt that my life would leave me stuck in this cycle of existence for some time to come but I may as well explore the options in the meantime.

I sat there looking at my map, and drew a line.

Drawing lines on maps has always been a dangerous affair with destiny, and a passion of mine. Drawing a line on a map is a commitment, as deep as any with a fellow human. Once drawn, there becomes an obligation that that line of intention be brought into actuality, that this intention of the future become a line of experience, accomplishment, and reward of the past. That line, be it with a pen on a map, or with a neuron in the brain, becomes the driving force regardless of what that line hides, what little that line knows of what lies beneath it. Lines on maps can cause all sorts of trouble, yet be the grandest thing that ever happened.

My line started at the small town of Dali, Yunnan province, China, a redeveloped touristy town, home of the Bai ethnic minority group in southern China. My line ended in Kargil, a Muslim-dominant town very close to the India-Pakistan cease fire line in northern India. Along the way lay Tibet, its capital, Lhasa, and the Himalaya. I would start in the spring, mid-May, and hopefully be done before the snow would fly and the passes close in the autumn. Easy for me to say.

My future then was set, at least for the following eight months. Four months of part-time planning and four months full-time exploration, with the option of an extended period of detention at the discretion of the Chinese.

I could feel the pulse quicken just slightly.

2

EASTERN TIBET

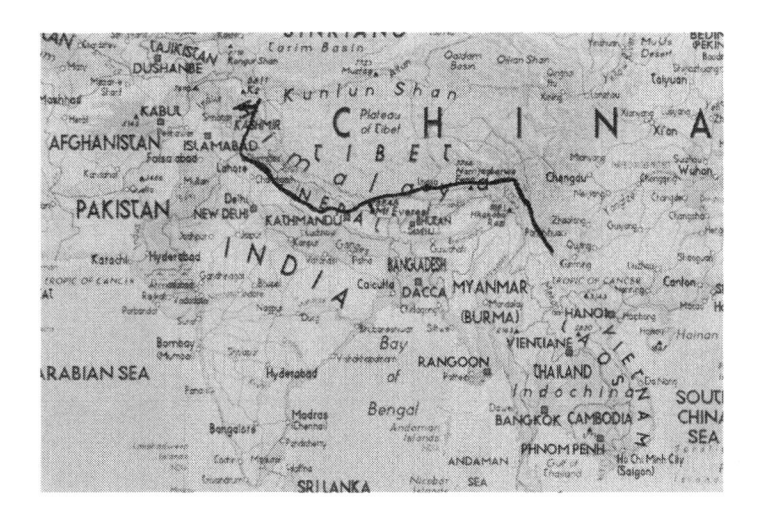

The journey is not about the destination, it was about getting to the start. Or so it seemed as I made my way across southern China. Multiple plane flights and long waits in airports brought me to Hong Kong. After a couple of days of organizing and sight wandering I took the train into mainland China, to Guangzhou East, into a shockingly different world. I had quickly gained acceptance of Hong Kong's clean modern efficiently organized chaos. It had a certain construction synergy. The mainland was instantly an unplanned mess of dirty crumbling high and low rise buildings, industry, fields and bare ground in various states of destruction and pollution. By the time I regained consciousness after three and a half hours sleep on the train heading west towards Kunming I was far out into the rural beauty of the Chinese countryside. Again, it was an altogether different world. Late day sun cast over gentle hills and rich green rice paddies.

Ten more hours of sleep later, the train began to climb into a dramatically hilly landscape. Rice paddies and terraces were tucked into narrow valleys bounded by near vertical cliffs, towers, and pinnacles of limestone, a karst landscape. Farmers were tending their fields by hand or with beast, in anticipation of the coming monsoonal rains. At times the landscape was a rolling land covered in fields, and others, a riot of grey limestone boulders and pinnacles that rose above rich brown earth. In others, deep valleys dropped to large rivers. Elsewhere, conical limestone towers rose above wide plains of fields and villages. The train gained altitude, forest and dryness as we continued. Periodically, but far too frequently, factories belched obscene clouds into what seemed an otherwise bucolic scene.

Inside, train life rambled on with immeasurable patience. Trolleys of food and drink passed along the aisles regularly supplying hot water thermos for instant noodle dinners that were slurped contentedly, or for tea that could be endlessly refreshed. Some folks played music or sung. Passengers wandered back and forth in ambivalent motion or lay on their beds in various states of chatter or slumber. After nearly 30 hours, the train pulled into Kunming.

At the baggage claim counter of the station I was told to return the next day for my bike as it was on a following train. For 24 hours I wandered modern, and mostly western, Kunming in the rain like an expectant father waiting for my baby to arrive and not being able to do a damn thing about it. Back at the luggage office the next day I held my breath in anticipation and rejoiced as my bike was wheeled out, happy and intact.

The rain escorted me west, my journey continuing on a crowded bus. The outskirts of Kunming were under construction. Building sites and half completed over-head freeways had turned the place into a mud bath. It was immeasurably unattractive. Further out the newly built freeway was a few centuries ahead of the fields and villages alongside it. Six days, two cars, three planes, two taxis, two buses, two trains, and four ferries from home I was finally in Dali and I could get on my bike for good. The real journey could begin.

******

Dali had been almost totally reconstructed. Lines of era-appropriate brick buildings housed touristy stores which bordered attractive stone walkway streets decorated with water features, lines of trees, and gardens. Young Bai ladies dressed in a variety of traditional clothing, added to the neat, old world, tourist-driven ambiance of the town. On one side of the town a piece of the old town wall had been rebuilt and I climbed up and walked along the crest, looking over the town to the range of mountains on the opposite side of the valley in the soft moist late afternoon light. By the time I came down from the wall the lights on the south gate tower had been turned on and it glowed in colorful brilliance against the darkening sky. The rain had eased, and there were even promising patches of blue, albeit small ones.

Near the gate I found a line of "point-and-eats" and ate big, relishing what was clearly China's finest attribute. On my previous journey in China I had discovered the route to a great cheap, and delicious, vegetarian meal. I would roam the streets until I found a small mum and pop restaurant stall with all kinds of ingredients displayed in glass cabinets. With the cook, I would point to the various foods I wanted to eat, while making a swooshing sound not dissimilar to the sound of veggies frying in a wok. A few minutes later that very sound would seep from the kitchen, and a few minutes after that a veritable feast would come through the door and onto my table. I was always a happy boy. I called these lovely places "point-and-eats".

Standing in the courtyard of the guesthouse in the early morning I tried to counter the distaste of cycling in the rain with my burning desire to finally get this show on the road. Motion won out and in the unpleasant wetness that ensued I completely forgot my tradition of taking the start photo, a picture of myself and my bike in front of something symbolic at the beginning of my journey.

Although the general direction of my journey was west, for the first 11 days I would cycle mostly north, more or less parallel to the border with Burma.

I started north following the wide smooth valley on an ample road filled with too many exhaust-spewing vehicles. I took a turn and lost much of the traffic, but it was no means quiet. Trucks did their best to fill the air with horns, exhaust, and their ominous presence. Yet it turned into a really pleasant ride. The rain had spent itself and it became warmer, drier, and brighter the further I progressed. The road cast in long arcs through a mellow valley covered in fields tended by fleets of locals busy plowing and planting with the help of slow plodding buffalos. Villages and homes dotted the landscape and steep, highly eroded, valley sides along the edge were testament to centuries of deforestation. The valley rose in steps, with a short steep climb to yet another round of fields and farmers, and then a final steep narrow pitch to a pass among pine forest.

At first I had balked at making the long 115 kilometers (71 miles) to the first town, and thus accommodation, after Dali, on the first day on the road. Better to work into this whole effort thing progressively. But by the time I hit the top of the pass I realized that camping spots were extremely illusive and it was, by then, a clean 20 kilometers (12 miles) of downhill to the town, Jianchuan. As

I sped down into the valley I found an altogether different environment. While folks were busy planting rice in soupy soil on the south side of the pass, others were harvesting golden fields of wheat from dry terraces on the north side. For 10 kilometers (6 miles) I wound through piles of wheat stalk piled on the pavement by the locals. It was a low-labor way to allow the passing vehicles to thresh it as they drove over it.

I pulled into Jianchuan hungry, thirsty, and tired. I found a hotel and later refueled at a "point-and-eat" across the street after a day of insufficient eating. Memories from my previous time in China came flooding back. The horns and exhaust of passing vehicles, the chaotic driving, the ugly towns, the periodically bumpy pavement, the unintelligible signs, the noisy do-it-all one cylinder diesel engine that powered half of everything that moved in China. I couldn't believe I was cycling in China again after I had been so happy to leave years before. Clearly I had checked my sanity in at the front desk.

As before though, cycling in China was also perpetually entertaining and insightful. There was always plenty to look at and think about. More often than not the landscape was some attractive, even beautiful, blend of natural and tranquil rural beauty, complete with the busy activity of locals making a living. I always had that feeling that I had the place to myself, that the next white guy was in the next country over. Love hate strikes again.

Horns and exhaust continued briefly the next morning. A huge ugly factory quickly sucked all the traffic from the road and the riding instantly became glorious. Gentle ridges covered in forest, mostly brown valley floors covered in corn, wheat or fields of long lines of plastic-covered mounds. Rising above it all ahead in the distance was Yulongue Shan, a 5,600 meter (18,400 feet) high glaciated peak standing bold and impressive with a cluster of clouds amid a deep blue sky. I was approaching the Yangtse River, the Chang Jiang. I crossed over a small pass and wound down to the river. Huge, wide, and deceptively placid at that point, the Yangtse is a river of superlatives. The longest river in Asia, third longest in the world, it rises on the northern and eastern flanks of the Tibetan plateau and by the time it empties into the East China sea, 6,400 kilometers (3,980 miles) later, it has drained one fifth of China's land area which is home to one third of the country's population. And it is the site of the world's largest hydro power plant. I expected that the point where I crossed it, at 1,860 meters (6,100 feet) above sea level, would be my lowest point til somewhere in Nepal, months down the road.

Following the river downstream I was aided by a handy tailwind. I was passed by a convoy of about 50 army vehicles (heading to Tibet for the summer?) and passed a curious, brand new, built-from-scratch, but totally empty, town. I passed by the entrance to Tiger Leaping Gorge. While short, a measly 15 kilometers (9 miles) long, the gorge is a narrow trench between two 5,300 meter plus (17,400 feet) high lofty giants making the gorge a strong contender in the deepest canyon in the world division. Even this relatively short day, that was mostly flat or downhill, had left me wilted and weary. The next day would not be so kind with nearly 1,525 meters (5,000 feet) of climbing to Zhongdian.

The smooth new highway started the climb through a steep forest-sided valley, past an assortment of small dams and reservoirs. Twenty kilometers up I took the guesthouse owner's advice and turned onto what must have been the old highway. I gave up smooth pavement and traffic for solitude and a road that oscillated between bumpy old asphalt and jumbles of rocks. The climbing was slow and laborious.

Not only did I have to accustom my body to the hard work of cycling, I had to train my mind to the slow progress of pedaling a heavy loaded bicycle, especially uphill. My bicycle with all its gear weighed in at over 55 kilograms (120 pounds). It took everything I had to lift it off the ground, and advancing, especially uphill, was tediously slow and laborious. Riding an unladen bicycle was like driving a sports car. Riding this beast was like driving a semi-trailer. I had to readjust my perceptions of speed and progress. Cycling was as much a game of the mind as the body. Patience and perseverance was as integral as leg strength and cardiovascular capability. Once adjusted though, cycling such a bike became second nature. The physical capability eventually caught up with the tasks set before it and the mind eventually settled down. Long tedious uphills became opportunities to look around, think and enjoy.

About 25 kilometers (15 miles) up the valley the road climbed more steeply and topped out on a pass decorated with a chorten and prayer flags. Somewhere along that climb I had crossed the boundary limit of the Tibetan cultural lands. Culturally at least, I was in Tibet, even if physically and politically Tibet was still a long way ahead. Even if Han China (the majority) remained totally dominant.

The Tibetans always decorated their passes. There could be a mound of rocks, prayer flags strung out across the land fluttering in the wind, or a chorten, a small stupa-like structure that contains Buddhist relics, often the remains of the deceased. It was one of many ways Tibetans paid homage to the gods, and said prayers. For the traveler it was a happy symbol of having arrived at the top of the climb, and added to the views of the surrounding landscape, and the proximity to mountains and the gods. It was a joy of Tibetan Buddhism, a festive feeling of colorful bits of material loaded with meaning and belief, strung out in haphazard abandon at the whim of wind.

The road dropped briefly into a gentle shallow valley. The land was dotted with typically Tibetan style homes. They were massive three story structures, thick stone or mud walls, tree trunk size support beams, and wood carving on balconies and eaves. Folks dressed in traditional clothes were out tilling their fields. The road of rocks turned into concrete and I picked up speed. I rejoined the new smooth wide highway for a fast, easy and flat last 40 kilometers (25 miles), across a broad grassland landscape, into Zhongdian.

Zhongdian was a figment of its former self. There was the ethnic minority center of narrow cobbled streets with an old-world feel, and the massive modern Chinese town that sprawled across the plain to the north. It was an indication of the dominance of the Hans, the Chinese majority that made up 93% of the country's population, over the local minorities, Naxi and Tibetan.

After a mere three days on the road I was sorely in need of a day off. I moved slowly and lethargically, wandering through the old town and up to a massive golden prayer wheel that sat on a small hill above the town. It was so large that it took me, and a few local ladies, to get it to spin. Snow-capped peaks lined the broad valley in the far distance. I took a bus out to Zongsanlin Monastery, but had left my visit too late for a peaceful visit. The place was awash with Chinese tourists. It was a far cry from the beautiful, meditative, contemplative, experience I had envisioned. I climbed to a hill behind the monastery and sat basking in the sun enjoying the view over the valley. I then walked the 3 kilometers (2 miles) back into town.

Later that evening I walked into town to watch the local communal dance. Periodically, on my previous journey through China, I would stumble upon this more enjoyable aspect of Chinese modern day culture. In the central Zhongdian town square about 300 to 400, mostly female, locals formed concentric rings around seven dance leaders. They all performed synchronized dance routines to recorded music at a variety of skill levels. As the music changed so too would the particular dance, and the dancers made the transition without a hiccup. Gradually the rings would migrate outwards, jamming those on the outside against the building walls around the square. Periodically the music would stop and everyone would move back towards the middle. It was local communal experience and exercise and it was immensely entertaining.

The quiet road slid north the next morning, out across the wide plain, out from under the layer of air pollution hanging over the town, and up into low forested hills and a pass. The gentle landscape abruptly came to an end. I rolled down from the pass into a vertical world of steep slopes of forest and rock. On the valley floor below, smooth green grass fields that accompanied Tibetan homes, provided a contrast in color and texture. The narrow paved road cut across the slopes clinging tenaciously, winding tightly, with continually exciting views over air and topography. The road climbed around the head of a side valley to a second pass and a view out over the abyss I was about to drop into. Below, a tight valley dropped thousands of feet to the out-of-sight Yangtse River. Far in the distance was a line of snow-capped peaks and a low point that was my pass for the next day's ride. Clearly the road was going for the maximum vertical possible. Rather than follow the Yangtse upstream from my last crossing, it had cut the corner and gone up and over. Rather than a long gentle ascent to that next pass, I would have to descend 1,000 meters (3,000 feet) to the river and then climb 2,300 meters (7,500 feet) the next day. Get used to it.

The descent was thrilling. I sped through tight curves into the valley. On one side was a vertical cliff face, on the other, air, and plenty of it. Once beside the creek, homes and small fields lined the road crammed into the narrow valley. I dodged donkeys, chickens, cows, and oncoming cars, meanwhile keeping an eye out for anything that might dart out from the side of the road, all while careening down the steep bumpy paved road. I was descending into a desert. On the pass there had been an open pine forest, part way down a low scrub, and further down valley from the homes the landscape was reduced to hot dry rocks and cliffs, a vertical desert. I crossed the river and followed it upstream, cutting across cliff faces and coming to the town of Benzilan, an oasis in the desert.

Benzilan, perched on a terrace above the Yangtse, was a quaint little village supplied with water via irrigation canals from the nearby side stream. It was a tranquil beautiful place. Even the main street, usually trashy in most towns, was pleasant and attractive. There were few, if any, vehicular horns and locals casually wandered all over the street.

Months later I would look back at Benzilan as one of the nicest settlements of the journey. After food and a room I strolled around the town, fields, and curiously, vineyards, and up to a small hill decorated with prayer flags.

The next day's task was the 2,300 meters (7,500 feet) of elevation gain in 50 kilometers (30 miles) to the next pass. It would take me the entire day. I climbed out of the comfort of Benzilan and into arid rock of the canyon. After 12 kilometers (7 miles) of solid climbing, the road topped out briefly at a minor pass. The inhospitably steep valley on the other side was home to a dispersed collection of homes and fields that perched almost precariously to the scrubby slopes and seemed like oases of calm in a tough vertical world.

The road contoured, giving brief rest from climbing, but then settled into another duel with gravity. I climbed through the canyon's vegetational zones, up into pine forest and cooler temperatures. Thirty four kilometers (21 miles) from Benzilan, the pavement ended, and what I received in exchange was cobbles. There had been no attempt to put the smooth side of the rocks up, nor to align them in any order. The result was a horrible, bumpy bouncy ride that was near impossible going uphill, especially so late in the day. On either side of the road there was a thin strip of gravel between cobbles and grass, the only place that was rideable. But the strip came and went with the curves of the road, and in places was too rutted or too loose to ride. I was continually having to cross the cobbles to get from one gravel strip to another. I still had thousands of feet to climb. Between spending all day cycling uphill, the deterioration in road quality, and my insufficient fuel consumption, I was exhausted. In the interest of durability I had given myself breaks every 7 kilometers (4 miles) for this climb. But these dwindled to every three (2 miles) going up the cobbles, and each time I just stood there slumped over the handle bars.

The top of the pass at 4,600 meters (15,100 feet) was smooth and round, bounded by snow-patched hills, with more impressive peaks rising into the clouds ahead. I was totally done. I couldn't even go downhill on the other side. I dropped off down the embankment on the top of the pass and camped, feeling vulnerable within sight of the road.

The tent carried a thin layer of snow in the morning. I was not done climbing, nor was I done with the cobbles. The road dropped, then contoured, then climbed high above deep forested valleys, over a small pass and then up to Yak La at around 4,250 meters (13,950 feet). I amused a local, while he waited for a bus, by taking a picture of myself in front of the pass sign surrounded by tired old prayer flags. There were mountains in every direction, including far beyond my next great trench, the Mekong.

With gravity finally on my side I suffered the cobbles for another 8 kilometers (5 miles). Pavement kicked in providing a grand swooping descent, curve after curve of blissful smoothness through forest littered with pink rhododendrons. I came to a viewpoint over a line of bright white chortens, to the vast glaciated spread of the 6,000 meter (20,000 feet) high Meilishan massif. I continued down to Dechen, a town stuck in the crook of a side valley as though it was hiding from something. It was a thankfully short day and I spent the rest of it eating, resting, and wandering the streets full of wild looking Tibetans in traditional dress. I stocked up the panniers with any food I could find.

My nemesis over the last few days, which would continue to be for several more, was tightly packaged in the Three Parallel Rivers of Yunnan Protected Area, a UNESCO World Heritage Site. Tectonic forces that pushed the Tibetan

Plateau up, and the river's energy that cut down, created this intensely topographic landscape where three of the great rivers of Asia; Yangtse (Jinsha), Lancang (Mekong), and Nujiang (Salween), are as little as 50 kilometers (30 miles) apart but separated by 6,000 meter (20,000 feet) high ranges. The 4,500 meters (15,000 feet) of local elevation difference and its geographic position gives it one of the most biologically diverse temperate areas on the planet. Much to my chagrin, excitement, and exhaustion, I was cutting across the grain of this amazing landscape. Up, down, repeat.

From Dechen I climbed briefly to another lookout over the Meilishan massive, then dropped into the gorge of the Mekong. Loss of pavement was another tragedy. I was left with rock and gravel. The road followed the fast flowing Mekong upstream. In between cursing the road I marveled at the landscape. I was in another vertical arid world, a kaleidoscope of geologic colors in huge geologic forms that covered vast canyon walls. Periodically, clumps of life, as solid Tibetan homes and smooth green fields fed by side streams and irrigation canals, survived and prospered in the otherwise inhospitable landscape. I cut across cliffs, dipped close to the river and climbed to perches on the canyon sides. At a small store I had a drink and picked up a companion. In spite of his 10 centimeter (4 inch) legs and 25 centimeter (10 inch) high body the little mutt dog followed me for 20 kilometers (12 miles), to the next settlement.

Part way up the Mekong I stopped for a drink at a small store, and the two guys offered a room upstairs. I was already cooked so I took them up on their offer.

Just 25 kilometers (15 miles) up the road was to be my first potential interaction with the police; checkpoint number one. My plan was to camp just before the town and roll through in the predawn darkness, while the police were hopefully getting a good night's rest. I wasn't unhappy about such a short day. I continued up the Mekong the next day at a leisurely pace, waving to folks harvesting on the other side of the river and enjoying the color of rock. I came to the border of Tibet.

While I had been in Tibetan cultural lands for five days, I had been in Yunnan province. There were also pieces of Tibet in Sichuan, Gansu, and Qinghai provinces. The Chinese had greatly reduced the size of Tibet and called it the Tibetan Autonomous Region (TAR). Although there was nothing autonomous about it, at least as far as the Tibetans were concerned. In the TAR, just as everywhere in China, Beijing called the shots. Down in the bottom of a massive trench, it didn't seem to mean much, other than now I was officially illegal. There was a huge concrete and tile sign announcing the border of the TAR. I took a picture of myself, feeling just a little bit criminal.

Three kilometers (2 miles) more I found a camp-spot hidden from, and above, the road. I relaxed and enjoyed the afternoon doing not much at all. It was a nice change. I gazed up at the canyon wall that ranged from the river through the arid rock, scrub, broad leaf forest, and pine forest layers, to the snow-patched mountain tops about 3,600 meters (12,000 feet) above me.

I packed in the dark the next morning, and cycled the remaining 4 kilometers (2.5 miles) to the checkpoint gate, my pathetic headlamp just barely better than nothing. As soon as the checkpoint came into view a truck pulled up to it from the other direction and blasted its horn to get the officials to open up. Just great! All this trouble and the cops were now awake. I waited a few minutes and continued through without hassle. Further along I came to a second checkpoint, again no problem and I continued through the town just as the first light began to filter into the canyon. A few kilometers on, the next big climb, 1,800 meters (6,000 feet) in 38 kilometers (24 miles), reared up to greet me. It went up the same side of the Mekong as I had come down. I would have to descend into and climb out of the Mekong twice. The Three Parallel Rivers were not making this any easier by making me cross every gorge twice.

The first half of the climb climbed up the side of the Mekong gorge. It was a surreal landscape in the early morning light. Patches of sun wandered across the barren gorge periodically illuminating areas of human endeavor that seemed smeared against the inhospitable slopes. The road turned into a major side valley and maintained its relentless grade. I entered the scrub zone but ironically the local human condition deteriorated. The well-built terraces, lush fields, clusters of trees, and solid Tibetan homes fed by glacial melt low in the gorge, were replaced by dry bare unterraced fields, and smaller more meager homes. This area didn't have the same feeling of abundance. These folks had shorter growing seasons, no irrigation canals, little surface water.

Higher still I began to wilt fast, my breaks became more frequent, my demeanor more desperate and focused. It had turned cold and inhospitable, with wind blowing into my face. I crested Hung La (4,400 meters, 14,400 feet) destroyed. Again.

My landscape changed anew. All was smooth and gentle, long low grassy ridges lined broad open shallow valleys. It was cold and bleak and it began to rain, making the road slimey, but the air fragrant. At a sign for a gompa (monastery) I turned uphill and hauled my bike up a rough track to the gompa.

The gompa was under major renovation with two new wings being added to the main temple, along with an entrance way, by a team of local men. Far from a quiet tranquil scene the place was a mess of wood beams and poles, piles of lumber, wood chips and rubbish. It was all a labor of love, from felling the trees, to dragging them onto the site, to trimming them, and making them into a gompa, all by hand.

About 15 to 20 mostly young monks lived there and most of them stood around me in bemused entertainment deciding what to do with me. They eventually took me inside, fed me Tibetan butter tea and tsampa (roasted barley flour) bread. We sat around doing something of a mime/

charades routine, understanding little of what each other was communicating. When I pulled out the map they nearly flattened me up against the wall in interest. It was all part comedy, part cross-cultural interaction. I began to regain my composure with the food. Later I had a spectator audience of several other monks and gompa workers even though it was late and my need for sleep was acute. A good experience comes at a price.

A couple of the monks fed me more tsampa and butter tea in the morning and helped me carry my stuff downstairs as the workers were arriving for another day of gompa building. The day's ride was one of the nicest of the journey thus far. It followed a valley north towards Markham. The road was gentle and smooth, there was a tailwind and the clouds parted to leave a lovely blue sky day. Even the landscape was gentle and smooth with the red brown of earth and the olive green of grass dotted with the large solid typically Tibetan homes in the same earth tone. It was a busy friendly valley. The locals tended fields or animals or were in the process of building or rebuilding homes or walls using packed earth and mud. Guys drove by on motorcycles, kids walked home from school and everyone waved, smiled, and called out Tashi Deleh (hello) with enthusiasm as I cycled by. I stopped to have a drink and had an onlooking crowd of about forty school kids. I stopped again to filter water and had three bubbly kids enthralled with rapt attention.

Forty-three kilometers (27 miles) up the road I bumped into Markham, my next checkpoint town. I back tracked a little and found a lovely camp-spot hidden from the road by an earthen wall and enjoyed a lazy afternoon in the sun.

By the time I had cycled through Markham and had my near death experience with the charging dogs in the dark the next morning, I had turned the corner. I was done with going north, it was all west to Lhasa.

From Lao La (4,420 meters, 14,500 feet) it was a long 37 kilometer (23 miles) dirt road descent back into the depths of the Mekong. Initially it was a beautiful grassland valley dotted with conifers, then homes and dozens of animals, goat, sheep and dzo (a yak-bovine cross) being herded by locals to higher pastures. Simple low brown homes turned to lush green fields and imposing white Tibetan homes lower down. Ahead, the next great range of peaks towered above the massive walls of the opposite side of the Mekong gorge. With the slow going of the rough dirt road it took hours to coast down into the arid gorge to the river. I had a meal at a rare roadside cafe, next to the river. I had bottomed out at 2,650 meters (8,700 feet). The next pass, Dungba La, was at 5,008 meters (16,400 feet).

The climb out of the Mekong River Gorge, the previous pass and descent visible to the upper right.

The road wound endlessly up the sides of the gorge, up out of the arid belt, and into a greener side valley. It wound around the head of the side valley then up through several banks of switchbacks. The grade was even and relentless, the views were continual and amazing. It may be a demanding environment to cycle through but to view and absorb it was magnificent and spectacular. Creeping along at about a fast walk, 6 to 7 kilometers per hour (4 miles per hour), I had time to look over the great brown muddy river, precipitous near vertical gorge slopes rising to lofty summits, homes perched on steep valley sides, and the view back over the tortuous road I had just climbed, to the valley I had descended that morning. It was grandeur on an immense scale. It was the most dramatic kind of sweet and sour cycling.

I climbed to a minor pass over a ridge jutting into the main gorge. I had wanted to camp but there was nothing level to camp on and I had no water. Fortunately, the road descended gently into a major side valley, to the village of Dungba. I found a rudimentary guesthouse with a beautifully painted roof, dust covered floor, an outhouse toilet that emptied directly into the clear creek out the back, and a gentle, kindly, round faced owner who made me a real meal of rice and fried cabbage. It had been a big day, a 4:45 am start, 92 kilometers (57 miles), almost 10 hours on the road, with 1,830 meters (6,000 feet) of ascent.

I still had 1,500 meters (5,000 feet) of ascent the next morning. The road followed a major side valley which gave itself to a more gentle grade than the climbs so far. Part way up the climb I was passed by a convoy of about 200 identical military trucks which kicked up dust and rocks and bombarded me with noise and horns. The valley curved westwards and rose above treeline to an environment of low bushes and grass. A head wind came down the valley against me and I suffered from a shortage of oxygen at the high altitudes. After five hours of continual ascent I finally hit the cold windy summit at 5,008 meters (16,430 feet).

The valley down the other side of the pass was steeper, the road a string of tight switchbacks that dropped quickly back into the forest. With the protection of the forest, and with a gorge approaching, I set camp.

I woke feeling weak and tired. It had rained during the night. About me steep valley sides rose into the clouds. A group of locals had found me and watched as I packed and headed back to the road. The road descended through a series of imposing limestone gorges and turned to pavement. I came into Zuogang, a large unattractive town strung out along the road. In a fog of low energy tiredness I cruised supermarket aisles and could find little that appealed. Even though my body was desperate for energy I had little appetite and the selection was poor.

I continued following the Wu Chu river upstream. Under normal conditions it would've been a great easy ride but I was exhausted, and drained. Minor hills left me wasted and downhills left me chilled. Forty kilometers (25 miles) up the river I stopped to rest. A local man on a motorcycle joined me and told me I could stay in the next village a few kilometers (2 miles) away. I continued on, found a simple guesthouse and immediately went to sleep.

I slept most of the way from 4 pm to 11 am. I had made a brief excursion downstairs and put in a game show of eating something somewhere around dinner time. And a few times I had to walk across the street to poop unseemly liquids through a disgusting hole in the floor boards of an outhouse. In the morning I asked the mama of the house to whip me up some tsampa bread. It wasn't nearly as good as the stuff at the gompa and I could barely get any of it down. I was roughly half way from Dali to Lhasa, struck with diarrhea, barely able to eat or get out of bed, illegal and half a planet away from help. Even years later I have never established whether I had exhaustion-aggravated diarrhea or diarrhea that caused extreme lethargy, or both. At least I had timed it well with the weather. It had been cold, grey, and rainy all day.

My composure gradually improved through the day. My rear end began to dry up, I was able to wash clothes, write, and eat a bowl of noodle soup. That night I was still so tired I slept most of the way through the noise of the village's party coming up through the floor boards.

After forty hours in my room I rejoined the road and tentatively continued up the Wu Chu. It was a beautiful ride and with pavement and easy uphill grades it was just the ticket for recovery mode. Snowline had dropped overnight and it was now only about 1,000 feet above the road. It made for an attractive scene, as clouds lifted to reveal snowy ridges above fields, grazing animals, friendly folks and enthusiastic kids. It was tranquil and peaceful, and the road largely empty. After the tracks I had been following previously, the road seemed so modern with retaining walls and guard rails. But it was already in the process of decay. I wandered around an assortment of rocks and boulders the size of bicycles that had been unhinged by rains and rolled down onto the road.

Higher up the valley, land use became exclusively grazing animals. In some areas every available piece of grass was dotted with animals in apparent disregard of stocking rates. Locals tended their animals, and after hearing their calls I would scan the slopes to find them as I cycled along. I stopped at Pamda Junction, an ugly collection of buildings at a road junction. It was a classic case of man taking something beautiful and turning it into something tragically ugly, something that man does so well.

It had been an easy day, which was exactly what the doctor would have ordered. I would go back to passville in the morning. After finding a room and a meal I climbed a small hill above the place. It was a sublimely beautiful valley. Animals by the thousands grazed on the vast grass expanse of the wide level valley bounded by tall imposing snow-capped ranges that extended north out of sight.

It was not good weather for climbing passes in the morning. It was cold and raining, the clouds barely cleared the valley floor. I started up anyway. At least it stopped raining and the cloud cover lifted so I could see where I was going. At one point I wound through a tidal flow of animals being herded down the road, and later was passed by the day's military convoy.

It was a short 14 kilometers (9 miles) up to the snow-covered slopes and prayer flags of Gama La at 4,618 meters (15,150 feet). I bundled up in tights, two fleece jackets, rain jacket, and gloves for the 45 kilometers (28 miles) of descent down into the Salween River gorge, my Third Parallel River. Yet three kilometers (two miles) down brought heart break; the pavement ended and I was down to mud and rocks. The road though had better things in mind. It cut in long gradual switchbacks across wide grass slopes, its long traverses visible ahead through holes in the milling clouds. It dropped into an ever-tightening arid gorge where it picked up most of the dozens of hairpin turns between summit and river. The road wound tightly and steeply in the cramped space of the gorge, flipping repeatedly from one side to the other, supported by copious amounts of embankments, bridges, retaining walls and culverts. It had all the makings of a great modern road, just not the surface. It was impressive enough as it was, with a little pavement it would have been a stunning descent.

Four hours of descent from Gama La the road came out above the Salween and turned upstream. Like the Yangtse and Mekong before it, the vertical gorge was arid rock, but even more so. There were no villages, no animals, no signs of life. It was steeper, more imposing, even intimidating in its rough imposing aridity. The road wound upstream to a bridge at 2,770 meters (9,100 feet) that spanned a short but narrow slot canyon through which the river thundered. With all the military convoys going along this road, this one bridge packed a strategic punch and two guards spent their days in total isolated boredom making sure that people like me didn't stop and purposefully blow themselves, or the bridge, up. The bridge went straight into a short tunnel and began to climb.

The road turned up a side valley with a stream the color of chocolate milk, into a canyon of vertical black walls. A shower passed briefly overhead and the road quickly turned to mud, adding a few more different shades of geology to my bike. The canyon opened up, the road turned to pavement, a settlement appeared. But still all the water, including that coming out of the villages taps, was brown. Concerned about finding clear water for a camp I continued on. Eventually a spring materialized beside the road and, soon after I camped in a nice hidden spot beside the river.

Happiness is a firm morning poop. My first since getting sick four days before. Health was returning.

The Three Parallel Rivers would be merciful this time. I would only have to cross the Salween once. And unlike the previous steep debilitating climbs, this one was long, protracted, mostly paved and took its sweet time gaining elevation.

After several periods of on again-off again pavement it kicked in for good and I came into Pashto. Usually able to communicate very well with locals despite a common language, I became totally flummoxed with the local food vendors in Pashto. I almost cycled out of the place empty-handed. I continued uphill, an increasing headwind attempting to make up for the wonderfully smooth road. I passed by settlements of full blooming trees rising from smooth lush green fields that had been harvested from the arid rock landscape of the valley. My daily military convoy came down the highway in the opposite direction.

Further up, a truck came flying around a corner, down the hill towards me. Not only did it swing wide around the corner and then fail to correct its path, it continued across my lane straight towards me. I abruptly veered off the road, narrowly missing being obliterated by about a foot. It could only have been a deliberate attempt to scare the crap out of a lao wai (foreigner) for a laugh. The driver had done well.

Further on still, I came upon four monks who were performing a ceremony on the side of the road. They walked in a circle while beating a drum and chanting, then drank unappealing water which they procured from a ditch. They stopped and walked up the road to their camp. A little later I camped also, hiding from the wind behind one of the many man-made rock walls.

It was cold and grey in the morning with the wind still coming down off the pass ahead into my face. The grade was gentle and I climbed steadily to high green meadows dotted with dark nomad tents and a lake nestled in the summit of the pass. Snow-capped peaks surrounded Ngaluk La, 4,373 meter (14,350 feet) pass. I passed the group of lamas I had seen the day before. Several others had joined them. I asked them if they were walking to Lhasa. They said yes.

Lhasa, the capital of Tibet, and its surroundings, is the homes to several of Tibet's holiest sites; the Potala, Jokhang temple and several large and important gompas. It was a highlight for Tibetans to make the pilgrimage to Lhasa, to visit these places, to make offerings, and pay their respects. Making the pilgrimage would generate great merit for themselves and bode them well in the journey to the next life and their larger journey to nirvana. The greater the effort and sacrifice of the pilgrimage, the greater the merit attained in doing so. Walking far outstripped catching the bus, and prostrating the entire way from home village to Lhasa was the ultimate commitment and attained the greatest merit. Devotees decorated in local hand made knee, elbow, and hand guards, and with a full-length abrasion resistant apron, prostrated full length along the road or trail. They stood up and moved to where their hands had reached and prostrated once again. They spent their days prostrating in a herculean act of devotion and belief, for hundreds, or a thousand kilometers to Lhasa. It is an act beyond the comprehension of most humans, a testament to the strength of these Tibetan people and the depth of their devotion.

From Ngaluk La it was a clear 250 kilometers (155 miles) of descent to the base of the climb to the next pass. The road followed a long series of creeks, then rivers, down through the mountains, converging towards the Indian border.

As I descended, the road dropped into coniferous forest and a tight gorge. The gorge opened a little and came to an opening decorated in many thousands of prayer flags. In long curving strips they were strung between poles, trees, bushes, and rocks, from a bridge over the creek, and up to, and across, the opposite cliff face. Long narrow flags were attached lengthways to tall poles that surrounded a clearing. It was a riot of color and motion as the flags waved casually in the breeze. Part way up the cliff a natural cave had been made into something of a small gompa, or lama retreat, and a lama sat outside. It was tranquil and quiet, peaceful and beautiful, and completely unexpected.

Downstream the gorge turned into a slot canyon barely wider than river and road. For about a kilometer the road went through a concrete tunnel, open on one side, to help keep the canyon side from falling onto the road. The gorge abruptly ended and emptied onto a broad flat valley around the town and lake of Rawok Tao.

This town was my last chance to rest before the final 800 kilometers (500 miles) over passes, and through more dangerous towns ahead, to Lhasa. I took an easy day of 36 kilometers (22 miles), taking the afternoon off to rest, eat and look around. In my hesitation on the street, deciding on what to do next, a man in a uniform walked up to me and said "Welcome to Rawok Tao" in English and continued on his way. I nodded and smiled, not knowing quite how else to respond. I was though, completely flabbergasted.

There was no shortage of uniforms in a variety of colors in eastern Tibet. But who were they all? Men and women in various shades of grey, blue, and green went by on motorcycles, cars, and trucks, wandered the streets of towns and villages, and usually left me alone. The secret was to keep moving, never staying anywhere long enough for some higher official to hear of my presence and order someone to go find me and bring me in. There were regular police, traffic police, military, PSB (the Public Security Bureau, my real nemesis, the ones I really didn't want to meet) and an assortment of others. I never quite knew who was who so I just cycled past all of them and hoped for the best. Ultimately I was going to be a pain in the neck for the average low ranking official since they wouldn't really know what to do with me. It was just easier for everyone to let me ride contentedly on. But there was always the element of the unknown and suspense. And this had kept me moving.

It had been my habit on my bicycle journeys to take frequent days off, to rest, explore the area, and hang out in colorful markets. But this inability to stop in towns, where officials could find me, kept up a speed, pressure and an inability to rest, eat and regain strength. And it was terrain where I most needed the time off. The cycling had been extreme: rough roads, mammoth climbs, and high altitudes. The food had been poor, unappealing and in low supply, and I had become sick which had weakened me and dimmed my appetite for a week or more. I had already been a skinny runt and now I had lost a lot of weight. I was permanently on the edge of my capability.

With each of my journeys I had progressively increased the challenge. As I gained skills I gained the ability to explore more demanding environments and conditions. But I was coming to a point where making life more difficult was becoming counter-productive. I was indeed traveling through one of the most spectacular environments. Beautiful, outrageous, jaw-dropping, scenes greeted every turn with incredible vistas over glacial peaks, valleys, gorges, deserts, forests, raging rivers, and a landscape full of friendly enthusiastic Tibetans who had created fields, homes and a livable environment sometimes from little more than rock. But I was barely able to enjoy it. So much of my energy was directed towards forward progress, to confronting the difficulties that were in front of me everyday. It was a slow hard pilgrim's-progress, a tough route to nirvana, but ultimately I wouldn't trade it for anything. It was my labor of love, my devotion to exploration and finding limits, of the world and of myself. It was my passion, my drive, my essential oil of life. My body was the engine, the landscape, the people, and the feat of having done it all by myself on a bicycle, the reward. I could relate to the Tibetan pilgrims.

I appreciated the official's welcome, and with a laugh went off to find a guesthouse.

The town along the highway was a typical ugly Chinese settlement, but away from the main drag was another world. The old town was quite unlike anything I had ever seen. It was a maze of low homes, alleys and walls made from piles of stones and old trees, all in such a jumble that it was hard to tell what was alley, or home entrance, yard, or home. Cows stood outside low wooden doors topped with incense burners. Standing on poles were elevated grain or animal feed storage structures. It felt ancient and medieval, a fairy tale kind of place in a gremlin sort of way.

I followed a path to a large chorten that sat on a small knoll in the middle of the wide flat valley floor. Dark fences criss-crossed the expanse of green grass. At one end of the valley was placid lake Rawok Tso. Surrounding it all were snow capped peaks shrouded in cloud. The sun came out. It was peaceful, gorgeous, and relaxed, seemingly far from the rigors of the road.

On the way back I passed the remains of a local party. A woman walked by with the last dregs of 40 liters (10 gallons) of chang (a thick milky looking Tibetan beer made from barley, the local home brew) in two 20 liter (5 gallon) metal drums. An old gent wobbled his way home.

It was a lovely ride along Rawok Tso in the morning. A couple of villages boasted prime locations with idyllic locations overlooking the aquamarine lake with towering mountain vistas. The lake narrowed, quickly picked up speed, and sped headlong with surprising ferocity into a lengthy spectacular gorge. The river, still aquamarine, dropped heedlessly below huge walls of rock, past tall thin waterfalls that dropped over cliff faces or through narrow chasms, and through lovely green forest adorned with billowing white blooming rhododendrons. The calls of birds mingled with the roar of water. It was the Parlung Tsangpo, the river that I would follow still another 200 kilometers (125 miles) downstream to the base of the next pass. It was such a lovely clean attractive river after all the muddy slurries of rivers I had been following for weeks.

I lost my pavement but like the descent from Gama La, all the road was there. Wide and built up, with guard rails, embankments, and culverts, it cut its way downstream across terrace, scree slope or rock wall. It was bumpy and rocky but at least it was downhill and I could coast my way through.

The gorge opened out and the pavement resumed. It was a wonderful ride down the continually dramatic valley, where mountainsides rose perhaps 3,000 meters (10,000 feet) into clouds, where the forest was thick, verdant and varied with conifer, deciduous and evergreen broadleaf species. Peeking up side valleys I could see glaciers drooping from the mountains. Under the heavy clouds, with the dark of forest, it all felt deep and mysterious as though I was descending into the jungle, which indeed I was. My route had bent south and closed in on the easternmost end of the Himalayas. Proximity to the south-Asian monsoon provided the clouds under which I was cycling and the rains for all this abundant life. Just over those mountains to the south lay Arunachal Pradesh in far north-eastern India.

I found a small gompa with thousands of prayer flag poles in long lines across the terrace surrounding it. Man-made fields were ablaze with yellow flowers, probably mustard. Homes made of wood with painted window frames and shingle roofs seemed like Swiss cottages among the grandeur of the mountains. The valley widened and I came to Sumozom with its line of newly built concrete stores opening onto the street, looking sterile and out of place, another Chinese developmental blessing. I rode another four kilometers and finished off one the nicest days of riding of the journey, with a camp and view of valley and mountain.

Wonderful scenic paved down-valley cycling continued the next day. The valley widened, the river became broad and braided, the opposite side of the valley now far away. There were fields of yellow, periodic settlements and homes with bright sheet metal roofs in red, green, but mostly blue. I stopped in Bomi and resupplied with food. It was a classically rebuilt Chinese town, with a long organized clean wide main street, with concrete from side to side, even lines of arching lamp-posts and cycle rickshaws to shuttle people along the only smooth level surface for 150 kilometers (100 miles). I met a couple of Chinese travelers who had driven their 4WD from their home in Beijing through northern Tibet to Lhasa. They were now on their way home. They even had the western tourist outfit down to a T, complete with quick dry travel clothes.

The valley narrowed, the valley sides steepened, the road clung impressively to near vertical cliffs 100 meters (300 feet) above yet another thundering river. A sign talked about the scenic spots of the Tibet Yigong Natural Geopark in Tibetan, Chinese and English. Another sign spoke of ancient landslides that had blocked the river and formed a lake. It was a good introduction to the next day. I camped in a forest that had become increasingly moist, tropical, and alive with the decreasing altitude. It was draped with moss and hummed with the sound of insects and birds.

It wasn't too far down the road the next morning to my first military convoy of the day and to the disappearance of the pavement and almost the road itself. The road was reduced to a single muddy track as it wound its way across an enormous landslide scar that poured down from 300 meters (1,000 feet) above the road. I took heart in the fact that if it could hold up a military convoy it could probably support me.

Pavement resumed on the other side and I came into the unappealing town of Tangmai, where another military convoy was just pulling in. Further on I came to a single-lane suspension bridge that crossed the mighty Tangmai River, a tributary of the Parlung. It was a flimsy wobbly bridge and could only take one vehicle at a time. Even with that one vehicle the bridge bent down under the weight of it, the dimple in the road bed moving along the bridge with the vehicle, like a mouse moving down the throat of a snake. Military vehicles were backed up on one side, private 4WDs backed up on the other. I jumped ahead of the queue and scurried across in between trucks.

Beyond the bridge the road ahead was a mess. It was one muddy unpaved lane that rose and fell in short sharp pitches that usually had me walking. It cut across cliffs directly above the river, occasionally supported by old wooden lattice structures. That this road was able to survive at all was part luck, part ingenuity, and part will of the gods. It was remarkable that the viability of the entire route from Yunnan and Sichuan to Lhasa, with all its convoys, rested on this one piece of very sketchy road.

After 200 kilometers of pavement it was a fun and dramatic novelty that quickly wore off. Twelve kilometers later, with a fanfare of prayer flags, I finally bottomed out on my 250 kilometer (155 miles) descent. I thanked the river for a wonderful ride.

A further 20 kilometers (12 miles) downstream the Parlung would merge with the Yarlung Tsangpo, one of the world's great rivers. Together they would enter the Great Gorge that would cut through the spine of the mountains, circling from east, to south, to west, forming the eastern end of the Great Himalaya, to spill out on the plains of India as the Brahmaputra, to pass through Bangladesh, and empty into the Bay of Bengal. A sign claimed the gorge of the Parlung, which I had just cycled, at 3,350 meters, (11,000 feet) deep, to be the third deepest in the world after the Great Gorge of the Yarlung (at 5,300 meters, 17,400 feet deep) and the Kali Gandaki in Nepal (4,400meters, 14,400 feet deep). My low point was 2,070 meters (6,800 feet) and now it was all uphill to my next pass at 4,515 meters (15,000 feet).

The road immediately settled into a smooth and steady climb, and followed the Rong Chu, another mighty stream, even if it was just a minor tributary. Twenty kilometers (12 miles) up it turned to pavement. It started to rain and was still at it as I pitched camp in the moist late day light. Rain was one thing, putting up my tent in the rain was something else.

In the grey wet gloom of early morning I continued my climb to Serkhyim La with only 60 kilometers (37 miles) of uphill left to go. The climb was largely uninhabited forest up a narrow valley, and later gorge, and then into a lovely, more open, pastoral valley with a pretty, almost Swiss-style village on the other side. A large locked gate and sign on the road to get to it aroused my suspicions that it might be a holiday resort for communist party officials..

Views extended as I climbed through more forest over the Rong Chu valley and the gentle ridges that surrounded it. Had the weather been clear I would've been able to see Namche Barwa, the 7,782 meter (25,531 feet) peak that has long been considered to be the eastern anchor of the Himalayan range set above the inside bend of the Great Gorge. As I had just found out the hard way, the peak may have been the easternmost end of the Himalayas, but it was not the easternmost end of the mountains. I finally climbed above treeline and arrived at the pass at 4:15 pm having been climbing since 8 am.

The pass was coated in an unbelievable number of prayer flags, hundreds of strings, thousands of flags, the whole hillside covered, the ground piled thick. It seemed that the flags were even rotting into the ground. I found a couple of guys in tents. They sewed prayer flags into strings and then sold them to passing tourists and travelers. There was a mob of Chinese tourists when I arrived, They were fresh out of the vehicles that had sped past me as I had labored uphill.

They took pictures of everything including me. It was a grey soggy uninspiring place with few views, a cold lonely place for the flag sewers.

For the first time on the journey I had uninterrupted pavement from the pass summit to the base of the descent.

The descent was a long series of swooping smooth curves, sublime exciting cycling as I dropped through a variety of spectacular scenery and increasing vegetation and warming temperatures. At first the road ran through a smooth hilly landscape, then through graceful curves into a long valley still above treeline. It then came out into a much larger valley, the base many thousands of feet below, distant ridges in fading shades of grey far beyond. It curled in upon itself repeatedly, sliding through road cuttings with curious colorful painted sculptures decorating the rock and concrete retaining walls. Closing in on the base of the descent I stopped to camp. Just ahead I had another suspect town to slide through in the early morning darkness. Again I was forced to put the tent up in the rain.

I rolled down the rest of the climb, past a couple of dark horses standing in the middle of the road, and through Nyingchi, in the dark, without a hitch. There was no checkpoint, no apparent reason for concern. I was joined by the early morning light. Low, flat, with plenty of rainfall and river water, the area was a major agricultural center and greenhouses covered the wide floodplain. I passed by the huge built-from-scratch urban apparition of bland Chinese architecture that was Bayi on a bypass road and started in on the next long climb up the Nyang Chu, a gradual climb along a very long valley. Nyingchi was at 2,970 meters (9,750 feet), my next pass was 4,720 meters (15,500 feet).

I spent the rest of the day cycling up a wide valley, below steep forested slopes, aided by a healthy tailwind, enjoying some of the most level riding of the journey. Already a long way from the rainforest the landscape was much drier than the Parlung valley. The further I went up the valley the drier the landscape became and the better the weather. I was diverging from the spine of the Himalaya, happy to be leaving its moist hinterland. But what I gained in easy cycling I also gained in traffic and I felt like I had returned to China as fleets of 4WDs and buses sped by, bound for Lhasa, an easy one day drive away. It was manic driving and horn usage all over again.

And apparently this part of Tibet was not exempt from Chinese construction mania. Dotted along the valley where strings of brand new residential communities. Each was comprised of rows of neat, huge Tibetan style homes, all identical, each row with its own bright roof color, all homes largely vacant, and all out in the middle of nowhere. Some of them had huge billboards along the road nearby with an artist's rendition of the community once finished, complete with paved roads, lighting and gutters as if some boastful representation of progress. Sometimes I would pass small rows of homes in construction progress right by the road, Tibetans busy with rock and cement.

It was all a ploy. The Chinese government had two things on their mind; dilution and control. In order to manage this far flung corner of the empire, and to exploit the resources of the land, the Chinese government was importing into Tibet, by incentive or force, thousands of Han people, the majority population of China, people who were far more sympathetic to, and controllable by, the government than the renegade Tibetans. They put the Hans into positions of administration, politics, and power and they had the controlling managerial influence leaving the Tibetans without control and a say in their own land. In order to gain control and sympathies of the Tibetans, the Chinese offered considerable sums of cold hard cash to the Tibetans to build themselves homes, but in locations the Chinese deemed appropriate. Tibetans, who for centuries, had lived wild nomadic lives far up into the mountains, and scattered out across the plateau, were flooding down into the valleys to live stable sedentary lives where the Chinese could see what they were up to, and have a controlling interest in what they could or couldn't do. This left the vast plateau open uninhabited territory the Chinese could then happily exploit. Building new homes then was a good deal for everyone.

With an early start and speedy progress I finished the day early in a village that was half under construction. I found a guesthouse and spent an easy afternoon eating, resting, washing clothes and strolling up to a small old gompa that had probably been destroyed in the Chinese Cultural Revolution. In spite of it being overgrown and crumbling it had a Buddhist image inside.

That night I had to battle it out with the local rodent population, and judging by the size of the poops the next morning, this was no little mouse. A storm had also rumbled though the night.

The road continued up the Nyang Chu, past fields of bright yellow flowers and many more of those brand new settlements with colorful roofs. Forty-eight kilometers (30 miles) up the valley I came to Kongba Gyamba. For the first time since Zhongdian I found bread, and even bananas, and left the town with gloriously full panniers. Bananas and bread had long been my staple and sustenance through many a non-western country. It had become standard fare for cheap, filling, safe, available, and tasty fuel. In Kongba Gyamba, through deprivation, the humble banana and bread combo had been elevated to the position of delicacy. I had the Muslims who lived in the town to thank.

Further up the valley I came to Jimba, a rough wild west Tibetan town strung out along the road with speakers blaring music over the town, outdoor pool tables lined up beside the road, and guys riding around on motorcycles. There were lamas sitting beside a store as they rested on their pilgrimage to Lhasa. I had passed others that day, walking by the road, some pulling carts, others camping. Just out of town I found a small terrace above the road and camped.

As I rose up onto the pass the next morning I finally started to have the feeling that I was on the Tibetan Plateau.

Hard Road To Nirvana

Climbing out of the last side valley of the Nyang Chu, there was not a tree or bush to be seen, just grass that coated the smooth and deceptively steep hills. The combination of gradual grade, pavement, acclimatization and weeks on the road getting fit made Mi La, my last pass before Lhasa, and second highest, one of the easiest. As soon as I was high enough to see around, it was clear that the afternoon thunderstorms were hot on my heels. I arrived on top to a round of applause from a 4WD load of white tourists who had just made the journey from Zongdian in only 8 days. It had taken me 24 days.

Surrounded by a few prayer flags on the summit of Mi La

      Mi La was trying to break the prayer flag record. Hundreds of strings radiated from the signs that hung over across above the road, coated rock walls and stretched out across the land. Mi La also had the best views, the best location, and the warmest weather of any pass summit so far.

I spent couple of hours soaking it all in, reveling in the fact that there were no more climbs between me and Lhasa. Time and the impending storm forced my hand and I rode down off the pass into the gentle smooth grassed valley with the looming doom rearing up behind me. The race was on to see who could get to camp first.

Yet the grass was not that smooth, nor was it all that dry, and there wasn't an ounce of protection to camp behind. My stops to find camp spots found only wetness, roughness, exposure and uncampable angles. With the storm almost on me I passed an abandoned building and headed over. It was dirty, dusty, and littered with garbage, but it offered protection. I found the cleanest room, put up my tent inside, and got in. It immediately started blowing and the rain continued until morning.

It got worse. As I continued downhill the next morning, the snow line, which had already dropped below the clouds hanging low on the mountains, dropped even further. I froze.

With time, distance and decreasing altitude, conditions improved. The sun appeared, clothing peeled, and a solid tailwind sprung up from the rear. I was soon scooting down the road, over-taking tractors, and eating up the miles down a gentle, ever widening valley. Late morning I hit the Kyu Chu. I had done 70 kilometers (43 miles) and it was an easy level 70 kilometer down-valley ride to Lhasa. It seemed easily doable by the end of the day. And I couldn't possibly stop only a few kilometers from Lhasa.

Symbolic of my arrival on the plateau, and unlike every other river valley so far, the Kyu Chu was kilometers across, a wide braided stream that casually made its way down the wide gentle valley. While the tailwind had eased some, I still made good time past steep hills rising from the flat expanse of the river. On south-facing slopes the hills were rocky and brown. On north facing sides they were smooth and green, while on the valley floor the fields were large and level. It was great rewarding cycling with little stress. But as I closed in on Lhasa, traffic increased, becoming thick and dangerous, tempering the thrill of homing in on my destination for 4 weeks. Staying alive became more important than reveling in success.

In the distance I caught glimpses of a hill in the center of the valley which had a sparkle in the afternoon light. The Potala was within sight. I crossed the bridge over the Kyu Chu and entered the city of Lhasa. Dicing it up with cycle rickshaws, I wound through city streets, to the Potala.

For decades I had been looking at photos of the Potala Palace, once the main residence of the political and spiritual leader of Tibet, the Dalai Lama. It is one of the world's most distinctive and iconic buildings, with its 13 stories, 1,000 rooms, and some 200,000 statues, and its stately position on Marpo Ri, Red Hill, in the middle of the valley plain. On the beautiful sunny afternoon I had arrived, the palace was radiant and commanding on its perch.

It had taken me 28 days and 1,990 kilometers (1,236 miles) to cycle from Dali, 533 kilometers (331 miles) of it unpaved. And 24,000 vertical meters (79,000 feet) of ascent, over 16 passes. It had been a hell of a damn ride, 28 days of hovering at the limit of my capability, and I wouldn't recommend it to anyone. It was though, absolutely amazing and one of the most spectacular and rewarding rides I had ever done. I had felt alone and isolated sitting on the edge of my resources and strength riding deeper into the mountains, ever climbing into a fabled land under my own steam in a landscape that gave perspective to the toils of a single man. Nirvana perhaps, was not the destination, but the journey itself.

For all the rewards I was glad it was over. I could finally take a day off and be at peace with going nowhere.

I took a few photos of myself and my bike in front of the Potala. Intermingling with the feelings of exhaustion, relief, and success, was a sense of the anticlimactic as the city and the traffic went by as if it was just another day, as it was, for them. Accomplishment was an internal thing, the satisfaction was all mine.

At least I remembered to get the photos at the end, if not at the beginning.

3

LHASA

My timing had been perfect. I had arrived in Lhasa just in time for Saga Dawa, the day of Buddha's birth, death and enlightenment. The saint was, at least, consistent.

The primary activity on the day for Tibetans was to walk the Lhasa kora, an 8 kilometer (5 mile) long pilgrimage loop through the streets of Lhasa, around the hill of the Potala, making offerings, giving alms, and spinning prayer wheels as they went. I left my hotel in the morning, set off down one of the city's main streets, and found a seemingly endless stream of Tibetans on their kora. I spent the next three or four hours doing the loop with tens of thousands of Tibetans on a mission of devotion.

The devotees were the whole cross section of the Tibetan community. While there was a plethora of older folks, there was everyone else too. Moms and dads carried infants on their backs, small kids held parental hands, there were teenagers, and multi-generational families. Some dressed in traditional clothes, some dressed entirely western, and some straddled the divide, mixing styles in a way only Tibetans could get away with.

Like many a culture caught somewhere between traditional and western ways it was the women who wore most of the traditional clothes. They wore a large wrap robe, a chuba, that extended to their shoes, tied around their waists with an often colorful sash, and a colorful, woven wool, horizontally striped apron in front that extended almost as long as the chuba. Underneath they wore a blouse, and over the top a cardigan, if it was cool. Many wore a scarf around their long dark hair that was curled around their heads in a braid. Some of the older men would wear a chuba also, without the apron and head scarf, but most men went about in some variation of western clothes: jeans, collared shirt, a suit.

Many of the devotees spun prayer wheels as they walked, multiplying the efficiency of their prayers. Prayer wheels were small metal cylinders, with a handle below, that contained rolled up strips of paper covered in written prayers. With every revolution of the wheel the prayers were said. The cylinders had a little metal weight attached to the outside via a short chain that helped in the momentum of the spinning. I particularly liked the large ones many of the men carried. The cylinders were almost as big as a man's head, the handle about two feet long, the end of which fit snuggly into a leather holster that hung at waist level from a strap over the shoulders. Tibetans could do almost anything while spinning a prayer wheel, it was almost a subliminal exercise, but done with the sincerest form of devotion.

It was a mostly quiet mob, many absorbed with their own states and thoughts, their walking, their prayers. But others chatted as they walked, and religious devotion didn't stop many from pausing to rest, eat, or shop, along the way.

Ironically it was the Muslims who were the caterers for the festival. All along the way, especially in the old town and along the walk beside the Kyu Chu, Muslims had set up stalls with tables and benches and were selling soup, bread, noodles and big pots of food.

The kora wound through the old town of narrow stone alleys and then flowed out onto the wider more modern streets of the town. Police controlled road crossings and kept folks on the footpath, even if the flow split onto both sides of the road. The kora followed the path beside the river. There were a series of large earthen incense burners (sangkang). Devotees would buy dried herbs from footpath vendors and toss handfuls into the openings of these white pot-bellied stoves. They also sprinkled water on the fire which served to maximize the plumes of aromatic smoke that drifted upwards and carried through the nearby trees and across the road and river. Some folks didn't bother with the burner and just added to huge piles of smoldering herbs sitting on the path. The smoke would engulf them, human forms among the pungent wafts.

Pilgrims make offerings along the Saga Dawa Kora

The kora turned away from the river and ran along a pedestrian alley. The entire 500 meter (1500 feet) length of the street was full of beggars, thousands of them. Giving alms was part of one's route to a better lot in the next life, and part of a route to redistribute the wealth of a community from those who have enough to those who have little. Giving alms was inherent in the Tibetan culture. The whole monastic society, a major component of the community, depended on giving alms. The recipients of alms both received and gave by giving the opportunity for those who were well off to gain merit. It was a mutually beneficial arrangement.

The recipients came in all shapes, sizes and ages from the very young to the very old, and included groups of monks and nuns who sat in small groups playing music, chanting, talking, or reading prayer books as money piled up in front of them. The monks wore the ubiquitous maroon robes characteristic of Tibetan lamas everywhere. Some recipients sat in long organized lines, others sat in big unorganized clusters. Many sat quietly and waited, almost nonchalant about the whole thing, others were more unruly with out-stretched hands, expectant faces, and beckoning with hand and voice. Some had shoe boxes into which people put the money, others kept their notes in neat wads in their hands.

The unit of currency for the alms-giving was the mao, one tenth of a yuan, the main currency of China, which in turn was one eighth of a US dollar. Folks carried around huge stacks of clean new notes and handed them out liberally. At 1.2 US cents per mao each donation wasn't a huge commitment, but the sheer volume was impressive and ultimately a lot of money was changing hands. It must have caused a minor headache at the bank, to have so many mao notes in one place at the same time, a unit of currency that was so small it almost had no value on the street. Notes piled up in boxes, on rugs, in laps, in hands.

The passing devotees squeezed tight between the sitting recipients. Everyone, including myself, was being pushed, bumped and jostled in our attempts at forward movement. Alms row, as I called it, and indeed the whole Saga Dawa event, was part human spectacle, and part continuation of a belief and custom that appeared to be alive and well in Lhasa.

The end of the street emptied onto a main modern city road and the alms-giving abruptly ended. There was space and movement and the route followed wide streets through the Chinese parts of the city that seemed bland, dull and inappropriate by comparison. At one point the route divided, with one route staying on the main street, and another following a narrow side alley, between lines of stalls, below the north wall of the Potala. The alley narrowed and I was soon back to a compressed mass of humanity being swept along with the tide, jammed in on all sides, taking lots of little steps. Things improved a little as the route followed a fenced path along a park. And then breathing space returned as it hit another of the main streets. The route turned back into the old Tibetan sector of the city and launched into another lap.

I spent three days in Lhasa. It was a great feeling not to have go to anywhere, and not to have to get involved in some superhuman effort to go there. I could enjoy some personal inside space and everywhere I wanted to go was a short level walk down the street. It was all so delightfully comfortable. And it was just a temporary thing.

The main attraction of the city was the Barkhor. The Barkhor was the central square of the main old Tibetan town of Lhasa. Not just the central open square surrounded by white three-story buildings with flat roofs and stores along the sides, but a whole complex of alleys and markets that surrounded the Jokhang temple, the most holy site in Tibetan Buddhism. The Barkhor is a place of endless activity, fascination and commerce. Tibetans sold yak butter, hardware, meat, fruit, vegetables, handicrafts jewelry, tourist trinkets, musical instruments, religious articles, cheap Chinese-made clothes, and tooth extractions. Colorful outdoor stalls displayed their goods laid out across the cobbled streets, reducing thoroughfares to barely passable alleys. Displays seemed to erupt out of stores onto the streets, small hills of clothing and shoes. Around the Jokhang ran the Barkhor kora, a short pilgrimage loop of a few hundred meters, that hundreds of folks walked repeatedly each day.

In front of the main door to the Jokhang people gathered, talking, praying, milling, sitting, but mostly prostrating, performing the oscillations between standing and lying face first on the ground, 108 at a time. Like the Lhasa kora, prostrating was done by a diverse crowd; young, old, male, female, dressed traditionally, dressed western. And there seemed to be no set format to prostrate. Some power prostrated, getting them fast and vigorously. There was the social approach, do a few, talk a bit, do a few more. And then there was the lackadaisical approach, do one, stand around and look around, do another, stand around some more.

I would return to the Barkhor repeatedly, mostly in the morning and afternoon, when the sun was low and less intense. When folks were out doing their laps of the kora, spinning their prayer wheels, touching their foreheads to the tall pole wrapped in thousands of prayer flags, or making offerings of herbs to the sangkangs outside the front of the Jokhang. When the shadows cast long and the sun gave a warm glow to faces already flush with the occasion. It was one of the most culturally beautiful places. It was clean, the Jokhang grand, the people busy with talk or religious devotion. It was much like many places in the world in the evening, where people gather to socialize and enjoy the cool evening air and the transition from day to night, to meet with friends, intentionally or accidentally. While in most of those places the focus was often on food, outdoor evening markets and restaurants, at the Barkhor it was on the religion, the kora.

I followed narrow dark alleys down behind the Jokhang into tiny mysterious courtyards and temples. In one temple devotees would line up to be blessed by a monk. He would pour water over their bowed heads, brush their heads with a long brush, and hold a dorje (thunderbolt) to their heads briefly. In another courtyard, hundreds of mostly women sat on cushions on the floor, twirling their prayer wheels, passing their retirement in a holy place. I wound along little aisles between them, out onto a roof, to find more folks doing the same under the shade of hanging tarpaulins. Indeed it seemed that every nook and cranny of this little maze of a temple complex had lines of older folks sitting and spinning. I climbed steep narrow stairs to balconies and halls and a little temple where folks donated mao notes, yak butter and alcoholic liquids to vessels, urns, and lamps. It was tranquil and spiritual, peaceful and beautiful. I felt so out of place, and so big.

I wandered over to the Potala. The former home of the Tibetan government, the Dalai Lama and high lamas, although currently occupied by the Chinese government, was still a holy place in the eyes of most Tibetans. Along the side walk, beside the road in front of the palace, a flock of Tibetans stood in admiration, and prostrating time and again. Around the base of the Marpo Ri, the hill on which the Potala stands, is another kora, much of which is lined with prayer wheels, along which Tibetans circled, paying their respects, saying their prayers. I walked up the ramp driveway, on the rear, north side of the hill, to the main gate of the palace. I arrived just in time for the morning's round of Chinese tour groups. I sat waiting for them to pass, to get a little relative peace in which to enjoy the palace by.

The follow-the-arrows tour was primarily through the 20 or so temples of the Red Palace that is so distinctly visible from in front of the complex. Each temple housed an assortment of images of Buddhas, Dalai Lamas and high lamas from Tibet's history, quite literally thousands of them. There were throne rooms and tombs, usually large golden chortens, for each of the Dalai Lamas. But after a while it all melted together. It felt like, and indeed was, just a museum, lifeless and stagnant, rather than a living breathing place of devotion, activity, government or scholarly pursuit. It was as much a reminder of what wasn't happening in Tibet, as a display of what was in Tibet.

It was the great irony that modernday Chinese tourists came far, and paid big, to admire the culture and religion of a people its previous generation had done so much to eradicate. Indeed, every time there was a Chinese government event that somehow involved the Tibetans, the Chinese would enlist Tibetans to do some cultural display of music and dance. Often such displays were watered down Sino-versions of real Tibetan cultures, which in turn helped the process of dilution and deterioration. It gave the misleading portrayal of a happy coexistence of mutually beneficial cultural appreciation. But it was markedly two faced to be on one hand promoting something, while working towards the destruction of that very thing. In some ways I would've been better off admiring the building only from the outside, as it, fortunately, has changed little. It remained an impressive and beautiful iconic building, an instantly recognizable symbol of a land and its people.

It didn't take me long, though, to want get out of the city itself and have a look around the surrounding hills. Three days to be precise.

I took a bus to the north side of the city and walked up past some yellow and green fields and out onto the warm, dry, rocky slopes of the valley. I came to Pabonka, one of the oldest gompas in Tibet, which had been rebuilt several times. Like many gompas it was a complex of buildings, with multiple temples, residences for the monks, and a kitchen. One of the temples was small and perched on a large boulder with one of its sides curved to fit the shape of the boulder. I climbed the stairs and found a tiny prayer hall with about 15 monks chanting their puja, (prayer). Eventually I was beckoned inside to sit. Two young monks soon arrived with large pots of butter tea. They poured the monks all a bowl when the chanting stopped. Large spoonfuls of tsampa were ladled into the bowls and the lamas kneaded the mixture into a doughy ball. The chanting had been replaced by slurping and munching. I left them to their culinary contentment.

I continued uphill, crossing a gully strung with dozens of strings of prayer flags, to the smaller Tashi Choling Gompa sitting on a small spur. There was a fine view over the surrounding hills and over the wide expanse of the Kyu Chu valley, the sprawling Lhasa, and the Potala, that from there seemed so small. I was welcomed into the gompa by a monk, who beckoned me into a lovely room decorated with rugged benches, ornate thangkas (painted scrolls of deities) and an awesome view over the valley, if the windows hadn't been so small and dirty. He showed me a couple of other temples and gave me some butter tea.

The quality of yak butter tea varies immensely. The tea is a staple of Tibetan life being consumed in huge quantity, providing warmth and caloric energy, ideal for the cold high altitude of Tibet. It is not usually for the foreign palate. It is made from regular black tea brewed with added salt. Once the tea is made and poured, a big ol' dob of yak butter is added to the cup, and forms a shiny film on top of the tea. Many Tibetans poured the tea and the butter together into a long thin wooden cylinder. With a plunger like handle they churned the tea to blend the butter with the tea which gives it a more even consistency and milky appearance. Modern day Tibetans often use a blender. Out in the country, or far up a hillside in a gompa, far from refrigeration, the quality of the tea hinges on the quality and age of the butter. Tea with rancid butter is a tough one to get down.

Outside the gompa, on the roof, the monks were busy making lunch. A pressure cooker sat in a metal frame structure about a meter off the ground at the focal point of two broad curving shiny sheets of metal, a solar cooker. Looking something like a cross between a satellite dish and a huge metallic butterfly it was extremely popular in Tibet, not surprisingly, considering the abundance of strong sun. I had seen them on roof tops everywhere, making tea, boiling water, or cooking up dinner.

Further up the ridge, past an area covered in a mess of old faded prayer flags, and another flag filled gully, I came to a cave hermitage of about eight tiny homes squeezed into a horizontal crook of a cliff. I was beckoned into a tiny cave chapel by one of several nuns who were busy chanting away. I was offered holy water from the spring in the back of the cave.

I came down the smooth grass hillside littered with round granite boulders to Sera Gompa, nestled at the base of the slope, one of the more important gompas in Tibet. I found the kora that followed the gompa's outer wall and came upon a collection of rock carvings and paintings, images of the Buddha, on smooth granite faces. Though I hadn't seen a foreigner all day, coming to the front entrance of the gompa there were instantly busloads of them. I went into the two main temples, both huge impressive halls with walls packed with gilded Buddha and high lama images and glass cabinets full of hundreds of prayer books. Bright streamers of colorful fabric hung from the red ceiling and on the wooden floor, a dozen rows of seats piled with maroon robes where the monks came to do puja, prayer.

Gompas were inherently atmospheric places. Monks scurried around, busy with errant missions or lounged in courtyards enjoying free time. Pious pilgrims did koras around temples and outer walls, and entered temples to pay respects and make offerings. There were temples and assembly halls where monks performed puja on a daily basis. The temples and halls were the focus of a network of buildings for monk and pilgrim alike. The solid, blocky, and mostly white exterior, hid well the dark mystery of the interior of the temples. Lucky to have a few small pokey dirty windows, often with the only light being from the butter lamps offered by pilgrims, the interiors were usually jammed packed with centuries of accumulated iconography that barely appeared in the resulting darkness. They were wild and beautiful places that instantly called for peace, silence and respect in their timeless devotion. They abounded with serene golden images of Buddhas and lamas from centuries before, in sizes that ranged from centimeters to meters, (inches to yards), decorated with robes and ribbons, with the offerings of butter lamps, rice, barley, and money lined up before them. There were protective demons that seemed more fierce and intimidating than comforting and reassuring. There were wall paintings and thangkas in a rainbow of colors and bewildering imagery.

Thangkas were painted or embroided on silk and depicted a Buddhist deity, mandala, historical scene, or retold myths associated with the life and times of Buddha, deities or important lamas. Often incredibly detailed and intricate, they are important teaching and meditation tools, and are used as centerpieces during ceremony or festival, all with the aim of bringing one further down the path towards enlightenment.

At the front of the temple were seats for head, and important visiting lamas. On the wooden floor were arranged the long low straight tables, and parallel rugs on which the other lamas sat, their books spread before them on the tables, where they did puja.

There was little in common between the interior of the temples and the exterior of Tibet, other than the Tibetans themselves, and the devotion that was everywhere.

Outside in a shady stoney courtyard though was this gompa's major lure for me. About 200 monks, dressed in their maroon robes, were in the process of religious debate. Each monk took their turn standing before one to four other seated monks. The standing monk would do his best to debate some obscure point in Buddhism in a technique that was as much dance as debate. He did most of the talking while rotating, bending, twisting, waving his arms in the air, and repeatedly lunging forward to stomp one foot and clap in the other monk's faces as if to hammer home the point. It was part exciting, part comical, part raucous, but mostly living, breathing religion and belief being learned, discussed, argued, absorbed, and handed down through the millennium. With so many monks all doing the same thing in a confined space it was a wonder they could hear each other speak. The main distraction were the tourists, many of whom had the disrespect to take photos of each other with the debating monks in the background.

Back in Lhasa in the middle of the night my health again failed me. The three course meal I had for dinner came out of both ends in a hurry.

I had spied Gyaphel Ri from both Lhasa and yesterday's hike. It was a big round mountain that rose 1,500 meters (5,000 feet) in one smooth pitch from the valley floor. And it was on the other end of an easy bus ride from town. It was also a low grade holy mountain, with Drepung Monastery at it base, a cave hermitage part way up, and a summit that attracted pilgrims. The night's stomach issues weren't enough to dissuade me from my plan to climb it.

From the end of the bus ride near Drepung Monastery I aimed directly for the mountain. I wound along narrow paths up gentle slopes and started climbing in earnest. Rather than take the more circuitous trail that climbed to cave and summit I went for the direct route. I could see the small cave hermitage about half way up the mountain and headed straight for it. Technically it was an easy hike but with the altitude and the relentless ascent it was physically demanding climbing. Nearly 900 meters (3,000 feet) from the base I came to the hermitage. I continued upwards, my speed and energy dwindling with altitude. I hit the summit ridge and rejoined the pilgrims trail. The trail was lined with cairns which grew with height and frequency as I closed in on the summit. I arrived at the 5,240 meter (17,200 feet) summit in that familiar feeling of self-destruction I knew so well from Eastern Tibet. It took me half an hour to get the energy to have a look around.

The broad smooth summit was a mass of cairns, prayer flags, and discarded clothing. The cairns ranged up to six feet high and were so numerous that they made walking around more of a scramble. The prayer flags were old and strewn across the ground. In many places they were melted and burnt. The strong sun against the rocks at this altitude was enough, it seemed, to melt the synthetic fabric of the flags. Leaving clothing behind was also a kind of devotional act by the pilgrims; leaving a token of oneself in a holy place. The flags and the clothing gave the summit something of a trash dump look which did little for the sanctity of the location.

Surrounding the peak though was only grandeur. Ridges and peaks by the dozen receded into the distance in all directions in fading shades of khaki. Far below, the broad Kyu Chu cut a wide level swath through the mountains. Lhasa sprawled out on one side of the mountain. On the other, the mighty glacial peaks of the Himalayas, somewhere in the vicinity of Sikkim and eastern Nepal, lined the horizon, far down and beyond the Kyu Chu. Clouds played with sun to produce beams that roamed through the mountains illuminating rugged slopes and smooth valley floors.

I returned much the same way I had come up. I dropped down onto the kora around Drepung Monastery and could hear the claps and voices of the monks debating within.

I was working my way outwards from Lhasa with my small excursions. I was happy to be leaving my bicycle in the care of the hotel and setting off to see Tibet on foot, far from those drivers with their dust, exhaust, and horns. It had always been like this.

On previous journeys, when the circumstances called, I would leave the bike to hike trails, ride trains, jeeps and buses, to climb mountains, and explore without it. It was a chance to add variety, to explore places too distant, too far off course, too remote or that would've been just too unpleasant or inappropriate to do by bicycle. Then by the time I returned to the bike I was so happy to see it, to jump on and head over the horizon under my own power. Variety was always a staple of life.

The next day I took a bus back up the Kyu Chu, the way I had first come in on my way to Lhasa. It turned off the main road after 30 kilometers (20 miles), to climb through a series of switchbacks, gaining 500 meters (1,700 feet), to Ganden monastery. I would walk through the mountains for four days, over two passes, to Samye monastery to the south.

Ganden Gompa had an idyllic location. It sat in the south-facing crook of a curving ridge, almost an amphitheater, as if to maximize its collection of sun. It was totally hidden from every direction but south. Tiers of buildings, big solid structures of temples, colleges and residences, some new, some little more than piles of rubble, perched on the steep slopes on the side of the ridge. I was amazed as to how much of the gompa there actually was.

Ganden Gompa was founded in 1409 and grew into the most important Gelugpa sect monastery in Tibet. At its peak, in the early 1900s, the monastery had around 6,000 monks. It had contained more than two dozen chapels, one of which could house 3,500 monks at a time. It had dozens of colleges and residences, and operated like its own self-contained world. By the time the Chinese arrived in the 1950 the numbers had decreased to 2,000 monks.

In 1950 the solitude and peace of the Tibetan people came to a crashing end when the Chinese army quickly moved into Tibet, completely overwhelming the meager Tibetan resistance. While not overtly changing much in Tibet, tension inevitably grew between the Tibetans and their occupying force, particularly when the Tibetans learned of a Chinese attempt to kidnap the Dalai Lama. The resulting protests and retaliation in 1959 resulted in the deaths of hundreds of Tibetans, and the wholesale destruction of Tibetan culture and architecture began in earnest.

According to the Chinese, they were liberating Tibet from reactionary forces, freeing oppressed serfs from monastic rule and ushering in a new era of equitable socialistic society. The Tibetans were getting liberated whether they liked it or not, regardless of the people's opposition.

Monasteries were looted, their riches stripped and destroyed, their scriptures burnt. Monks and nuns were forced out of the monasteries, were tortured, forced to marry, work at menial jobs and treated atrociously. Monasteries by the hundreds, like Ganden, were bombed into piles of rubble.

The surrounding countryside fell victim to Mao's Great Leap Forward, a demented and totally misguided attempt to propel China into the modern age. Part of the 30 million people who died as a result were about 70,000 Tibetans who were forced to stop growing the barley that grew well at altitude and had sustained them for centuries, and grow wheat and rice instead, crops completely unsuited to Tibet's high altitude.

The cultural genocide of Tibet continued with the Chinese Cultural Revolution that started in 1966. The real purpose of the Cultural revolution was for Mao to consolidate his own power within the Communist party and over the country. But he used the guise of removing the capitalistic, traditional, cultural and religious elements from Chinese society in order to enforce Communism in the country and Maoist orthodoxy in the communist party. He formulated the Red Guard, a force of young violently impassioned, radically Mao youth, that grew into the millions, that ran a path of cultural, religious, humanitarian, and societal destruction, with governmentally sanctioned torture, violence and murder.

Within months the Red Guard entered Tibet and desecrated and destroyed every religious and cultural thing they could get their hands on. The more than 6,000 monasteries that once thrived in Tibet were reduced to a handful, monks and lay people were tortured and forced to destroy their monasteries and commit inhumane acts at gun point. Many more died from further asinine and misguided agricultural reforms. What little of Ganden that had survived and been rebuilt from the 1959 rebellion was bombed again. Ganden had been reduced to lifeless piles of rocks. While Mao would declare the Cultural Revolution to be over in 1969 it would continue on with less ferocity until his death in 1976. Over the 30 years of Chinese rule, 6,254 monasteries had been destroyed, 1.2 million (one in six) Tibetans had been killed, 100,000 Tibetans were in labor camps, two thirds of Tibet had been absorbed into "mainland" China, and there had been extensive deforestation and environmental destruction.

With some relaxation of Chinese rule, and the general recognition by the Chinese government that their policy in Tibet had been wrong, reconstruction of Ganden, and other of Tibet's monasteries, began in the 1980s. By the time I arrived, there were a couple of dozen buildings, mostly largely finished, on the exterior anyway, and others were in the process of being rebuilt. It would be a process that would go on for decades in an ongoing labor of love.

I got a room in the gompa guesthouse and set off to walk the high kora. The trail climbed steadily to the crest of the ridge that rose up from the impressive mass of buildings of the gompa in its most improbable of places. I worked my way slowly along the ridge, back toward the gompa, over a succession of small bumps decorated with thousands of prayer flags, with a continuing panorama of mountains and valleys. Directly below was the Kyu Chu with its wide grey expanse of gravel and multiple curving channels. Around it was a diorama of grass-covered ridges and mountains in various shades of green and khaki and above, an endless sky that was as expansive as the landscape below it.

I descended slowly back along the ridge to the gompa. It took me hours to find someone to let me into the temples. They were all new and shiny, and lacked the dark age-old atmosphere of other Buddhist temples I had visited that were stained by yak butter and the countless hands of passing pilgrims. Still I was excited to see them there at all, that belief and devotion had been regaining strength in Tibet, and astounded by the faith that rebuilt the hardware after such a series of catastrophes.

Later, I returned to the ridge above the gompa in the late afternoon light, the light low, the shadows long, the landscape brilliant and dramatic. Coming down in the last light I heard the raucous voices and clapping of lively monk debate and found over 100 monks going at it with gusto in a courtyard. I sat and watched, the only lay person there, as sun faded and lights came on. One particular debate became quite heated, all five monks standing with a lot of pushing and shoving, all in jest and spirited debate. I left them to it and I could hear them still at it when I went to bed.

My route to Samye followed the ridge up from Ganden, south over several ridge points, past a couple of large cairns set in the ridge saddles. I dropped off the ridge into a valley. Passing a couple of nomad tents I was invited in for tea by a couple of girls who appeared from one of them. Mama was waiting for me inside.

The tent home was made of the typical dark yak wool of Tibet's signature animal. It had a mud hearth in the middle, three benches to sit or sleep on, and an assortment of stuff including a trunk, music speakers, harnesses for the yaks, and a pile of dried yak pies for fuel. Occasionally mama would get up and churn yak milk in the long thin cylinder in which the locals made yak butter, while I sipped the butter tea she had given me. We made some small talk, very small talk considering we had not a word in common. She had three girls, with one away in school. There was no husband evident but he was probably up on some far hillside tending animals. Mama gave me some cooked potatoes to take with me as I walked out the door.

I followed the valley downstream, past a small shrine, getting some directions from locals, and later turned up a side valley to start the 1,200 meter (4,000 foot) climb to the next pass. The trail faded and I was left to walk over a rough wet tussock grass, past grazing yaks, sheep and goats.

While goat and sheep are herded by the Tibetans, it is the yak that is the domesticated animal symbol of the land. Related to cattle, but larger and bulkier, they are uniquely adapted to high altitude living with a thick long fur that often hangs skirt-like almost to the ground. They have larger hearts and lungs, and greater hemoglobin than their low land cousins. They have a thick layer of subcutaneous fat and a complete lack of sweat glands. They suffer from heat exhaustion at temperatures above 15 degrees C (59 F) and easily catch disease at low altitudes. They are a docile and friendly animal that allows for easily handling by the Tibetans.

Yaks form the mainstay of nomadic culture. The animals provide meat and milk for consumption; wool for clothing, tents and ropes; bones and horns for tools; dung for heating and cooking; hide for clothing, rugs and accessories; goods for trade; and act as the primary beasts of burden for load-carrying and field-plowing. Yaks are often crossed with cattle to form dzo, male hybrids, or dzomo, female hybrids. It can be sometimes difficult to tell a dzo from the full-blood yak.

Yaks are found across the Tibetan plateau and the Himalayan regions, and into Mongolia, in domesticated and wild forms, at altitudes between 3,000 and 5,500 meters (9,800 and 18,000 feet). They are inextricably linked to Tibetan and Tibetan Buddhist culture and are an emblematic symbol of a country or region, like the kangaroo to Australia, the panda to China, the lion to Africa, the llama to the Andes, the bison to North America.

While the yaks were peaceful and approachable, I gave nomad tents a wide birth. The only thing I feared in these mountains were the huge Tibetan dogs that guarded the animals and tents of the nomads. As their reputation preceded them, I was prepared to sacrifice some more of that wonderful hospitality to avoid the nasty confrontations I was almost certain to lose. As I would find out later, it was a well-founded fear.

With about 800 meters (2,600 feet) still to go to the pass I camped. I received visitors as I sat there, a young girl, and later an older man, both taking breaks from tending animals. It was another gorgeous afternoon at 4,450 meters (14,600 feet).

The long grassy ascent continued the next morning, past grazing yaks, all the way to Shug La (5,250 meters, 17,200 feet). With only a short day, I left the pack and took a side trip uphill onto the surrounding ridges and a small peak at about 5,550 meters (18,200 feet). The summit brought beauty and distress. Mellow, narrow, rocky, but easily walked ridges, extended in all directions far into the distance. I could see Lhasa and Gyaphel Ri, and glaciated peaks in the far distance in many directions. But about 5 kilometers (3 miles) to the east was a big piece of earth-moving equipment cutting a road across an isolated ridge at about 5,000 meters (16,500 feet). Most probably it was the Chinese building a road to access terrain for geologic exploration or mining.

I returned to the pass and followed a wide rocky trail down into the next valley, converging with the valley floor. I followed the valley upstream, dodging nomad tents to a set of exquisite shallow lakes at about 5,000 meters (16,500 feet), surrounded by grazing yaks and smooth grassy peaks. Several waterbirds hung out around the edges of the lake. I camped.

Climbing resumed the next morning following a long curving valley to the next pass, Chitu La (5,100 meters, 16,700 feet). Without a trail, the going was deceptively difficult over the deeply tussocked grass and boggy ground. At the pass I left the pack again and climbed to higher views over the two lakes on the south side of the pass, over a few surrounding peaks, and down the valley I had just climbed to the lakes at last night's camp.

The route down from the pass entered a short narrow gorge. Below the gorge scrubby vegetation resumed and I passed a yak caravan carrying huge bundles of evergreen brush the locals had hacked from bushes further down the valley. It didn't bode well for the local vegetation. Further down I was beckoned over to a camp by the family outside. I sat around on the lovely front lawn, enjoying salt tea (no butter), with the warm friendly family trying to make conversation with few words in common.

Further down I descended into thickening vegetation and camped in a meadow in the shade of small trees, by a clear babbling brook, in a quintessentially nice scene that was so unlike the camps so far. After camping at 5,000 meters (16,500 feet) the night before I felt positively low camping at just 4,250 meters (14,000 feet).

The transition down the valley continued the next morning. For a while the landscape became greener, more luxuriant, more inhabited. I came upon the first of a series of small villages linked by the stream and lovely green and yellow fields that were surrounded by rock walls. The villages became larger, the fields wider, as the valley grew broader. Then hillside vegetation became drier, more stunted, the going hotter and less appealing. I had dropped from altitude into a zone of optimal growth, where man and nature could live and prosper, where temperature, growing season and rainfall were just right. I dropped out of that zone into another that was too hot and dry for most of the local natural vegetation to grow, and man could only grow crops and grass using irrigation canals. Most of the last hour I walked through a hot desert with the central building of Samye Gompa visible ahead. I followed an irrigation canal into the lush man-made green of the fields around the gompa.

Established in about 775 AD, Samye is Tibet's first Buddhist monastery. It was the first incursion of Buddhism into Bon-dominated Tibet. Many of the rituals, symbols and practices of Buddhism have their roots deep in Bon, an animistic and shamanistic religion that had been alive and well on the plateau for at least two 2,000 years. The buildings of the gompa have been destroyed repeatedly by fire, earthquake, wars and invasions, and repeatedly rebuilt. The gompa sits on the side of the vast arid plain of the Yarlung Tsangpo river but is surrounded by the lush green fields made possible by irrigation canals and hard work. The gompa is modeled after a mandala and has a long circular outer wall. Before the Cultural Revolution, there were 108 buildings on the inside of the wall. I counted 38 scattered across the dry and dusty grounds of the gompa.

After resting and refueling I set off to walk around the interior side of the outer wall. I spun prayer wheels housed in long alcoves in the walls, and in wooden structures with little roofs that ran along the walls. I took a turn into each of the ten temples that were spaced along the route. Each temple was similar yet unique. Some were entered through a pleasant courtyard, decorated with flowers and trees, that felt a bit like someone's home, as it may well have been as each temple had a caretaker, usually a wizened old man cleaning butter lamps. As usual for a temple they were solemn, peaceful, cool dark places with dozens, or hundreds, of Buddha or lama images, sitting, standing, and looming out of the darkness.

Outside the walls of the gompa construction was rampant. I wound through it and climbed a small hill, Hepo Ri, a holy place. It was here that Padmasambhava, considered by the Nyingma tradition to be the second Buddha, triumphed over the massed demons of Tibet, a symbolic representation of Buddhism's victory over Bon.

The Yarlung Tsangpo was perhaps 8 kilometers (5 miles) wide, a vast barren expanse of roaming streams, sand dunes, gravel beds and bush dotted desert. Steep arid hills rose abruptly from the plain to high ridges. I could see far up the valley I had walked down earlier. Coming down the valley was a tongue of lush, verdant, canal-supported green that broadened and swept around the wide circle of the gompa wall and carried down into the valley before eventually dwindling into the gravel. Strong winds kicked up dust storms that swept across the Yarlung. The tall central temple of Samye stood imposing and inspiring, the monastery looking so much more attractive from above. The low sun cast deepening shadows across the textured mountains and valley. It was a magnificent spot. I returned for another dose in the morning.

Lhasa was about 140 kilometers (87 miles) upstream, along the Yarlung Tsangpo and the Kyu Chu, from Samye. It took 6.5 hours by bus. First we had to go in the opposite direction for an hour to get to the only bridge across the Yarlung. It then returned upstream to Tsethang, a spiritless could-be-anywhere-in-China city that seemed so ugly and out of place in Tibet. We then went south, again away from Lhasa, to visit a couple of gompas. One was Yumbulagang, considered to be the oldest building in Tibet, even though it had been rebuilt, a tall slender tower of a building that sits on a craggy ridge above the green fields of the valley.

After almost four hours we were finally level with Samye and getting closer to Lhasa. The road ran alongside the Saharan-like expanse of the Yarlung. Along the edges of the river flats millions of trees had been planted in an attempt at stabilization and reforestation. The trees on the south side of the valley did well, growing to about 15 meters (50 feet), while the trees on the north side were either stunted or dead. Sand dunes sprawled out across the valley floor, and curiously, perched on the sides of the mountains as high as 900 meters (3,000 feet) above the river. Excitement mounted as we approached Lhasa airport. The locals were totally thrilled to see a couple of planes sitting on the tarmac.

Soon after arriving in Lhasa it began to rain for the first time in almost two weeks. The rain continued through the night and the next day. The south Asian monsoon had snuck over the Himalayas and was paying Tibet a visit. I spent much of the day catching up on life, winding down from the last outing and gearing up for the next. A few hours into it I set off to visit the holiest place in Tibet, the Jokhang. I had missed the Jokhang on my previous time in Lhasa. Every time I was ready, it wasn't.

The place was mobbed. The Jokhang saw an almost constant flow of wide eyed and adoring Tibetans who came from all over the Tibetan cultural lands, to the mysterious dark interiors, to honor their deities and gods with offerings. I passed between the statues of the Four Guardian Kings into the inner courtyard, entered the inner prayer hall, and turned left to circle the hall clockwise, in the custom of Tibetan Buddhism. The hall was surrounded by a collection of chapels, each displaying and honoring particular deities, bodhisattvas or Buddhas: Guru Rinpoche, Maitreya, Chenrezig, Tsongkhapa, Tsepame, the Buddha of Infinite Light, the Eight Medicine Buddhas, the Nine Buddhas of Longevity. Each tiny chapel, barely big enough for the single file line of devotees to circle around inside it held a few, a dozen, a hundred, images of these revered beings, figures in gold, draped in elaborate cloth, housed in glass cabinets, in poses of great significance. It was a confusing pantheon of characters that had always bewildered me, especially since they all looked remarkably alike, all very Buddha-like, all serene, golden, and at peace, only a nuance of pose, or clothing setting them apart.

But that wasn't the point. It was the devotion used to create these beautiful images and their surroundings. It was the tranquility, the concept of inner peace, infinite wisdom and timeless presence they symbolized. It was the loving lifestyle, the life's purpose, they silently promoted. It was the constant flow of Tibetan devotion that circled the hall paying their respects, the shuffle of those humbled pilgrims as they threw seeds as offerings, touched their foreheads to revered statues, cabinets, walls, and pillars, who made offerings of mao notes or of molten yak butter to thousands of lazily burning lamps. It was the slimy floor covered in a thin layer of dripped yak butter, and the door frames worn smooth and greasy by countless caressing hands. It was ritual, reverence, the heart and soul of a people and their belief.

I climbed stairs to the upper floor to another round of chapels that would make about 30 altogether. The Jokhang was not a place for the claustrophobic. I climbed up onto the roof.

A Tibetan mother cradles her infant in Lhasa

The roof was delightful, partly for the views out over Barkhor Square and the city, partly for the wonderful arrangement of windows, potted plants, cloth window fringes, colored walls, golden spires, and open space. The other part for the team doing reconstruction work. Tibetans sung for just about everything they did. They had songs for planting and harvesting, for ritual, for parties and ceremonies, for babies and kids, and for doing work on the roof. A group of about ten workers were armed with broom-like paddles. They stood in a lined formation and stomped their feet and paddles in time with their singing in order to compact the mud like roofing material. It combined practicality with fun and beauty. It was especially beautiful with the large golden bell figures beside them and the Potala on the hill behind them.

My plan was to visit Nam Tso, a large holy lake about 240 kilometers (150 miles) north-west of Lhasa, for a few days. Getting out of town soon turned into a pain in the neck.

I caught a rickshaw to the bus station in the morning. But it was the wrong bus station, so I caught another rickshaw to the right station only to find that the drivers going to Damzung, the nearest town to the lake, wouldn't take me. They feared that traffic police would catch them with a foreigner in a closed area, and they would be in serious trouble. No amount of reassurance that Damzung was open to foreigners would placate them and they left without me. Mildly frantic I did a round of the tourist agents, hoping that I could hop on a tour just for the transport to Danzung. But I would have to pay the full two day tour cost just for the ride. I went out on the street and hailed a taxi. The driver looked a little shocked at a 200 kilometer (125 mile) fare but was up for the drive.

The road to Damzung was the Tibet-Qinghai highway, the main route between China and Tibet from the north. It was also the route of the controversial, brand new, never used, railway line from mainland China.

There was no doubt that the railway line was an expensive engineering marvel. It crossed over a 5,072 meter (16,640 feet) high pass, spent nearly 90% of its distance above 4,000 meters (13,000 feet), and necessitated a cooling system to prevent the permafrost, that half the track rested on, from thawing in the summer. The section I followed was a long series of elevated bridges above the valley below. One bridge was long enough that it had 66 towers (they were numbered) holding it up. Another section avoided a gorge in the valley by a tunnel about 5 kilometers (3 miles) long. There were stations in the middle of nowhere, cell phone towers, huge cuttings and enormous embankments.

What was not so certain was the impending impact on the Tibetan people. While decreasing transport costs for goods by 75% it could also deposit in Lhasa 2,500 Chinese tourists and immigrants per day, leaving the Tibetans feeling even more marginalized and outnumbered than they already had been. The Tibetans had seen little benefit from the building of the line, as less than 10% of the workers were Tibetan, and in operation, few of the workers on the train would be Tibetan. The $4.1 billion spent on construction was more than the Chinese had spent on Tibetan hospitals and schools in the 50 years of occupation. It was a further, and very significant, step in the dilution and degeneration of the Tibetan culture and people.

The highway rose up onto a vast lonesome grassland plateau. It ran alongside the 7,000 meter (23,000 feet) high Nyenchen Tonglha Range that spilled glaciers far enough to be seen below the low-slung clouds. The driving though had been perpetually horrific. Like the driving in many non-western countries, the only rule was that there were no rules. It was fast, and alarming. When I got out in Damzung I gave a sigh of relief that I was still alive.

Nam Tso lay on the opposite side of the Nyenchen Tonglha from Damzung and my intention had been to walk over a high pass via a dirt road that carried yak trains. But progress had preceded me and the road was now paved. I was so set on completing the loop hike over two passes to the lake and back to Damzung I just kept walking anyway.

The landscape expanded even further to the north as I rose up west towards the pass. On an immense river flat thousands of animals grazed, black dots disappearing into the distance. It was easy to imagine the expanse extending the thousand kilometers to the north side of the Tibetan Plateau. The road climbed steadily over smooth grass slopes and then into a narrower gorge. The skies cleared, the road was empty and I waved to friendly road workers doing meaningless tasks. At about 4,950 meters (16,200 feet) I found a camp spot of yak mown grass below the road, by the stream, with a fine view down the valley.

Thirty minutes of hiking in the morning and I was on top of La Ken La at 5,190 meters (17,030 feet). I became the center of attention of a small group of Tibetan fellows who sold prayer flags to passers-by. I left the road in the pass and followed the valley down the other side and climbed a small hill to a great view over the surrounds. On the summit were prayer flags, blond yak hair, and a pile of yak horns. Nam Tso, 70 kilometers (43 miles) long and 30 kilometers (19 miles) wide, was an ocean of deep blue surrounded by dry ridges, hills and mountains. Far in the distance was my destination, the small isthmus of Tashi Do, protruding into the lake. I soaked in the view for an hour.

I set off down into the view, cutting a line straight across the wide expanse of grassland between the Nyenchen Tonglha peaks and the lake, past yaks and nomad tents. An intimidating thunderstorm loomed up behind me on the range. Fortunately it stayed in the mountains, eventually moving to reveal peaks covered in a new layer of snow. The only glitch in my straight line progress was a bay of the lake which disappeared once I dropped onto the flat plain. I walked over the grassland, that alternated between smooth grass and the rough tussocks, into increasing wetness. A lady, who came out of her tent in response to her barking dogs, told me that I would have to take a long detour around the bay. I followed the edge of dry grass but was soon in a big marsh and hopping from one tussock to another above the goopy standing water. The irritating tussocks were finally showing some benefit. I came out on the other side of the marsh to a greeting of endlessly chatting nomad kids and three big ugly mastiff dogs. They eventually tired and left me to peace as I walked the last few kilometers to Tashi Do.

The settlement at Tashi Do was instantly a raging disappointment. It was another clear case of man taking something beautiful and creating something repulsive. It was a collection of camps, half-assed construction, piles of junk, and haphazard organization amidst sky, lake, mountain range and hills that came to together in an otherwise awesome spectacle. I walked away from the place and camped. It was a gorgeous clear afternoon; late sun caught the central high white peak of the Nyenchen Tonglha. I sauntered along the rocky beach and sat on a rocky point near a mani wall decorated with yak horns.

I wanted to explore the area free of the weight of my pack. I swallowed my sense of aesthetics and checked in at one of the Tashi Do camps, solely for the secure pack storage, and set off to enjoy the lake. First I climbed 200 meters (600 feet) to the higher of the two hills of the isthmus, Tashi Do Chen. Armed with my lightweight camping seat I sat on the summit for three hours soaking in the scene. Thunderstorms quickly grew along the crest of the Nyenchen Tonglha, fueled by monsoonal moisture from the south and the lake below. The line of storms hung for hours on the range, moving slowly to reveal peaks coated in new snow. The lake was left cloud-free, leaving two oceans of blue, above and below, separated by brown grasslands, white glaciated peaks, and the dynamic clouds of the storms. Eagles glided by, small birds darted among the bushes nearby.

I returned to lake level and set off on the short kora around the end of the peninsula. I moved at a snail's pace and then sat for an hour at the end enjoying the solitude and beauty. I returned along the opposite side of the isthmus, to a long mani wall.

Afternoon storms roam the skies above Nam Tso

Mani walls are a typical and traditional feature of the Tibetan Buddhist landscape. They are walls, two meters to over a kilometer long, made of rocks and earth and faced with inscribed stones in an elegant sanskrit script. The script is a repetition of the primary Tibetan mantra, "Om Mani Padme Hum", "Hail to the Jewel of the Lotus." Mani walls are built along roads, trails, rivers, lakes, and in passes. They should be always be passed on the left side, in keeping with the clockwise tradition of Tibetan Buddhism, in accordance with the rotation of the earth and the universe. The size of the script, the rock, and the wall can vary immensely, and they can be painted as well as inscribed. The act of carving or creating a mani stone is an act of devotion, the act of passing it, an act of respect to the gods. It was also a symbol of the piety and devotion of the Tibetan people in general.

Like the prayer flags, I found the mani stones festive, a beautiful way of connecting land with spirit, deed with prayer, natural elements with devotion.

I climbed the lower of the two hills, Tashi Do Chung. The skyscape had evolved through the day as a succession of thunderstorms wandered out across the sky only to dissipate in the dry air, or to rain as virga. Later in the day, a solid line of dark clouds had built above the low range to the north of the lake. A stiffening breeze seemed to be pushing it towards me. A large black vulture rode the currents above me, below me an immature vulture sat on a ledge keeping a weary eye out for me.

The next morning I set off to walk back to Damzung. I would take a different way back, climbing over the spine of the Nyenchen Tonglha at what would be my highest pass so far, Kong La at 5,410 meters (17,750 feet). I would be lucky to have a trail of any kind.

I followed the long sweeping beach that joined the isthmus to the mainland. There were geese, other birds, and the early morning light. I returned to the grass and climbed the almost imperceptible grade of the alluvial fan that radiated out from the mouth of the valley that led to the pass. The mountain's cloud was already growing, ahead it appeared ominous, while behind me, back over the lake, it was just another glorious sunny day.

I began to receive visitors. Two kids ran down from a nomad camp to greet me. Their initially shy demeanor soon changed and they began to ask for edible handouts. Soon after those fellows gave up and went home two others joined me. They didn't even talk to me, rather they just followed me and made the same unintelligible high pitched call over and over, which was both puzzling and irritating. They followed me a long way before I gestured that I wanted them to go.

The valley narrowed, steepened, the going becoming rougher. I stopped and was joined by three young herders in traditional clothes. Unlike their down-valley counterparts these fellows were curious, innocent, and undemanding. They sat and watched but asked for nothing. They pulled out pouches of moist tsampa from inside their chubas, repeatedly offering me some. We smiled and enjoyed hanging out together without the unpleasant demands and endless chatter of the kids below.

Further up I came to the last place to camp before the pass. I considered stopping but the clouds had all moved out and, by this time, I was only 250 meters (800 feet) below the pass. I made hay and continued on with the anticipation of doing something big late in the day.

The pass was so wide, level and long that it had two summit cairns, one at each end. There was a fine view to a line of craggy peaks down the valley on the other side. Shortly after starting down I heard singing and whistling and was joined by a couple of young nomad men in chubas and cowboy hats. We talked and continued down the river together. They stopped to smoke and I went ahead. The geology had changed as I crossed the pass, the red bands of rock had changed to grey, the landscape was steeper, rockier, the peaks craggier and more glaciated. I was running out of light.

I was rejoined by one of the nomads and he began asking for things; medications, photos of the Dalai Lama, a look through the binoculars I did not have. I found a camp with a grand view over the impressive valley of peaks, glaciers, and nomad camps far below. After hanging with me for a long time, I asked my nomad to leave so I could camp in peace. He refused and continued to stay. The tension began to increase as I repeatedly asked him to go, and he continued to stay. There was no mistaking my desires but I could not understand his motives. In retrospect I should've just held my ground in spite of my increasing heat, but I picked up my pack and headed further down the valley, although it meant getting closer to the nomad tents, something I wasn't too happy about.

By the time I hit the next water and level ground I was between two nomad tents and was almost immediately surrounded by a group of curious nomads. They later left, but after I had dinner, another group took up position. They stayed for a while before leaving me in peace.

Initially I thought that the motive of my nemesis concerned warning me about the poor camp site I had selected. Later I came to realize that what he wanted was for me to continue, to camp next to the nomad tents so that everyone in town could come down and check me out. I had fallen for his plan.

I had chosen a method of travel that did not involve a lot of privacy. From the moment I got on the bike, or put on my hiking shoes, to the moment I got off, I was in the public view, fully immersed in the environment and totally available to anyone along the way. It was much of the appeal. Indeed it was the point, the lure and attraction of cycling. But I drew my lines.

After a long day on the road, hard up against the landscape and its people, I did just want a little peace, to rest and regain sanity and calm. This is usually not a problem in western countries. Western people know about privacy, indeed they can be pretty stiff and focused, absorbed in their own worlds. In non-western countries they have a different relationship with privacy. Huge populations, vast extended families, and cramped living conditions, leaves most non-western people with minimal needs for personal space, or at least a totally different concept of it. That many of them live simple, uncomplicated lives, with low sensory impacts, and little knowledge of the world beyond their own leaves them inherently curious, especially of rich white folks with all sorts of fancy equipment, clothing, and gizmos.

Camping was one of the riskier aspects of travel. It involved a lot of time in one place, so I was always went to a lot of trouble to find the best location possible, one that ensured safety, but also peace and solitude. I didn't want to be the center of attention for the entire village. Camping to me was like drinking. When I camped alone, I preferred to be by myself.

It rained through most of the night and I woke concerned about river crossings without bridges I was sure I would have to make. Snowline had dropped to about 1,000 feet above the camp. Environmentally my decision to cross the pass yesterday had been a good call. Culturally, it was a different story.

The walking was rough over boulders and tussock grass, as I followed the stream, which was easily forded after all, below huge cliff faces that rose into the low clouds. Lower down I found a trail which contoured out of the valley to avoid a canyon further downstream. I came out on an undulating meadow with views out over the wide valley surrounding Damzung. I was joined by another young nomad, this one was peaceful, quiet, friendly and non-demanding. Tibetan nomads varied as much as any other type of people. There was far more variation between individuals than between peoples.

I walked down off the ridge and cut as straight a line as possible across the gentle slopes for Damzung, scattering dozens of pikas back into their holes as I went. Plowed fields, irrigation canals, and fences forced me off my line and on to an old airstrip, which I followed into Damzung.

An hour on the main highway and I had a bus all the way back into Lhasa. It was relaxing and easy, the land slipping by to the tune of western-style Chinese music videos that were indistinguishable from sappy teenage pop songs in the west, except for the language. And it was a whole lot less frightening than the taxi ride out from Lhasa. I just traded that fear for a kid throwing up in the opposite seat.

Spaced evenly along the nearby railway were guards protecting the track prior to the train's grand opening in a few days.

I spent a couple more days in Lhasa which, like many a town before it, had undergone a transition for me.

With time, and my subsequent visits, it made a progression from a new exciting novelty, with most of my time devoted to enjoying the new sights, people, atmosphere, to that of a service center. With services and supplies that would be completely unavailable anywhere else in the country, it was a place to get things done, to clean and wind down after the last forays into the country, and prepare and wind up for the next round. And the next round would return me to the bike, to continue the journey west on a converging course with the Himalaya.

The most important item on the list was food. Food had been major issue in Eastern Tibet, where poor supply had left me wilted and drained, the energy burnt far outweighing the energy consumed. With a selection of large supermarkets and stores, I was able to find an assortment of palatable options. By the time I was done buying, my panniers were bulging, more than enough to get me to the next significant town of Gyantse.

With everything ready for the ride west I wandered down to the Barkhor for one last kora and a soak in the late day pilgrim parade. Like all the other visits it was a magical experience of peaceful exercise and devotion, of purpose and spirituality. After two weeks of being in and out Lhasa, the town had quickly taken on the role of home base, assuming a certain comforting familiarity in a world of wild, exciting and different. With my imminent departure the next morning, the pendulum was quickly swinging back the other way and I was already missing what tomorrow would be, behind me. It felt like the whole adventure was beginning again. I was setting off anew and I had to go through a whole other round of pre-adventure apprehension and nerves. It was a gentle tug of war between the desire to stay with the homey and familiar, versus the desire to reach out into the exciting and new. It had happened many times before, I knew it well, and the familiar always lost out. It also happened on the few occasions when I would meet friends, either new that I had met along the way, or those that came to visit me from the past. After a few days of being together there would always be this slump in my psyche on their departure, when the solitude and loneliness would slap me in the face. It would take a day of travel down the road for the strong world adventurer to overcome the emotional romantic. Then I would be fine and cruising across the world, loving what I did.

4

Central Tibet

I cycled slowly out of Lhasa, past the Potala and the pilgrims that lined up out the front, prostrating to the palace. I followed a long wide boulevard of a street through the characterless and Chinese west side of Lhasa. It was clearly a big day. Lined along the road were police, one every 200 meters (600 feet), both sides, all the way to the edge of town. Tomorrow the first train ever to come to Lhasa was scheduled to arrive. Today the president of China, and a fleet of high ranking officials, were flying in from Beijing in preparation for the occasion.

I passed under an enormous 12 meter (40 foot) high sign that stretched across above the eight lanes of the road. Against a panoramic scene of the brand new railway bridge across the Kyu Chu was written in three languages, "Qinghai---Tibet railway---a road of happiness, hope and harmony and golden opportunity". How ironic I thought, for everyone but the Tibetan people.

It was clear that the Tibetans just wanted to be left alone, to herd their yaks, do their koras, have their own commerce, progress into the future in their own good time, and to have the Dalai Lama alive and well and ruling Tibet from the Potala. I too really wanted for that, for these humble, friendly and devoted people to have rule over their own land and lives. But I really didn't give them much of a chance, ever. The arrival of the train signaled a whole new era in commitment and control over Tibet and its people by the Chinese. And the Chinese weren't about to throw that away or hand it over.

The Free Tibet movement had been alive and active in Tibet, India and the west for decades. There were the bumper stickers, the Tibetan national flags, the Tibetan prayer flags that decorated the homes and communities of those few people who knew or cared. There was the Dalai Lama who toured the world to give lectures, to attend meetings, and give speeches about Buddhism, the Tibetan plight, what could happen in the future, and what he wanted for the Tibetan people. But the Chinese had rapidly gone from isolationist and untouchable to incredibly powerful and untouchable. They had propelled themselves into being the second biggest economy, the second most powerful nation on the planet, and they even owned a lot of the debt of the most powerful country. It wasn't a democratic regime that could eventually change and take a different course. Tibet , a country with just a few million people tucked away on some remote corner of the planet, had no power, no oil, no reason for anyone of power to do anything powerful in contradiction against its most powerful overlords. The Chinese had sunk billions into Tibet, building roads, railway lines, homes, towns, a new Lhasa. They had the opportunity to milk billions from its resources.

Humanity has always been, and always will be, a work in progress. It is in a perpetual state of flux. It is the very embodiment of the adage that the only constant is change itself. And the history of humanity has always been the history of man's inhumanity to man. Humanity has been aggressive, and violent, and self centered, since it dropped out of the trees. History is the story of one act of aggression, one war, one act of violence after another, separated by periods of peace and growth. Thousands of years of so-called civilization has not seemed to help humanity come to grips with its hard wired sense of aggression and brutality; the 20th century was by far the most violent in history.

In the process of development, humanity has ebbed and flowed, civilizations and cultures have come and gone. They have been created by desire, strength, greed, expansion, and technological innovation. They have been destroyed by over population, invading cultures and environmental deterioration. Ruins all over the world are testament to lives, cultures, civilizations and stories that modern cultures learn about, but refuse to learn from. Man has not learned, nor will it ever, that there might be a better way than the millenniums of injustice, violence and aggression that has characterized its history. The innocent and the powerless have always been the victims of the behavior and actions of the rich, powerful and influential, be they women, children, the poor, animals and ecosystems, or quiet unarmed cultures like the Tibetans. The Tibetan situation was just another brick in the wall of man's continued egotistical progress at the expense of others. The Chinese, considering their violent history, could learn from the Tibetans' peaceful life of devotion on top of the world, rather than trying to destroy it. But then, that just wouldn't be human.

Cycling out of Lhasa I came to the intersection between the road north to Golmud and the road west to Nepal. It was swarming with police and I thought that they may not let me continue. I just kept cycling. Vehicles were prevented from entering the road and those on the road were forced off. I had the road to myself, which seemed like a good arrangement. It was only temporary. Five kilometers (3 miles) down the road, passing police told me to get off the highway. The authorities were clearing the entire road, 75 kilometers (47 miles), of everything that moved, from the Lhasa airport in the Yarlung Valley, to Lhasa. I joined a group of vehicles and folks parked on the side of the road. Half an hour later, a twenty-vehicle motorcade came whizzing by. It was the dignitaries, the Chinese president and his buddies, coming into Lhasa to officially welcome the train. It would be a big Communist Party picnic bash. Once they passed, everyone quickly jumped back on the road.

I waited for the resulting blitz of traffic to pass, and lost even more traffic with the turnoff to the airport. The rest of the day was a peaceful ride along quiet roads. I intersected with the Yarlung Valley and continued upstream to a long narrow bridge over the river, complete with guards. Further up, kids from nearby villages rushed up to the road to greet me. Some ran along side, grabbing my panniers, some stood alongside the road with hands extended hoping for a high five, others stood in front of my on-coming bike, some were naked having just run up to the road from an unappealing muddy swimming hole.

After I left the kids the road began to climb. I had turned off the main road west from Lhasa, that ran through Shigatse and on to the Tibetan border, the so-called Friendship Highway, named for the supposed alliance between China and Nepal. I would take the scenic route over a couple of high passes and through Gyantse to rejoin the Friendship in Shigatse. For the time being anyway it looked like I was going to have smooth pavement clear through to the top of the first pass, Kampa La. The road wound up the side of the Yarlung Valley. It was hot going in the intense sun. I camped above the road, out of sight, part way up.

With the new smooth pavement it was a relatively easy climb, two hours more, to the summit. Along the way I was passed by fleets of the day's tourist vehicles. At the top, at 4,990 meters (16,370 feet), there was a log jam of them madly taking photos. I sailed down into the view on the other side. Below me was Yamdruk Tso, one of the four holy lakes of Tibet. The road dropped to the water's edge with a delightful, easy smooth ride along the shoreline, past homes nestled behind alcoves of the lake, across steep brown grass valley sides, and above the curving arm of deep turquoise water.

I climbed away from the lake only to rejoin it soon after, another arm of the lake curling around a hill to meet me. The town of Nagartse was a horrible mess. The whole place was under construction, the road covered in dust and dirt. Part way through I heard a thwak from my real wheel and stopped to pull a two inch nail out from my rear tire. My flat-free ride through Tibet had come to an end. I fixed the thing with an audience of locals and continued on, only to have to stop again. The nail had made a series of holes and I had to replace the tube.

The road ran towards the mountains, from the gentle slopes around the town, and into a valley heading to the next pass. The pavement ended, and for a while I had smooth comfortable dirt. But then I hit construction and I was down to walking my bicycle around boulders, behind newly-built retaining walls, machinery and men. It occurred to me that the empty road since Kampa La was because the road was closed due to this construction. The valley narrowed, the sides steepened, the road climbed. By the time I found a camp I had views across the valley to minor craggy peaks and hanging glaciers. After dinner a herder came by with his 200 sheep. He stopped to visit, a gentle, smiley, undemanding fellow.

In the morning I continued up the pass, and through periodic construction. The peaks gained in stature, in a variety of earth tones, above the smooth grassy valley, and the glaciers gained in volume. On one side of the 5,000 meter (16,500 feet) pass was a long ridge, over 6,000 meters (20,000 feet), that was an interrupted wall of suspended, yet falling, ice.

I had a feeling there would be trouble ahead. Barely had I gotton off the summit of the pass when I hit a mess of rock and torn up road. There was a tiny settlement where a lady tried to get me to take her baby goat. She was joking. The next 8 kilometers (5 miles) were terrible as construction had laid the road to waste. I was walking often, over rocks, across creeks, down rough tracks; on what was left of the road. I came down a valley and out into a broad high basin dotted with isolated villages and surrounded on one side by smooth ridges, and on the other by an imposing glacial peak. The road improved some, but every culvert, and there were plenty, was gone and I had to walk a narrow, dusty, muddy track around all of them.

The road dropped into a narrow valley and the road deteriorated further. For the next 40 kilometers (25 miles) the road wound down the valley in various states of destruction.

I was well familiar with the Chinese method of road rebuilding. They ripped up 100 kilometers (60 miles) of road at a time and then slowly rebuilt the thing, in no particular order, other than doing all the easy bits first, leaving the more difficult sections, like the bridges and culverts, to the end. Periodically the road was quite decent and I could make reasonable speed, but mostly it was just one piece of ripped up road and rough detour after another.

There were thousands of people working on this road, hundreds of dump trucks carting rock back and forth, and hundreds of various pieces of heavy equipment, air compressors, jack hammers, concrete mixers, generators, tractors and horse-drawn carts. These people were working in appalling, unbearable, conditions, in perpetual clouds of dust, next to machines producing ear piercing noise levels, sloping around in mud, covered in dust, mud, cement, or dirt, lumbering enormous loads of rocks and bags of cement, digging away in caves or holes. They had no hard hats, no ear plugs, no dust masks, no steel-toed boots, no concept of safety. I found it intolerable just to cycle by and these guys were in it all day, every day.

Yet for all this I was greeted by thousands of hellos the entire way down the road. I was the only excitement in the day, a white guy going by on a bike, and they responded the only way they knew how, with the only word of English they knew. And all they got back from me was little more than ignoring. I had soon dropped into a survival mode of interior-focused strength. It was all I could do to get me and my heavy bike through the mess and destruction and intolerable impact. Covered in mud and dust, there was no way I could camp, which meant getting to Gyantse by the end of the day. There was little left over for gazing at the view or social pleasantries. At best I gave them a wave.

Part way down, the road rose to contour above a large reservoir. Track hoes and jack hammers cut away at the cliff face and set explosives. One man helped carry my bike around a machine above a 100 meter (300 foot) drop directly into the water.

Below the dam the road improved and I picked up speed and ease passing gorgeous bright yellow fields below craggy brown cliffs. Even so, every damn culvert was gone and I had to walk rough dirty detours for everyone of them.

I finally came into Gyantse with everything covered in mud and dust. I found a guesthouse where it took four of us, pouring bowls of water over bike and panniers, to get it clean.

Like many a good day off from the road I literally walked a fine line between doing as little as possible and getting out and roaming around the town feeling the atmosphere and experiencing the sights. This usually consisted of walking very slowly and taking lots of long breaks.

Gyantse had a sizable gompa, noted for its even more sizable, and extremely elaborate and detailed chorten. The chorten was the biggest in Tibet, with six stories, dozens of chapels in its walls, 35 meters (115 feet) of height, a rooftop view, and a golden-spired crown. I wandered through the assembly hall and the chorten, and then up the hill behind. Part way up the hill was a large temple, and on the crest was a stone tower with a large blank rock wall from which the lamas hung enormous thangkas on festivals and auspicious occasions. From the tower two crumbling, crenulated, ochre-colored walls ranged down each side to the plain. The wide level valley floor was a sea of green fields that spread from one side of the valley to the other, in total contrast to the surrounding low, almost vegetation free, hills. On one side of the hill was the old Tibetan town. I had walked through the town on the way to the gompa. It was an atmospheric place, narrow alleys radiating out from the gompa, with cows lined up outside the walls of the whitewashed homes, dogs wandering the streets, the place full of atmosphere and charm, rustic and dirty. Beyond the old town was another hill, on the summit of which was the old dzong, fort, and beyond that the new Chinese town, clean organized with its usual lack of character and attraction. Two completely different worlds, cultures and philosophies, just down the street from each other.

The next day's ride to Shigatse was a direct contrast to the ride to Gyantyse. Flat to gently downhill, paved, dry, with an increasing tailwind. It was fast, smooth, fun, and the least topographic ride and scenery of the journey so far. It followed the ever-widening valley downstream with little traffic, and friendly folks. I came out into the Yarlung valley, although I could hardly tell, the expanse was so flat and wide. I was done with the 95 kilometers (59 miles) by 1 pm.

The next morning I set off to do the short kora around the large complex of the Tashilhunpo gompa. Like many a gompa lingkor (sacred path), the kora followed the gompa's exterior walls. It was short, about an hour at most for the average pilgrim. It had such an atmosphere of happy devotion I stretched it out for two and a half hours. A nearly constant procession of pilgrims wound up around the wall spinning their individual prayer wheels, as well as the hundreds of brass-colored prayer wheels built near the wall along the way. They walked by, and under, thousands of prayer flags, passed paintings of Buddha images on boulders, climbed over rocks, and through a tunnel, to the 13-story white tower wall on which were hung massive thangkas during festivals. I looked out over the monastery and its own little town of monastic quarters, temples and busy narrow alleys. Pilgrims made offerings of tsampa at appropriate spots along the kora, bowing to touch their foreheads to auspicious rocks as sheep happily ate the tsampa on the boulders above them. So much of what happened in traditional Tibet was a mutually beneficial arrangement.

Tashilhunpo was the traditional home of the Panchen Lama, the second highest ranking lama in Tibet, after the Dalai Lama. The Panchen and Dalai Lamas have strong influences in the nomination of each other's reincarnated successor. The ninth Panchen Lama died in 1937. With Chinese domination over Tibet in 1951, the Chinese government had forced Tibetan delegates in Beijing to endorse their own selection for the next Panchen Lama, hoping for a puppet Panchen. However, after the Tibetan uprising, and resulting destruction of Tibet by the Chinese, their chosen Panchen Lama spoke out against the Chinese, presenting the Chinese with a 70,000-word manifesto that listed Chinese atrocities in Tibet, and calling for increased freedoms for Tibetans. He spoke out against the Chinese at public gatherings and stated that one day Tibet would reclaim its freedoms. The Chinese rewarded their once - puppet lama with 14 years in jail complete with torture and abuse. After his release in 1978 he continued to speak out against the Chinese, albeit more quietly, until his death in 1989.

His successor was named by the Dalai Lama in 1995 but was promptly arrested by the Chinese. The Chinese then ordered the lamas of Tashilhunpo to choose a government approved candidate, one who was the son of communist party members. Controlling the Panchen Lama was a route for the Chinese to control the successor to the Dalai Lama, putting the Tibetan people under deeper Chinese control.

In the afternoon I climbed the long slender ridge directly behind the gompa, Nyizer Ri. It was a straightforward trailless climb, from the edge of town in the hot sun, over a succession of rocky bumps, to the summit. I spent two hours on the summit enjoying the views up and down the Yalung valley and up the valley that lead to Gyantse. Shigatse, Tibet's second largest town sprawled out over the plain of the Yarlung 400 meters (1,300 feet) below. Closer to the ridge were several clusters of low, dirty white irregular homes of the old Tibetan town. Beyond were the modern high rise, grandiose buildings, long wide avenues, and rows of identical apartment buildings of the Chinese new town.

Pilgrims make the kora around Tashilunpo Monastery, Shigatse spinning prayer wheels as they go.

     I dropped straight down off the south face of the ridge, a tricky winding descent, past upended strata cliffs and gravelly slopes, down to the gompa. On the way back to my accommodation I bought food and money for the next two days ride to Lhatse.

    In Shigatse I had rejoined the Friendship Highway to continue west. I cycled uphill out of town the next morning to the gentlest of passes. It had already rained that morning, and the landscape had a fresh fragrant wetness, with deeper, more vibrant colors, typical of a moist landscape. Gentle cycling continued down into an even broader landscape of fields, massively eroded hillsides and a huge wall of black intimidating clouds dead ahead. A thorough dousing seemed certain. It was great cycling till I caught up with road works. For the next 15 kilometers (9 miles) I fought it out with dump trucks, dust, and bumpy roads. Meanwhile the impending doom of the storm casually moved aside, and I made it through without a drop. Storms abounded as I cycled through central Tibet, but they always moved aside just in time for me to cycle by unscathed.

    I had chosen the summer, and the monsoon, to cycle in Tibet. There were logistical reasons that revolved around work and seasonally-based time off. But most important was that I had to do this entire ride from Dali to Ladakh in the spring-summer-fall season when it was physically possible to do it unencumbered by freezing winter conditions and snow-bound passes. Logically this placed me in Tibet in the middle of summer. The fall may have had better weather than the storm-plagued conditions of summer but I was quite happy to be riding my days periodically dodging storms. The storms added a compelling dynamism to Tibet's vast skies, an excitement to the ride ahead, a feeling of uncertainty of my immediate future, and a powerful beauty to the already astounding scenery. The warmth and long days of the summer brought snow melt, brilliant green and yellow fields, and locals that were out and active, doing koras, tending animals, working in the fields. The life and activity provided the contrast of man's created environment against the stark, yet colorful, dryness of the surrounding hills, mountains and topography. It made for some spectacular cycling.

Pavement resumed and I passed through Gyading, another town under the ugly construction that made it a place to get through as fast as possible. The road wound through hills of muted earth and grass tones, and came out into a broader valley that revealed the road climbing to the next pass on the opposite side. Too late in the day for another round of toil and stiff climb, I found a camp on a river flat, with a wonderful view, and several friendly inquisitive locals who came by to visit. Yet another storm rolled in and I retreated into my tent feeling like I should've gone for a more protected site to camp. The tent flapped in the wind, and danced in the rain, and then the storm was gone.

It was a short easy day to Lhatse, 7 kilometers (4 miles) up to Tropu La (4,440 meters,14,570 feet), and down the gentle valley on the other side. Lhatse was immediately disappointing. I kept thinking, kept hoping, that just once I'd meet a nice Tibetan town that was cute, neat, clean, not under construction, a kind of place that you may just want to stay and not run away from. Almost two months in Tibet and I was struggling, although strong contenders were the old town areas of Gyantse, Bomi, Pasho, Rawok and Benzilan, most of which were encountered long ago. Lhatse was appalling. It was dirty, with revolting pools of water beside the road, areas of mud, rubbish, stinking toilets, and ugly old Chinese buildings lining the streets. Fortunately the guesthouse was the opposite, and since it was arranged around a courtyard, it focused inward.

It was an unfortunate fact that in Tibet there was rubbish scattered across the ground anywhere humans gathered in quantity. I could tell I was approaching some kind of settlement just by the quantity of garbage on the ground, or blowing around with the wind. And it didn't take much, even out in the middle of the grassland, nomads threw cigarette boxes, wrappers and butts on the ground just about anywhere.

Tibet was not alone. Garbage was an almost elemental part of the non-western country landscape. In most of these countries there was almost no environmental ethos, no concept that garbage strewn across the landscape was unhealthy or unattractive. Few places had anything resembling trash cans, or municipal garbage collection. Local people just threw garbage out the window, or off the horse, with no thought to a better way, or correct disposal.

There was a time when it wasn't so different in the west. Being environmentally correct was a learned habit.m Many people had to be trained to dispose of garbage thoughtfully and government bodies had to develop mechanisms and laws to deal with the ever increasing mounds of trash. And people still throw garbage out the window, and drive down deserted tracks to dump trash in the woods. Trash, after all, is an invention of the west.

There was a time when there was no trash. All the byproducts of society were made from easily biodegradable natural products, animal and plant parts, that quickly blended in with the ground and surroundings, or eaten by other animals. It wasn't until a much more modern society that learnted how to make durable trash from plastic, glass, metal, and paper, materials that could last centuries and outlast civilizations, that waste management even mattered. Yet the mindset of that previous millennium still prevailed, people still threw garbage around like it would quickly disappear. Coming to grips with the problem of its own creation took time. The more organized west had developed systems and laws that controlled the populace and managed the waste. The non-west had only barely begun to appreciate that it was even a problem.

Of course the true mark of development and civilization is not to create durable trash in the first place. One parameter of civilization was its relationship with its own environment, to be able to exist in harmony with its surroundings, and the other beings on the planet, while maintaining a level of modern human condition, and environmental health. By this measure humanity had been going backward for quite some time.

I started up the road at 5 AM the next morning. Apparently there was a police checkpoint not far from the edge of town and I wanted to pass early and in the dark. Beyond, it was a 1,200 meter (4,000 foot) climb to a high pass and I wanted to summit before it became too hot. The road was under construction and an early start would minimize dust-coating work and traffic on the lower sections.

There was indeed a checkpoint, there were police, but it was for traffic, not for foreigners, and the guys let the gate up for me to pass. False alarm. Pavement came and went for about 5 kilometers (3 miles) before finally settling in on a doable dirt, rock, and gravel road that ran to the pass summit. I gave up on the headlamp with the increasing light and settled in for the 30 kilometer (19 mile) climb. With the light came the workers and I was soon riding along a road to a continual string of hellos. The road followed a stream as it climbed through a gorge and out into a vast basin dotted with nomad tents and animals. I took a break at half way, then at 5 kilometer (3 mile) intervals.

Gyatso La (5,220 meters, 17,126 feet), was the highest cycling pass of the journey, and of my life. While a good solid 5-hour climb, it was far easier than the 4,000 meter (13,000 feet) passes early in the journey in Eastern Tibet. I had acclimatized, I had days off, I was eating, I was feeling normal, I wasn't sick.

A huge sign over the pass announced that I was entering Qomolungma Nature Reserve and dozens of prayer flags extended to tundra festooned with flowers. The morning had dawned totally clear, unusual for the recent days.

Qomolungma, or Chomolungma, ("holy mother" or "goddess of mountain", depending on who is doing the translating) is the Tibetan word for Mount Everest. I had been hoping for my first glimpse of the illustrious peak to the south from Gyatso la, but it either wasn't in line of sight or the distant light puffy clouds of the mid-morning were sitting on the peak. The view to the north felt very much like the Tibetan plateau. It was a long thin horizon of a view, over countless small ridgetop bumps of grass and rocks, that were really mountains shrunk by distance, that extended into the distance for 150 kilometers (100 miles) or more. It felt like it went on forever, in all directions, as though the plateau was limitless, smooth enough that I could just walk into it and go for months.

I rolled the bike off the road on the south side and lay on the grass for an hour enjoying the view and warm sun. I could've easily done another hour.

It was to become another construction-destroyed descent, although not nearly as bad as the road to Gyantse. The road probably went through about 50 unexplainable surface changes, alternating between a variety of rough rock and dust, and something that was quite smooth and enjoyable. I passed legions of workers and was passed by vehicles that sent up clouds of dust and sometimes forced me off the road.

The valley into which I descended had more variety than the usual, with smooth slopes, long cliff bands, eroded gullies, and broad side valleys. Lower down villages appeared, there was a nunnery, and a hermitage at the base of a cliff. Located high above the valley on cliff tops and lofty perches, were many small ruins, probably forts. I stopped for the night at a settlement at the turn off to Shegar.

The next morning I left the luggage at the guesthouse and rode up to Shegar on a delightfully light and zippy bicycle. Seven kilometers of pavement brought me past the Chinese part of the town to the old Tibetan town nestled at the base of a steep rocky hill. It was a quintessential old-world Tibetan town, a timeless place that seemed unchanged over the centuries. It was a tight cluster, a maze, of clean white homes with piles of cut and split firewood and yak dung cakes, that fueled cooking and heating stoves, sitting atop tall walls. Twisty, narrow alleys led to hidden doors decorated with images of sun and moon.

The air was filled with the smells and aromas of people and animals, dung and wood. Folks sauntered along rubbish-free alleys on errant missions. Rooftops, places of storage and family activity, were clean and organized

I followed a path that was cut into the cliff, climbed past a colorful Buddha image painted on the rock, walked through a couple of arching entranceways, to a gompa perched in a cup of an angled ledge on the side of the hill. The gompa was a collection of white buildings and an ochre-colored temple that was catching the early morning light. Friendly monks directed me up the hill to the dzong. I climbed up the rocky slopes to the first of a series of ruined stone towers and walls that stretched up the slope perhaps 300 meters (1,000 feet) to the summit fortress that sat atop a band of cliffs on the spiky crest of the hill. I wound up through the ruins perched on the 60 degree slope, in the brilliant morning light. I climbed past the towers, each of which was about 6 to 15 meters (20 to 50 feet) tall, past the remains of old buildings and crumbling walls to ever-expanding views. Part way up, I looked to the south and there, sure enough, was the white triangle of Everest, along with its brother Lhotse, looking grand and distant. Sun had crept into the valley below. A smooth valley curved gracefully north, a gentle inclined plain covered, earth-tone hill to earth-tone hill, in lush green fields with clusters of homes and villages. It was all spectacular and perfect. This indeed was the Tibet I had been looking for.....rough, wild, beautiful, the elements and the humanity combining harmoniously, all at the same place, and at the same time.

I slowly made my way down through ruins, the monastery, the old town, and out into the fields of the valley to look up at the white gompa, and the ruins that blended into the hill side. I rode back along the road passing little wooden carts pulled by over-worked ponies with red woolen tassels on their heads, with cute families, or piles of kids, in the back.

I reunited with my load and continued on. Not far down there was a checkpoint, there were police and they looked at my passport. Strictly speaking, as far as I could make out, I was supposed to have a permit to be on this road. And, as before, there was no way I was going to get one as a solo foreign cyclist. So I had just loaded up and rode down the Friendship anyway and avoided the checkposts where I could. So far it had worked out well, one arm of the authorities didn't know what the other arm was doing, and I had made it this far without a hassle, other than a few early morning rides in the dark. The fellow returned my passport and let me though. Another few kilometers down the road I passed the turnoff to Everest base camp and was happy to see the end of the tourist traffic that had periodically plagued me.

I entered a long valley that was drier, less vegetated and less hospitable than almost anything so far on the plateau. The valley alternated in greenness between wide meadows, sparse fields and dry baking valley floor. There was the significant river, the Ra Chu, and series of lakes, that created green and made life possible. There were horses, yaks, goats and villages that seemed to eek out a living from nothing at all. There were even a few villages of brand new concrete Tibetan style homes. I often wondered about those Han Chinese that had been relocated from mainland China. They had spent their life in a lush wet green landscape in one of the heavily populated eastern provinces, and then uprooted to a place that was a lonely, remote, barren outpost, thin on water, life, people, and air. Perhaps they felt like some poor soldier in the French Foreign Legion, who wakes up to find himself stationed at the end of the world, perhaps wondering what they had done wrong to deserve this.

A long way up the valley I rounded a corner into the wide plains of Tingri. In the distance was a line of massive glaciated peaks rising into the clouds, the main spine of the Himalayas. Tingri was a typical, uninspiring, windswept, wild-west Tibetan town.

The guesthouse in which I stayed was little more than lines of rooms arranged around a football field sized dirt courtyard. The toilet was the typical Tibetan dire and unappealing hole in the ground that was more a thing to be endured and was always the low point of the Tibetan home/guesthouse experience. The dining and common living area, on the other hand, was the apex, the joy, of finding oneself in the local's home environment. These rooms were large magnificent places, lined with benches that were covered in plush rugs and cushions on which folks sat. On the floor parallel to these benches were elaborately and brightly painted coffee tables. The walls were painted with circular designs and bands of color and decorated with paintings and wall hangings. There may be cabinets, also brightly painted, and this one in Tingri had a huge imposing iron stove. They were places that beckoned, that invited prolonged enjoyment, to eat, write, relax and watch the family relate. Too bad Tibet had such a poor relationship with plumbing.

The view south from above Tingri, across the Ra Chu plain to Cho Oyu

Sensing a good view I woke at the first light of the next morning and walked up to the top of Gangyar Ri, the low ridge that rises from the edge of Tingri. I sat on a wall that was some part of a display by the nature reserve. The early sun slowly cast its mellow glow over the plain and the peaks beyond.

Directly below the hill a stream of livestock was being herded lazily out to the well-grazed grasslands of the valley. Extending south was the wide plain of the Ra Chu, a patchwork of green and yellow fields. Growing out of the plain were several small bumps that cast long shadows across the plain. In the distance, smooth hills led up to the peaks. Directly to the south of me, and straddling the Tibet-China border, was Cho Oyu, one of the world's fourteen 8,000 meter (26,000 feet) peaks, a triangle of white against the subdued skies. Further east and looking smaller was Everest. The panorama was sublimely magnificent.

Tibet was not short of a contrast. Scrappy little towns sat in a landscape that swung between starkly barren and arrestingly beautiful. Warm, friendly people created wonderful interior environments that lulled one into lingering, but made towns that promoted speed and exit strategy. Life and growth, lush and green, sat just on the other side of irrigation canals from parched aridity. The complexity of monastic Buddhism with its bewildering deities, lamas, images and poses competed with the simple elemental life of the Tibetans, surviving with animals, grain, family and a tough unyielding environment. It was a land that went on and on, vacillating between repetitive similarity and a new view, a new idea, a new experience, with every bend.

I repacked and re-sorted, eliminating everything I couldn't live without for a few days. I lightened my load for what was sure to be some of the roughest going yet, the ride up a four-wheel-drive track to Mount Everest base camp. I removed enough gear that I could eliminate the front panniers. I moved the tent to the front but while I was much lighter I was also very unequally balanced. I had almost always ridden with front and rear panniers, and internally scoffed at cycle travelers I had seen with only rear. Having only rear panniers meant that all the weight of the luggage, most of the weight of the human, and the drive force all sat on the rear wheel. Bad for the rear wheel, lousy for the handling, and even worse for managing the bike when you weren't on it, the whole thing just wanted to fall over backwards. Still at this point I couldn't do anything about it. It was quite a long way to a bike store. I loaded up with food and set off.

For a while I made good time up the edge of the Ra Chu plain, at the base of the barren hills. There were river crossings, sand, and rocks that were manageable and a tad easier with less baggage. I came to a signless fork and hesitated, even walking back and forth between the choices further up the track. Fortunately the one I chose was the correct one. I climbed to a small ridge with a view over the river and the vast angled plains and hills of glacial debris that the river, and past glaciers, had brought down from the Himalayas to the south. I was back to a stark inhospitable landscape.

I turned up a side valley, the grade increased, the road deteriorated, and my speed dwindled. Progress was hindered even more by the dreaded afternoon wind that came down the valley. I could see the track coming down the broad slopes ahead. At one point I had to ford a deep, fast-moving side stream, as it raced over a rough alluvial fan of jumbled rocks. I walked it, bracing bicycle and legs against the flow. Further up I took a short cut, that clearly the 4WDs were using, and had to walk that too, the angle slowing me down and forcing me to stop every 20 meters (60 feet) to regain composure. I climbed to a lip in the valley, thinking that it was the pass summit, only to find that it was a step in the landscape. The track swung wide into another, higher, gentle valley for a whole other round of climbing. Eventually the track climbed out of the valley and onto the wide smooth expanse of the pass at 5,060 meters (16,600 feet).

I looked around at the austere geologic wildness that surrounded me.....remote, vast, windswept, high, cool, dry and unfriendly. Beautiful but tough, a place to feel small and meaningless. Just to the south, three glaciers hung on a small peak. Above and beyond, Cho Oyu rose into the clouds.

The descent was very gentle and the road surface improved the further I went. About 6 kilometers (4 miles) down I camped, sheltered by a small ridge with views to two glaciated peaks.

Scattered out across the landscape, inhospitable as it was, were the camps of the drokpas, nomads, living in their yak-wool tents. And at every one of them, where I saw people that were close enough to the track, the folks had their hands out begging. It had been a common occurrence along the Friendship Highway. In Lhasa it had been almost the norm and I had gotton heartily sick of it. But it hadn't occurred at all in eastern Tibet. Considering that there were plenty of foreign tourists in Lhasa, along this track, and along the Friendship Highway, and very few through Eastern Tibet, I presumed that it was the presence of tourists that accounted for the change in local behavior.

Giving gifts to the locals in Tibet, and similar poor non-western countries, is a surprisingly thorny issue. Foreign tourists often feel that they are contributing to the plight of these people, who are so much worse off than themselves, by giving gifts of usually money, sweets or pens, as they pass by. The recipient gets a present, the tourist feels like they are contributing, the act of giving providing a short-term fix, placating any guilt they may have at the disparity in wealth as they pass by on their hectic tour schedule. But these gifts have unwanted side effects. It had the strong tendency to turn the locals, particularly the kids, into a bunch of annoying beggars. Many years previous I had trekked through the Nepalese Himalaya. In so many villages along that route I was accosted by kids, sometimes in packs, with their hand out, yelling "One pen, one pen". I called it Himalayan One Pen Disease. Clearly tourists had gone by handing out pens to many of the kids, and handing out the expectation that all tourists would walk by and hand out pens. Giving out a pen had a short term benefit of the kid having a pen to do schoolwork or to draw, but kids then saw tourists as little more than bearers of gifts. Giving out sweets to folks who probably didn't have a toothbrush, toothpaste, and perhaps only the most basic appreciation of oral hygiene ,was just promoting dental decay issues.

It was a bit like foreign international aid. While satisfying the immediate need of feeding needy people, foreign aid created the expectation in the recipients that foreign countries would always feed them. All the locals had to do was just sit around waiting for the next handout. It has become widely accepted that foreign aid as handouts was rarely a good long term solution, it just created a culture of dependency. It was far better that the aid take the form of providing mechanisms whereby the local people could feed and house themselves, such as irrigation, micro-hydro plants, or education.

Tibet though was a culture that included the giving of alms, as I has seen on the Saga Dawa kora. Wealthy Tibetans gave to poor Tibetans as happens in India, Nepal, even in western countries. Until humanity could figure out a better way, poverty and disparity was an inherent part of society. The poor did what they could to survive even if it meant begging. Some rich felt compelled to help those in need, even if it had some unpleasant side effects. On a grander scale the wealthy supporting charities, the arts, and a host of humanitarian and environmental organizations was a basic component of western society. Without these donations such organizations would not exist. Where does one draw the line?

Traveling through these societies, my experience was inevitably tainted by begging experiences. My interaction with locals was always richer if there was no expectation or expression of wanting something, other than an exchange of words, ideas, companionship, or goodwill. With begging I just wanted the people to go away. Without it I could hangout, communicate any way we could, and I walked away with a warm glow of cross cultural interaction. I'm sure that the tourists who handed out presents had no idea of the repercussions of their actions. It seemed to me that the benefits and rewards of a fine experience between two people of vastly different backgrounds was far more valuable than the short term fix of a material gift.

I continued down the valley in the morning past the village of Zomphu, with its chorus of roaming barking dogs that had me off the bike and skirting the place. I came to the Dzakar Chu, the river that drains the north side of Mount Everest, and joined the main dirt road that followed the valley from the Friendship Highway up to the base camp. The road was instantly a bummer. The next 15 kilometers (9 miles) was horrible, the road a mess of rocks, corrugations and 4WDs that flew by without any consideration, respect, distance, or the clouds of dust they sent up around me. Rounding a corner I came upon Rongphu Gompa, and a large Chinese Hotel.

Rongphu gompa was an iconic landmark that sat on the edge of the valley with a view of the mammoth north wall of Everest at the head of the valley. The scene of gompa, chorten, prayer flag, and mountain graced many a Himalayan climbing, photography and guidebook for half a century. But the hotel, another ugly building below the gompa, and the tourists stole from the sense of arrival and grandeur. Fortunately vehicles were prohibited from going further up the valley. I shared the track with the horse-drawn carts that took the tourists up to base camp.

Part way up to the camp I came upon 23 bharal sheep, the first wild animal I had seen in Tibet that was bigger than a marmot. They seemed placid, if a little skittish. The track climbed around some moraine hills and came out at Everest base camp. I was instantly crushed. It was Tashi

Do all over again. Lining the end of the track was a line of makeshift tents that housed trinket stands, tea stalls, sleeping quarters (labelled hotels), with folks outside touting their goods. There was garbage on the ground, ugly toilet blocks nearby, and clusters of tents on the opposite side of a shallow pond. Surrounded by rough moraine, steep valley sides, and rules prohibiting further progress, I had to join the tents.

The next morning I left the tent and set off to wander up the valley. Passing a sign proclaiming a $200 fine for anyone going up the valley without permission, I wasn't quite sure how far I would get before being turned around by some overzealous park ranger. I walked across a wide expanse of gravel on the valley side, then up the narrow ablation valley between the mountain side and the long thin ridge of the lateral moraine. I climbed up onto the crest of the moraine, with continual views of Everest, and out over the wide expanse of the Rongbuk Glacier. There was nothing clean and white about the glacier that curled down from the west side of Everest. The glacier itself was buried beneath a chaotic mess of mounds of rocks, curving walls of dirty black ice and small lakes, some dirty and brown, others in various shades of turquoise. Yet the glacier was moving and alive. Periodically rocks rolled off mounds, down icy cliffs, and into the lakes, the sound reverberating around the steep mountain walls.

I turned up a side valley, the East Rongbuk, following a narrow trail that climbers used to access Camp One and the route up the north face of Everest. I climbed quickly across the rocky slopes above the dirty torrent of the creek. The view of the Rongbuk Glacier shrank behind the narrower valley but grew to include Pumori, a significant peak also straddling the Tibet-Nepal border. Pumori, with its bulky triangular form was, in some ways, more impressive than Everest. I was, by then, right under the massive north face of Everest. It rose 3,600 meters (12,000 feet) in one pitch to the summit. The climbers hiked to the base of the eastern end of the wall, followed a well-placed natural ramp onto the face and climbed onto the summit ridge, which they then followed west to the summit. Easier said of course. Far up that face were the dead and frozen remains of many a climber, including Mallory, one of the peak's first climbers.

I came to a flat area where rocks had been cleared for tent spaces. I was still far from Camp One but it felt like progress at around 5,500 meters (18,000 feet). I turned around and wandered back down valley as the afternoon's clouds built up on the peaks. Back at the gravel flats above base camp the stream I had casually hopped across in the morning had turned into a torrent with the warmth of the day and snow melt. I gingerly waded across with bare feet, gravel being swept down the stream bombarding my skin. Most of the tents that had littered base camp were gone. I had a peaceful late afternoon in the sun.

I climbed the moraine ridge behind the camp for the morning sunrise show on Everest. While impressive enough, from that angle most of Everest was back lit and in shadow.

I started down valley on the bike for the ride back the same way I had come to Tingri. While the descent down the valley had the gravitational advantage, the road was no smoother, and the 4WDs were no more respectful. When one gave me the horn I thumped my fist on a side window as it passed. I was only too happy to get the hell off that road and onto the smoother, quieter, 4WD track.

I climbed back up the valley, verbally fought off two dogs in Zonphu, and labored up the roughening track to the pass. The landscape around the pass was equally inspiring, dramatically beautiful, and as intimidating as it had been the first time. At a creek down the other side of the pass I filtered water and was joined by a couple of drokpas, a mother and daughter. They were upbeat, smiling and spinning wool while we exchanged pleasantries. They were lovely, and the exchange sweet and undemanding, as wonderful as other exchanges had been unpleasant. Repeatedly kids ran out from their camps on my way down the valley. They were grubby little things, yelling over and over, intent on touching my bike and everything on it.

Further on I came to the creek crossing I had waded on the way up. The flow had grown with time and fortunately a local came by and gave me a hand, the two of us a match for the strength of the flow.

I came down into the wide expanse of the Ra Chu valley and picked up a healthy tailwind, my speed increased considerably. Further down I caught sight of a bridge over the river that offered a different route back via the village of Choling. Always being up for something different, I took it. It was a terrible mistake. It started out smooth enough, passing the cute village and its green fields. But later it intersected with a raised gravel road that ran up the main valley directly towards Cho Oyu. The road's surface was a mess of river rocks that had been just dropped on the road and graded level. I bounced and jostled the last 7 kilometers into Tingri for a long frustrating hour, emotionally crushed after a long day, having sacrificed my smooth cart track for bicycle agony. I was only too happy to see the lonely streets of Tingri, where dust and garbage were being blown around in the wind.

I took a well-deserved day off in Tingri and spent it eating and organizing, cleaning and repacking, writing and resupplying. The mundane activities of life were a pleasant way to fill up a lazy day while giving the feeling that forward progress was still happening. I poured over a map and analyzed my route. Judging by my map I was almost exactly half way along my journey from Dali to Kargil. and about halfway from Lhasa to Kathmandu. In a few days I would leave Tibet to cross into Nepal into a completely different environment. It was time. Tibet had been outstanding in so many ways, especially the people and the environment, but it had also been incredibly demanding, physically and emotionally, and I was ready to trade in some of the grandeur for something new, different, and perhaps something a little less draining.

Everest and Cho Oyu were there to greet me as I rolled out of Tingri and crossed the plains to the hills to the east. I was soon chased by a dog who took some personal exception to my presence. Two others joined it and I rode out of town hounded by three barking dogs until I was far out of their territory. After 6 kilometers (4 miles) I ran out of pavement, but the surface that followed was the best unpaved road in Tibet. I passed three tractors that were blading the road smooth, but the road surface didn't help with the traffic and there was an irregular stream of disrespectful, speeding 4WDs.

I couldn't believe that I was cycling across Tibet, the rooftop of the world, on crappy unpaved roads, having traffic problems. Was there no place left on earth where a guy could go cycling without being hounded by vehicles? I had thought, in planning this journey, that out in this lonesome isolated place, I would at least have the road largely to myself, that traffic would not be an issue. It wasn't just that the vehicles existed, but it was mostly that they just blasted by, barely moving aside, or slowing down, and as a result left me a cloud of dust and flying pebbles.

In Tibet the main form of travel was 4WDs. Public bus transport was limited to Lhasa and the roads to Shigatse, and north across the plateau to Golmud. Train travel was only just being introduced. There just wasn't much choice. So officials and tourists, western and Chinese, and anyone who could afford it, hired 4WDs that were mostly brand new white Toyota Landcruisers, driven mostly by Tibetans, who I had seen at stops along the way. I felt a certain irony and duplicity in these guys. Being Tibetans they wanted the concern and sympathy of the west and outside world for their plight against the Chinese. But when it came to show a little respect and concern for others it seemed in short supply. I grew to hate these guys, as strong as that sounds, the whole experience of them flying by so contrary to the peaceful ethos of Buddhism and so completely unnecessary.

Long after I was done with the journey, and home, I met up with a friend who handed me a magazine article that she had saved. It was the short story of a tour group that had travelled by commercially organized 4WDs through Tibet. Their driver drove so fast that they eventually asked him to slow down. He did for a little while, then the speed increased, and soon they were ripping along again. They asked him repeatedly to slow down, but every time it was a short term response. Eventually they fired their driver, leaving them stranded in some small village out in the middle of nowhere. They reasoned that that was better than dying in the middle of nowhere. I was not alone in my disdain for these drivers.

The road followed the valley north, then west and then south. The scenery for the entire day was littered with ruins, on hills and valley floors, mostly as tall lumps of wall remnants, but sometimes as more complete towers, complexes, or compounds. There must have been one hundred individual structures, and mostly all once formidable buildings, if the height of the ruins, the wall thickness, and their solid construction was any clue. I stopped for food in the wonderfully named Gutso. The Han storekeeper drew me a map in the dirt showing me passes, distances, and places to sleep on the way to Nyelam, even though I hadn't asked.

Heading south I picked up what had become the predictable afternoon southerly wind. There were a string of villages that were little different from others in Tibet except for the unique and delightfully colorful wall paintings on the homes. The usual whitewashed walls had ochre colored stripes down each corner, around the windows, doors and along the roof edges. Between the windows were two more vertical stripes, one of ochre, and one of grey. It was simple, yet attractive, and gave the villages a little pizzazz out there in the wilds of Tibet.

Out of one of the villages came another trio of terrorizing dogs until a couple of local ladies helped me out.

Further up the road, with the climb to the next pass looming up, I pitched camp, hiding from the wind behind a low ridge of rocks.

It was not the weather for climbing two high passes the next morning. The overnight rain stopped and I rose up the pass towards the low cloud, climbing out of a valley onto the broad, wet, unspectacular, and unfriendly La Lung La (5,030 meters, 16,500 feet). I stopped long enough on the summit to put on my rain jacket and continued down the other side. A short descent brought me to a small settlement of drokpa camps, a road workers depot, and a small house. A friendly old fellow directed me into the house. Inside a stove warmed me and a lady gave me butter tea. She played a cassette tape of a speech of the Dalai Lama. I was at 4,900 meters (16,000 feet) in a tiny house, in the middle of the clouds, on the Tibetan plateau, listening to contraband.

I climbed up onto the mother of all broad expansive passes, Thong La, (5,120 meters, 16,800 feet). An arch of prayer flags went over the road, a little structure of wind-driven prayer flags sat off to the side, appropriately located considering the brisk wind coming out of the south. Two guys lived in a tent selling prayer flags.

I stood essentially on the crest of the Himalayas, on the edge of the Tibetan Plateau, on the divide of two great rivers. To the north was the vast emptiness of the plateau, 1,500 kilometers (900 miles) of dry brown grass, ridges and isolated nomads. To the north, water drained onto the Yarlung Tsangpo, a river that flowed through a Buddhist high altitude desert, to cut through the mountains, to flow out into Hindu India as the Brahmaputra, and then through Islamic Bangladesh into the Bay of Bengal. To the south the water flowed through the Himalaya into a lush, warm, green landscape of abundance and plenty, out onto the teemingly populated plains of Hindu India, to the Ganges River, and into the Bay of Bengal. It was a startling transition, a potent place of delineation.

The so-called longest road descent in the world, from 5,120 meters to 958 meters, (16,800 feet to 3,140 feet) started with 13 kilometers (8 miles) of twisty switchbacks down into the first valley. At the bottom, the grade relaxed enough that the day's afternoon wind became a consuming opposition. It didn't really feel at all like the descent the numbers would have you believe; a rough dirt road, periodic uphills to skirt cliffs and alluvial fans, and a fight into the wind wasn't exactly a thrilling free-wheeling descent. As the 4WDs reappeared it occurred to me that a whole new round of devotion was fueling the traffic. The vehicles were full of Indian pilgrims heading to Mt Kailash in far western Tibet. Kailash was an important Hindu, as well as Buddhist, holy mountain. Devotees of both stripes made the pilgrimage to the mountain to pay their respects and do the kora around its base.

I came down the valley to Nyelam, perched on the side of the Gyu Chu valley, sitting on the cusp between the brown landscape above and the green landscape below.

My last hurrah for Tibet would be a hike up the nearby side valley, the Tsondi Chu valley, to Dara Tso, a low-grade holy lake. The Tsondi Chu led to Shishapangma, the only 8,000 meter (26,000 foot) peak completely in Tibet.

I followed road, then trail, up the valley to Phulok, a collection of stone buildings and fields cut from a boulder field. I climbed a hill to find a wide smooth trail, more akin to a trail in a US national park than in Tibet, and followed it uphill away from the creek. The day's cloud had lifted to reveal a wall of peaks, part of the Jugal Himal, along the crest of which ran the Nepalese border. Glaciers hung from the peaks and moraine ridges ran down into the valley from the base of the wall. I really didn't know where Dara Tso was but the trail followed a valley towards the wall which was fine by me.

I approached the white tent of a nomad, but was still at least 100 meters (300 feet) away, when my presence alerted two guard dogs by the tent. They bolted towards me, unrestrained by rope or owner. One particularly was fast, furious, and bore down on me, teeth bared, unperturbed by my commanding shouts or the couple of rocks I feebly threw at him. He came straight at me and went straight for my leg. The force of the impact pushed me over and I was instantly on my back, squirming to get my legs between him and me, totally prone to whatever the dog wanted to do next. The dog seemed content with his one impact and backed off. By this time the drokpa man had come out of his tent and followed his dog. I got up, the drokpa grabbed his dog and carried it back to the tent. I turned around and gave up on the view of the wall of peaks.

    I immediately went down to the creek and washed my leg. Fortunately, against my usual habit of shorts, I had been wearing pants and the dogs teeth had not cut through the fabric. Instead he had left five holes in my leg, one deep. I put rabies shots on my list of things to do in Kathmandu. Clearly I had been bypassing drokpa camps for good reason.

    I left the wide trail and climbed a moraine ridge to find the surprisingly large Dara Tso peacefully cupped on a wide terrace high on the side of the main valley. Backed by glacial peaks the lake was spectacular in of itself but what held the appeal was the ground around it. My route over the last day of cycling had brought me south towards the Jugal Himal. The monsoon lapped over the mountains, bringing with it a regular supply of rain that didn't make it very far beyond the first valley north of the spine of the mountains. The entire ground surface here was green, with grass, low shrubs, and wildflowers, the air full of the scents of life. After months of barrenness and earthtones the walking was wonderfully colorful, soft and smooth underfoot. I dropped to the water's edge and followed it around, doing a lap of the lake. I passed an area with an impressive collection of prayer flags at the far end of the lake. I followed the moraine ridge that separated the lake from the main, Tsondi Chu valley. This valley was long and straight, and lined with the tallest moraine ridges I had ever seen, rising about 300 meters

(1,000 feet) above the stream. Upstream, huge cliff faces rose into the clouds and beyond, concealed by the clouds, was Shishapangma.

I followed the ridge down through an alpine garden of flowers, shrubs and boulders strewn artistically across the ground. The air was fresh and moist, the views surprisingly spectacular. Being a holy lake, devotees had walked up to the lake and left articles of clothing scattered across the ground as offerings to the deities. While holding some spiritual appeal it looked more like ugly trash.

I wound down to the unappealing town of Nyelam and set to work on my leg, finally putting the small first aid kit I carried to good use.

It was time to go to Nepal. The road climbed briefly out of Nyelam and from there it was all downhill, 2,100 meters (7,000 feet) of descent in 48 kilometers (30 miles) and take the entire day.

The landscape was green right from Nyelam and only gained in lushness and vegetative depth the further and lower I went. The unpaved road cut a gentle, relaxed grade down into a gorge that sliced through the backbone of the Himalayas. The road was cut into the near vertical sides of the gorge with constant views that had me repeatedly stopping to admire the scene and soak up the dramatic change in my surroundings. Moss, grass, bushes, and forest clung to near vertical cliffs and slopes in luxuriance unrestrained by verticality. Long slender waterfalls fell through every nook, crease and fold and in the gorge walls. Some were tiny and wispy and had the most minuscule of drainages, some were thunderous white torrents. Some fell onto the road, one fell over the road entirely, the road cut into the cliff face behind it. Directly below the road, cliffs dropped to the Phu Chu that plummeted over a continuous series of falls and cascades. The gorge sides rose 1,500 to 3,000 meters (5,000 to 10,000 feet) to peaks and visible glaciers. The weather had cleared entirely, the gorge bathed in bright light, the vertical world a brilliant green.

I was agog. The spectacular grandeur of the gorge was accentuated by the sensory explosion of green, life and wetness after months of dry geology. I stopped probably 40 to 50 times in the first 30 kilometers (19 miles).

The gorge relaxed some, the cliffs receding to just plain steep forested valley sides. I came into Zhongmu, the border town. I hit pavement and wound through tight bends through the town that seemed precariously perched high above the valley.

The streets of the town were lined with trucks most just waiting patiently for the next load. Others were in the process of international trade, loads being transferred between Indian TATA trucks and Chinese Dong Fengs. I changed my last Chinese yuans to US dollars and Nepalese rupees and rolled down to immigration. It was painlessly simple and I was soon in the no-mans-land between China and Nepal. I had spent two months in Tibet and for all of it, except for the area around Lhasa, I should've had a permit. I had passed on the permit, preferring freedom, possibility and skullduggery, and made the entire journey unscathed by officials and supposed rules. It was always nice when you could beat the system.

Below immigration, the road was jammed with parked vehicles and hundreds of meters of parked TATA trucks. I had to walk between the lines of vehicles to get through. The road then lost its pavement and dropped through a series of steep switchbacks into the valley. It was clearly the worst road surface this side of Lhatse and I walked down several steep rocky pitches. Was the condition of the road indicative of the Chinese-Nepal relationship, rocky? It was hard to believe that all those trucks came up this road.

I went though one more passport check and crossed the Friendship Bridge over the Phu Chu, the actual border into Nepal. I checked into Nepal at immigration, although they didn't really seem to care, and then made my way down the rocky street crowded with people, lined with cheap ramshackle buildings, across streams that ran across the road. I made it to Tatopani, five kilometers down the road, and called it good. It had been an exhausting day going downhill. I made it into a guesthouse with seconds to spare before the afternoon thunderstorm filled the steep valley.

By dropping 3,300 meters (11,000 feet), crossing a mountain range, and a frontier, the world around me had become a different place. Earth tones had become green tones, aridity had become luxuriance, parched had become saturated, concrete had become wood and brick, the religion had become Buddhist and Hindu, the complexions and faces had become more Indian, the traditional dress had become lighter, more colorful, the air thicker, moister, warmer, and full of the scents of life, decay and spice. I had crossed a frontier, and crossed a road, to cycle on the other side. I had set my clock back two and a quarter hours from the Beijing time that ruled over all of China and Tibet. I had moved on - the joy and sadness of travel. I had the joy of greeting the new and unknown, and the sadness of leaving the makings of great memories behind. In travel, change was guaranteed. Sometimes the transitions were slow and gradual, sometimes it all happened at once.

5

NEPAL

I was not done going down and wasn't unhappy about the situation. The only issue was the road. I continued down the valley that had become the Bhote Kosi as it crossed the border. The road was a muddy rutted mess through Tatopani and out to the first of the day's landslides. In the 20 kilometers (12 miles) between Tatopani and Berebise, the next town down the street, there were 12 to 15 landslides, places where the road became a muddy rocky mess, with steep pitches up or down, and where I was often walking. Add a little water and the mountains became mobile.

The road crossed the river at a short narrow gorge. Pavement appeared on the other side, although it was on again, off again, for another five kilometers as landslides diminished in size and frequency.

With progress down the valley the population density increased, and the amount of natural forest decreased. Around Tatopani the valley sides were steep and imposing, ranging skywards for thousands of feet through an assemblage of cliffs and thick luxuriant forests. With distance, the slopes relaxed, the cliffs receded into the general incline, the forest became more dissected and interspersed with agriculture. By Berebise there was nothing left of the forest at all, the hillsides had become a mix of narrow terraces of corn, rice, and grass and what looked like sparse regrowth. Scattered across the hillsides were the homes of the locals, in clusters or alone. Generations of human existence and deforestation had resulted in a forest that was thin to nonexistent, had immeasurable difficulty regrowing, and was largely monocultural.

Homes lined stretches of the road and folks of all ages hung out on door stoops, in stores and along the road, doing little more than chatting and watching the world go by. The road was the social center of the valley. And the people were all extraordinarily friendly. They waved, smiled, yelled hello, their greetings sincere and joyous. After the grubby munchkins of Tibet, the kids in Nepal were squeaky clean and ran up to the road to watch me go by with huge smiles and waves. There were no shortage of beautiful women in colorful outfits. Berebise was a real town, lined with dozens of stores, and I loaded up on fruit and cookies.

With continuous good pavement and no landslides, the ride down valley from Berebise was wonderful, even if the scenery was less spectacular. The raging Bhote Kosi had mellowed considerably, becoming a smooth, wide brown river that was casually making its way down to the plains. I got my second flat of the journey from a shard of glass, and I had a small spectator crowd watching me repair it.

About 30 kilometers (20 miles) down from Berebise the road started a short 2.5 (1.5 mile) kilometer climb up the valley side to climb over the ridge separating the Bhote from the Sun Kosi. That was plenty enough, the sun was intense, and by the top I was pulsating from the heat. I dropped an equal amount to the Sun Kosi and Dolaghat.

Dolaghat was a scruffy little settlement gathered at either end of the large bridge over the Sun Kosi. It was as much a road town as anything, where small restaurants fried up little 10 centimeter (4 inch) long fish for passing road users and folks took their bags of rubbish out to the center of the bridge and tossed them over.

I got a room three flights up at one of the restaurants, cum hotels, called the Fish Fry Hotel, and I sat on the porch watching the world go by as I did a little work on my bike that couldn't wait another day to Kathmandu. While I had a river view, I didn't have the end of the road tranquility of Tatopani. The plentiful buses with roof racks bulging with people, blew their horns as they rounded the sharp bends approaching the bridge. At the set time in the evening the hotel served up Nepal's national dish, dal baht, a plate with measures of white rice, overcooked vegetables and a thin lentil stew. It was no Chinese "point-and-eat" experience, but it was endlessly replenishable, and one never left the table hungry. I had never been a fan of dal baht, nor of eating soupy food with my fingers, which is how the locals ate it. In Nepal I carried a spoon and ate dal baht when there was no other choice.

In Dolaghat I had bottomed out. I was at 958 meters (3,140 feet), just 4,162 meters (13,650 feet) below Thong La at the edge of the Tibetan Plateau. I was back to going up.

I didn't feel that well in the morning and the thought of a 900 meter (3,000 foot) climb did not thrill me. Still, the first 7 kilometers (4 miles) were wonderful as the quiet road climbed gradually up to a minor unexpected pass through a small valley with luxuriant terraces and cute houses with porches. I rolled into a larger valley, through a town, to a far more serious climb. I climbed to ever-expanding views and met up with little kids on their way to school. School kids in Nepal wear uniforms and all the kids wandering along the road looked totally dapper and adorably cute with clean brushed hair, freshly cleaned and ironed shirts, ties, shorts, socks and polished shoes. English is taught in schools from an early age so that most young folks can speak English to some degree. I chatted with the kids who were outgoing and eager to talk.

Further up I stopped at a store and downed a couple of sodas. The bus population had long since skyrocketed. There was a phenomenal number of buses and I couldn't figure out where they were all going. They chugged up, or barreled down, and I held on tight hoping that one wouldn't swing too wide, or lean too far, and take me out on the way through.

By the time I reached the top at Dhulikhel I was destroyed. I sat on a wall, over-baked, exhausted, lethargic, and incapable of further movement. It was a feeling familiar from my sickness halfway between Dali and Lhasa. Dhulikhel was an unappealing bus stop town and it was downhill, or level, clear through to Kathmandu. I rallied.

I rolled down the short hill off the pass and was soon in the maelstrom of Banepa, an ugly, frenetic town of vehicles and unattractive brick buildings. On the other side I climbed gently to a minor pass and then dropped into Kathmandu Valley proper.

It was chaos and survival cycling all the way to Thamel, the foreigner's tourist ghetto of the city. The scenery was ugly development, the road was narrow, the traffic thick, and set on self-destruction. It was all horns, insane overtaking, and close encounters with streams of cars, trucks, buses and thousands of motorcycles. It was scary shit. I finally made it onto the map of Kathmandu and wound my way over to Thamel. I was instantly besieged by hotel touts. I finally let one of them take me to their hotel. The destruction was complete. It was all I could to go out for food hours later, and I returned feverish, sweating, and dizzy.

It had always been a part of the plan, to spend a week or two in Kathmandu. I knew from a previous visit that it had enough cultural interest to keep me occupied, enough services to be comfortable, to be able to get things done, and enough food options for me to be happily well fed. It would be an opportunity to rest and recover from the journey to date, and prepare for the remainder of the journey ahead. I could hang out in the city, and if I got restless, I could take small excursions to places around the valley.

The hotel I had been escorted to for the first night was hardly ideal. It was dirty, and only my exhaustion had allowed me to sleep though the all-night dance club directly out the window. Rested and composed I set out the next morning to look for more congenial accommodations. I ended up outside of the tourist enclave of Thamel, in a quiet leafy area, in a friendly, peaceful guesthouse.

I spent the next couple of days in recovery mode, alternating eating with working on a to-do list of chores and errands. I washed everything from clothes to bicycle, panniers, cooking pots, tent. I repaired panniers, spent hours in internet cafes, cut my hair, and worked on the bike. I bought a guidebook for India, and the necessary visa for the country, which took five days, three visits, and many hours of standing around. I got a rabies shot, and when stomach issues resurfaced and refused to go, I bought some drugs and took them.

There was some irony in this situation. At home or when traveling, I avoided medicinal drugs like the plague. I suffered through, opting to build natural immunity and allowing the situation to pass of its own accord. This had worked well, through years of travel, and a whole gamut of dicey environments and water and food situations, I rarely got sick. But I did draw my lines, and the last time had taken drugs to fend off a stomach bug was in Kathmandu, 16 years before.

I also compiled my trip data to give me a record of my progress so far. Armed with cycle computer and altimeter I recorded all the information at the end of each day. It was a valuable tool in gauging progress, provided a record of achievement, and it was just fun to add it all up and see what I had done. In the 74 days since Dali I had cycled 3,195 kilometers (1,985 miles), climbed 34,000 meters (111,500 feet) of vertical ascent over 27 passes. Of the distance, 35% was unpaved, and I had been above 5,000 meters (16,500 feet) 14 times. I had also hiked 464 kilometers (288 miles) climbing 11,700 meters (38,400 feet). This probably accounted for why I was so tired.

I also met Kendon, a like-minded Australian cyclist and traveler, who had been on the road, or ocean, for four years. He had been in the banking industry for five years and hated it. He finally gave it up and set off for the world. By the time he reached Kathmandu he had been going for 4 years, combining cycling across countries with hitching rides across oceans on sailing yachts. He had stalled out in Kathmandu, having been in the city for a month, but with the intention of continuing back to Australia. By the time I left Kathmandu 11 days later, Kendon still hadn't moved. He had not gone out of the city, not even to the main Durbar Square in the city center.

Kathmandu seemed more chaotic, more congested, and the touts more aggressive than I remembered. Outside the quiet calm of the guesthouse the general street scene was loud, confused, congested, and packed with vehicles, rickshaws, bicycles, and motorcycles, all making slow progress. It was an unpleasant and demanding experience with a continual bombardment to the senses, and risk to life and limb. I was constantly fending off salesman while dodging people and vehicles, being passed by mere inches by horn-blasting conveyances.

Apart from that, Katmandu is an exhausting and wonderful mix of old and new world architecture, residential activity, of color, activity, goods, and folks busy going about their day or waiting for the next sale. Narrow streets, and more open squares, are lined with stalls and vendors and punctuated with small Hindu shrines or much larger piles of garbage. Similar goods and similar services cluster in particular parts of town, or parts of a street. There are streets full of brassware, or blankets, or electronics, or shoes, or jewelry, or fruit and vegetables, or fabric, where everyone is selling the same thing at the same time in some form of Asian tradition of like-attraction.

Small openings between stores led to tranquil courtyards of Hindu temples. In larger squares and courtyards folks fed flocks of pigeons into which ran excited little kids, lifting the birds into the air. Terraced temples made handy displays for blanket sellers who created walls of soft warm color. Women sat on the ground behind big piles of flowers or vegetables hoping for a sale. Men stood at street junctions with two dozen handbags slung around their necks. Small stalls sold little plastic bags of boldly labeled spices and herbs. Multi-level temples sat quietly in partially forgotten corners as the world sped by around them. Beautiful women in dazzling saris glided serenely through the chaos, talking to friends, doing quiet deals with vendors. It was beautiful and busy, frustrating and reassuring, so Asian, so entertaining, so chaotic, so picturesque. And often so unexpected.

Walking down a street I found a group of folks gathered around a human figure made from long stalky vegetation. The figure was pushed over and an old man, with a bare torso, painting on his back, and flaming torch of dried vegetation in his hand, sat on it. He and the vegetative figure were then dragged by a group of locals about 100 meters (100 yards) down the street and around the corner, with various stops for traffic and equipment malfunctions. The old man then got up and walked away. The vegetative figure was set standing up in the middle of the intersection and the draggers and spectators all went home. I was later told that the act was the figurative and spiritual dragging of health problems away from the home.

Wandering through the central Durbar Square in the afternoon I came upon a temple that was a hive of activity. Some men, but mostly women, swarmed around the small temple waiting to go inside, lighting little candles in tiny disposable clay cups on the railing around the temple, or being blessed by various men who sat outside with various powders and liquids in various colors. It was a busy colorful scene, a whirl of people, smoke, and devotion in the late light of day.

I could only spend so much time in the city itself so, after almost a week, I set off for a hike out into the countryside.

It took me over two hours to get out of the city itself and into the countryside, which was my real destination. This was partly because I took the longest straight line route possible, but partly because Kathmandu had grown enormously. The city was like a living, breathing, consuming mass that was expanding in all directions, devouring the lovely green countryside as it went.

Women and kids light lamps at a temple in Kathmandu

Across the non-western world people constructed boxy look-a-like multi-floor buildings by creating a concrete framework of thin pillars and slab floors. They then filled in the walls with bricks. They could extend upwards as far as they wanted, needed, or could afford. Sometimes they would plaster, and then perhaps paint, over the outside walls or just leave them as raw brick and concrete. It was cheap, utilitarian construction, and would probably come down like a house of cards in an earthquake. It was also unattractive, characterless and cultureless. It was mostly this type of building that was eating into the rice paddies of the Kathmandu Valley.

What was left of the green valley was caught between the encroaching development of the city and the surrounding ridges of the valley's rim. It had become a thin band of bucolic green terraces, that rose up the gentle slopes dotted with homes and trees, to steep slopes, covered in pine or broadleaf forest, that rose to narrow ridges. I left the road and frenetic civilization and climbed a trail, then a thin paved road, up the side of a pine covered ridge. The winding road followed the ridge into a saddle. Two men sat beside the road making metal deity images. Using a charcoal fire and a hand-powered forced-air fan they liquified a silver-colored metal and poured it into a sand block cast. Continuing on a trail I dodged barking dogs and rain showers, wandered through pancake stack-like terraces, past older cute brick homes secluded in the greenery, and among thick forest, with views out over the brilliant green of rice paddies to the sprawling mass of Kathmandu. I came out on a road and followed it uphill to Budhanilkantha.

Budhanilkantha is the home of a huge reclining image of the Hindu god Vishnu as Narayan, the creator of all life. He had a particularly comfortable spot sleeping peacefully on the coils of the huge 11-headed snake, Ananta, who symbolizes eternity. Ananta was made from one slab of black rock hauled by hand from the surrounding hills. The snake was set in a pool of water, which symbolized the cosmic sea.

My next foray into the country was to the summit of Narajun, a prominent forested hill beyond the edge of the city. I followed a dirty, chaotic artery of the city and found the base of the hill's east ridge, guarded by a few military chaps whiling away the day behind their machine guns. The trail up the ridge was slick, slimey, hard-packed mud that had on-your-ass written all over it. It ascended steeply and I was soon a hot sweaty mess. The grade tapered and I passed several guys who looked relaxed but packed sizable weapons. I could only think that the government considered this strategic hill, with its commanding views over the city, to be prime position for the Maoists to lob a few bombs into the city.

It was remarkable how a peaceful, joyous people could become violent. Traditionally Nepal had been ruled by a monarchy, but by 1989 the people had become weary of the abuses and inequalities of the aristocracy, and its inability to improve conditions for the people. They called for democracy. Peaceful protests were greeted with gross government violence. In the end the King was forced to assume a constitutional monarchy role over an elected government that turned out to be corrupt, and still failed to improve the conditions for the people. A communist party splinter group, the Maoists, started an insurgency, a "People's War", which grew into an ever-increasing cycle of violence and retribution with the government. Fueled by rural poverty, disenfranchisement with the government, and resentment against the caste system, Maoist numbers grew to 15,000, with an additional 50,000 militia, and conflict covered the entire country. The war rattled on for a decade, with its executions, abductions, torture, and child conscription on both sides. It destroyed the meager infrastructure of the country, diverted government funds away from needed programs, suspended foreign aid programs, killed 13,000 people, and left half a generation of Nepali kids without an education. Nine governments ran Nepal over the ten years. In 2005 the king dissolved the government, only to be forced to restore parliamentary democracy a year later after massive demonstrations. The parliament reduced the king to a figurehead which was enough to bring the Maoists to the negotiating table and a peace accord was signed.

Peace and recovery was speedy albeit incomplete, with local racial tensions, continued political squabbling, and Nepal remaining one of the poorest countries in the world. I had been to Nepal both before and after the war and the people had always impressed me with their peaceful gentle demeanor, their tough work ethic, and their joy regardless of meager resources. While the vast majority were not directly involved in the war it was clear that push anyone far enough and they may just push back.

It is a similar scenario the world over. As is so often the case, especially in non-western countries, the government is the people's worst enemy. So often governments, organizations that were intrinsically created for the good of the people, became corrupt self-serving instruments of the people within them. These governments became means for officials toward self enrichment, for inflated egos and power thirst at the expense of the people they were supposed to protect and enrich. In a repeated reverberation of Orwell's "Animal Farm", governments born from a people's revolution, end up effectively turning against the people, on the one hand exorcising the country of an old oppressive regime, only to eventually replace it with an oppressive regime of their own. Time and again, majority led revolutionaries have overthrown colonial authorities as the people's liberator, only to end up being far worse to the people than the old colonial powers. Decades after the first revolution, another is needed and often occurs, in what becomes a cycle of violence and upheaval that keeps many of these countries poor, the people disadvantaged, the landscape abused. Resources are squandered on corrupt officials and on perpetuating the violence. It is often the government itself, and its failure to govern for the good of the country and its people, that keeps these countries firmly imbedded in the poor non-west. Although this scenario was not restricted to the non-west, it was just most pronounced there.

I continued up the ridge through the thick dark forest that pulsed with insect life. The cacophony they produced reached a crescendo the higher I climbed, the sound a cross between a band saw, radio static and really bad techno music. I intersected with the road, which wound up the opposite side of the hill, and followed it to the summit. The summit had a lookout tower, a Buddhist temple, and hundreds of strings of prayer flags that ran between every tree on the summit. Below was a commanding view of the entire bowl of Kathmandu valley. The grey-brown of angular concrete and brick of the Kathmandu coated the valley floor, occupying almost all of the level land. Surrounding it was the thin band of the agricultural terraces, what remained of the valley's rural landscape and lifestyle. Forming the perimeter of the valley were the steep dark forested ridges that rose to monsoonal clouds which obscured the line of white mountain monarchs that I knew lay beyond. City haze mingled with encroaching rain showers.

I dropped off the peak, down steep grass slopes, heading directly towards the city. There was no trail, I just hoped there would be one by the time I needed it. Faith had its rewards, and as I entered the forest I found a trail. Further down I came upon groups of bare-foot ladies who were cutting wood and carrying huge baskets of sticks and branches down the slick trail. Since we were in a forest reserve I could only surmise that what they were doing was illegal. I dropped out of the forest, past homes, along increasingly wide and eroded trails, onto the road. I turned towards the city and soon passed a large home with a spectacular hilltop location, with high fences, guard towers, and men in bunkers with impressive guns. It was clearly the home of someone important. I skirted the hill of Swaynambunath, following an exceptionally long line of prayer wheels built into the walls.

I was being systematic about my forays into the countryside around Katmandu. First to the north-east, then the north-west, and the last was to the south-west.

I followed the streets out to the Vishnumati River which ran south down the west side of the city. Apart from the river itself being disgustingly polluted, the banks were the local rubbish heap and assorted toxic waste depository. At least the muddy dirt road that ran alongside it was calmer than the average Kathmandu street. The road took me away from the river and I inadvertently walked through a dump and recycling area of town. Over a dozen locals sifted through the huge mound of garbage looking for anything worthwhile. The hike was off to a scenic start.

I found my way to Tribhuvan University. It was large, with ample open space and greenery, but like so many public spaces in non-western countries it was tired, run down and tatty. It hardly seemed like a place for higher learning.

I climbed onto a low narrow ridge upon which sat the village of Chobar. The village was an interesting tangle of narrow streets surrounding a temple, Adinath Lokeshwar, sacred to both Hindus and Buddhists. The temple was clearly a place for newly-weds. Upon every surface of the temple, and attached to bits of wood and jammed behind temple struts, were hundreds of pots and pans placed there by young couples hoping to secure a happy life. I was approached by a group of happy kids who delighted in telling me all their names and asking mine.

I dropped off the ridge into the road through Chobar Gorge. Since it was a long way down the valley to my next destination I hopped on a bus and joined a group of folks on the roof for a fun ride down the winding road. I got off at the end of the road, at Daksinkali, a temple to the goddess Kali.

Kali, consort of Shiva, is the Hindu goddess of time and change. She is a fierce blood-thirsty goddess of darkness but also a benevolent mother goddess. She is commonly represented as having blue or black skin, largely naked with a skirt made from human arms, a necklace made of human heads, with red eyes, matted hair, a drooping tongue, multiple arms, standing with one foot on a lying Shiva and one hand holding a severed human head. She is death and destruction, a viscous slayer of demons, the supreme mistress of the universe and, with Shiva, creates and destroys worlds. She's quite the gal.

Yet, all this just underlined the complexity of the Hindu religion. Every aspect of Kali and her visual representation had a deep spiritual significance and specifically related to the various aspects of life, personality, human emotion, and the world and universe as a whole. The various legends and traditions of Hinduism portrayed different manifestations of the same goddess, highlighted her different qualities, gave a variation on the iconography. Her form and personality was as complex and varied as the humans that idolized her, and the universe in which she ruled. The often repugnant representations of Kali allowed for Hindus to gain a better understanding of human nature and the universe that surrounded them with the aim of self-improvement. Kali, on the one hand, gave a sense to it all, but on the other hand created an altogether new complexity that took a being Hindu to figure out.

And Kali was not alone. She lived alongside a pantheon of Hindu gods: Shiva, Vishnu, Brahma, Ganesh, Hanuman, and is the foremost of the ten fierce Tantric goddesses, the Dasa Mahavidyas. If that wasn't enough many, of these gods had multiple forms. Kali was the dark violent incarnation of the peaceful Parvati, consort of Shiva. The gods had goddess consorts, the gods had vehicles, usually animals, on which they rode, they had symbols to which the people prayed, and they had aspects of life which they governed and represented. Shiva, Nepal's most important god, is the reproducer and the destroyer, he represents masculinity, and is pure consciousness. He carries a trident, is represented by the phallic lingum, lives at Mt Kailash in western Tibet, and rides a bull. Shiva has benevolent forms and fearsome forms, he is depicted in deep meditation and slaying demons.

To complicate matters still further, Hinduism and Buddhism have shared parallel beliefs and have existed side by side for centuries. Indeed Buddhism grew from Hindu origins and many of the concepts of Buddhism are identical to those in Hinduism. Buddha is an avatar of the Hindu god Vishnu, and traditionally Hindus believed that Buddhism was one of the many strains of Hinduism. Yet many differences exist between the religions with regard to meditation, gods, the relationship with attachment and detachment, rituals, rites, caste and cosmology.

By comparison, the monotheistic religions of Christianity and Islam seemed downright simplistic. And a whole lot easier to understand and assimilate for the masses. Just one big god that took care of everything. Phew!

On particular days Hindus come to Dakshinkali to make sacrifices to Kali, bringing with them animals that are beheaded at the temple and then cooked into picnic lunches which they enjoy on the grass nearby. I walked down the path past lines of vendors selling marigolds, coconuts, and offerings to Kali. I had arrived on the right day but was too late for any sacrificial activity and all that remained were the contented picnickers on the grass. Music played, people ate, it was a bit of a party. Down at the temple it was relatively quiet, folks came down to the temple, located in a cleft in the forest, and made offerings and lit oil lamps. It was a peaceful meditative place.

It was a curious aspect of Hindu temples that the images at the center of the temple themselves were often relatively small and difficult to see. To me it amplified the mystery of the gods that they be in relatively small dark alcoves deep inside elaborate temples or temple complexes. And then the images were covered in the offerings of the devotees, red, orange or yellow powder or liquid, rice, flower petals, ribbons. It was such a contrast to Buddha or Christ images that always seem to be large, elevated and prominently displayed. In Kathmandu there were images all over town. Many sat inside large stone temples and the buildings made them impressive. Others sat beside chaotic streets, naked and unprotected to the passing melee. Often they hardly seemed like holy images at all, or treated as such. Perhaps such positioning just made the religion and deities more accessible, more a part of daily life rather than remote and distant. It was an interesting combination of revered and commonplace.

Mother and child at Swaynambunath Temple above Kathmandu

I climbed a path up through the forest and came out into the rice paddies nearby. Locals were out planting rice, or crouched on paddy walls, resting from the backbreaking work. There was a gompa nearby. It seemed that every time I ventured into Katmandu's hinterland that there was a plethora of gompas. They were often large, new and clean. They were a product of Nepal's own indigenous Buddhist community, but also grown from the flood of Tibetans who had fled the Chinese rule of Tibet. Monks in their maroon robes hung out in Pharping watching the soccer game with the local lads. I caught a bus back into Kathmandu.

It was time to move on. The road called, I had still a long way to go. I spent my last day mostly doing errands and getting the last things for the ride west. In the afternoon I walked across the river and climbed the long stairs up to Swaynambunath, the monkey temple, set on a hill that rises from the level valley. The whole hilltop is crammed with temples, gompas, walkways, prayer flags and wheels, chortens, burning incense, and butter lamps in a complex melange of Hindu and Buddhist iconography. Folks came to pay their respects, to make offerings, to do laps around the temples, and to get their hands painted with intricate designs by a man with squeeze tubes of chocolate colored liquid, perhaps henna. The air over the valley was brilliantly clear and many folks just hung on the walls enjoying the contemplative peace and scenery.

I had left Lhasa on the last day of June, I left Kathmandu on the last day of July. It was a rude reintroduction to cycling as I climbed gently out of the city, and the valley, to the low pass on the rim, dueling it out with traffic, horns, and exhaust. I was following the main highway that linked Kathmandu with most of the rest of Nepal and India. Just about everything imported into Kathmandu came up this road. My journey would continue west, parallel to the main spine of the Himalayas, to Pokhara, the country's second largest town. At the top of the pass there were views down into the deep, green valley into which I was about to descend, and a line of white giants of the Himalayas rising above the valley sides.

The descent off the pass was eye opening. It was narrow, winding, bumpy pavement with an irregular stream of trucks that crept slowly upwards towards me. The trucks had no hesitation about overtaking even on the blindest of curves. It wasn't unusual for me to come around a corner to find two trucks heading towards me, side by side, taking up the entire road. It was lunacy at its finest. I sat on the brakes all the way down the pass.

After the initial descent, the road undulated down the Trisuli Valley lined with homes, villages, fields, terraces and some small areas of forest clinging bravely to existence. With time and distance I lost altitude and gained heat. The mere act of me getting on the bicycle after 11 days in Kathmandu was enough to bring out the sun in force and I was soon baking under a cloudless blue sky. I bottomed out in Mugling and traded the traffic of the main highway for the long involved climb to Pokhara. It was instantly quiet cycling but I made it only another 8 kilometers (5 miles) before I found a hotel. The heat had done its work and I was a wilted exhausted mess by the time I was done.

With little traffic and the cool moist air that followed the early morning rain, it was a lovely ride up the Marsyandi Valley the next morning. The valley was gentler, the hills lower than the Trisuli Valley, the folks were friendly and welcoming, and I had the energy to reciprocate and enjoy. The road left the river, climbed to a low pass and dropped to the wide gravel stream bed of the Mardi Khola. I picked up some traffic and then climbed again to another low pass, with another decent, to the Seh River. By this time the clouds had parted, the sun was set on bake mode and I faded fast as I made the long incessant climb up the Seh, 22 kilometers (14 miles) to Pokhara. I stopped repeatedly under the shade of large arching trees. The locals had built wooden platforms under the trees that became social focus points where folks could relax, enjoy, watch the world go by, or wait for a bus.

Near every roadside village, they were simple, wonderful places for rest and communication on overheated summer days.

The afternoon's thunder clouds had waited too long and I was already installed in a room near Phewa Tal, the lake Pokhara sat beside, by the time they obscured the sun.

I felt slow and lethargic the next day as I wandered through the quiet early morning streets of the tourist strip of restaurants and guesthouses the next morning. I gazed out over the lake, past colorful canoes the locals used to transport themselves and paying tourists, to the surrounding tall steep valley sides. I casually wondered if it would be possible to do a nice, easy, level walk around the lake. It only stood to reason, there were people and trails everywhere in Nepal. I set off clueless as to what I was getting myself into.

I followed the wide level trail around the north side of the lake, past dwindling guesthouses, to the paddies, forested slopes, and homes of the locals strung out along the lake. After about an hour I passed the top end of the lake and wound through a wide marsh. The marsh was mostly paddies, groups of folks were out tending their crops, dots of moving color in the expanse of green bound by tall forested slopes. It was tranquil and quiet, bucolic and beautiful.

I came to small village of fish restaurants and found a trail that led through the marsh, along a rough wooden elevated walkway and rickety bridge, that gave me access to the other side of the valley and the route back. I spent about 20 minutes at a cluster of homes trying to find a trail back along the valley. Asking a woman for directions all I got was a demand for money. I spotted a trail following a power line up the steep valley sides, so rather than return the same way, I followed it. It was hot sweaty work climbing the well-built trail, that was as much a long stone stairway, up through the forest. I passed a couple of isolated homes with unnerving unruly dogs that were soon restrained by owners. Two thousand feet above the lake I hit the top of the ridge and was quickly in a totally different environment. I stepped over a neat man made stone wall onto a bald hill of buffalo-mown lawn, surrounded by rock walls, a large in-ground water tank, elevated resting platforms and incredible views down into the valley, Phewa Tal and the surrounding hills.

The walk down along the ridge was superlative. I followed an assortment of roads and incredibly well-built trails with steps, large flat stepping stones, and lined with rock walls. I passed a variety of traditional style neat clean and organized homes that were surrounded by well-made stone walls and accessed by stone stairs from gates along the trails. I passed park-like grassy areas with in-ground stone lined water tanks, rock walls as fences, and large trees that rose from man-made rock mounds. Built up roads linked villages but had no traffic. The level of development on this isolated steep hillside, was impressive and the continual views over hills and ridges into the distance, wonderful.

I dropped down to the World Peace Pagoda, a large white monolith surrounded by four golden Buddhas, that commanded a stellar position on the ridge directly above Phewa Tal. I continued down the ridge into the forest and came out at the small dam at the mouth of Phewa Tal and returned to the guesthouse 8.5 hours after my lazy start to the day. So much for the rest day.

After traveling through a plethora of the world's cultures I felt the need to get some perspective on the relative frames of mind of the peoples I passed by. There had been movies and sociological studies of people's happiness but I wanted to encompass their peace of mind, their countenance, their outlook and love of life. I decided that one measure must surely be described as the "Kid Factor".

The kids in Nepal seemed incredibly happy, playful, joyous and open. They seemed to spend an incredible amount of time having fun, laughing, and making up fun and trivial ways to play. They also seemed very open to outsiders, easy to smile and wave, and confident in approaching strangers. While they seemed to have carefree childhoods they also appeared to go to school and assume responsibility at young ages. At ages unheard of in the west they tended the family store, cooked food in family restaurants, tended the family animals, did household chores, and baby sat siblings only two or three years their junior.

I am continually amazed by the capability and responsibility of kids in Nepal, and in many non-western countries. And continually appalled by the incapability and dissatisfaction of western kids. Kids in many of these non-western countries just seemed so much happier than their counterparts in western countries. Poor and happy seemed to be legions ahead of rich and unsatisfied.

What had gone wrong in this societal progression towards wealth? I had to look at the way the kids in non-western countries grew up. They spent much of their first couple of years close to their parents. Infants and toddlers in non-western countries were carried by their parents wrapped in cloth against back or chest. They went everywhere with their parents, working in the fields, about the home, traveling on public transport, and seemed remarkably content and placid in spite of rough conditions, crowding, and handling. They felt the familiar warmth and movement of the parent that was not that different from the womb.

In contrast, western cultures tended to distance themselves from their kids. Right from birth in hospitals, new born infants were plucked away from the comfort of their mother and kept mostly in separate rooms. Parents travelled with the kids in strollers, alone and disconnected from the parents. They slept in different beds, and hung out alone and detached, while parents worked, cooked, played. As kids grew older in the west they were bombarded with external sensory input via radio, TV, computer, and quickly assumed complex restricted lives that relied ever increasingly on outside input. Non-western kids, on the other hand, lived simple elemental free lives they mostly made up for themselves with little exterior input outside of parents and friends. They created their own reality rather than having it created for them. With a secure and comforted infancy, non-western kids felt more secure, and had a better grounding which enabled them to continue into life assuming those responsibilities that parents gave them. Resource-strapped non-western parents needed the help of their children for the family good and the kids were better able to respond. Resource-heavy westerners kept their kids physically distant but mothered them to much older ages. Given the right background and the right input, kids were far more capable than westerners gave them credit.

It was, of course, not all peaches and cream for non-western kids and many at the poorer end of those societies lived relatively desperate lives that involved overwork, abuse, hunger, and disease.

My time in these countries, and in the west, left me wondering if we hadn't just simply missed the boat, that in our hunger for progress and modernity we hadn't actually alienated ourselves from each other, including our own family, and our own inner humanity. Modern society had gained and had lost, as so often happens, regardless of our best intentions.

I finally did get my lazy rest day and I spent the cloudy day wandering about the town and sitting by the lake. Late in the day the clouds began to part and some of the grand peaks nearby, the sharp spire of Machepuchare, and others, appeared through the clouds.

Whether I liked it or not I had to leave the mountains for the plains. There just wasn't a road continuing west through the mountains. Forward progress meant that I spend time on the hot plains of the Ganges in Nepal and India, moving parallel to the Himalayas, until I could turn back north and climb into the cooler climes of the mountains of northern India.

I was out of Pokhara in a few minutes and climbing along the Siddartha Highway that took an involved path over the foothills of the Himalayas down to the Terai, the plains. It started with a pleasant climb, with little traffic and cooler temps, for the 18 kilometers (11 miles) up to the first pass. The day's ride turned out to be one of the best of the entire journey. Totally paved, the road was quiet with only the occasional bus or truck. It was constantly winding, rising and falling, but largely contouring across valley sides of forest, terraces, homes and villages with almost constant views. The folks along the road were effervescent and lively, with copious hellos and Namastes (the Nepali traditional greeting). Well into the day the road climbed high up onto a ridge, passed through a saddle to the other side, and took a long curving descent down to the Kali Gandaki River. Nearing the bottom I spied a sign for a hotel and stopped. The term hotel completely overstated the nature of the building. It was more home with spare room and restaurant downstairs.

Later I took a stroll down the trail behind the hotel. I was far from the regular tourist path and many of the locals looked quite amazed as I walked by. I came upon a group of folks working on planting their paddy and they beckoned me over. The family of seven had three terraced fields, which provided enough rice in the six month growing season to feed them for a year. It took them all about four hours to plant each field with the men plowing the soupy mud with bulls in preparation for the women to plant the seedlings. While standing calf deep in watery mud they complained that this year's monsoon had been dry. One of the kids took me down to the river for a look then escorted me back up a different path towards the hotel as folks with huge piles of grass or corn stalks climbed slowly up the path towards home in the late day light.

Great riding continued in the morning as I descended to the Kali Gandaki and made the gentle climb across steep slopes to the next ridge. Once on the ridge the road contoured along it for some easy view-filled riding above a broad gentle valley covered in rice paddies. The road then descended, winding down into a steep narrow gorge, down into heat, sweltering humidity, and increased traffic, with the rosy glow of friendly folks and beautiful scenery waning dramatically. The road came out onto the plains and immediately came into the unattractive, cycle rickshaw-filled streets of Butwal.

After 83 days from Dali I had finally left the mountains. While I was happy to be temporarily free of my constant duel with gravity I knew that the cycling ahead would have its own considerable challenges. My timing was anything but good and I had arrived at the lowest point of the journey, at the hottest time of the year, in the middle of the monsoon. With flat terrain my speed and daily distances would increase, but the summer, that had been good for the mountains, would be my nemesis on the plains. The flatness would be welcome but it would come with a price. Not being much of a fan of heat I had just made a trade of challenges. There would be, though, the lure of a difference in scenery, culture and, just down the road a week, the heavy impact of India.

I took a wander around Butwal in the cooler late day. The old part of town had a quiet antiquated, and strangely unfriendly feel. I passed a building with a large room full of hand-operated looms. Their operation produced a clackety clack sound that carried out over the street. I wandered down to the large suspension bridge over the river. Kids by the dozen swam in the waters below. While the males were free to strip to briefs to swim or wash in Nepal, women were stuck wrapped in a colorful piece of fabric that extended from armpit to ankle to do the same. I attracted a group of kids that stood around and watched me as I watched the Nepalese world go by. Back on the main street it was still chaotically busy at 7pm. There were almost as many cycle rickshaws lined up along the roadside as there were people on the street.

I rode west along the relatively narrow strip of plains between the foothills and the Indian border, the Terai. To the right the hills were barely visible through the haze, to the left the Gangetic plain extended for 1,000 kilometers (600 miles) choked with people. The road cut through an alternating scene of forest and largely developed areas of home, villages, and rice fields. While the fields were often attractive seas of green that stretched off into the distance, the homes were unattractive concrete and brick structures, the villages less pleasant roadside strip developments.

But my perception of my surrounds was severely clouded by the heat that quickly rose to suffocating levels. The riding itself took almost everything I had, there was little left over for friendly interaction with the locals, admiring the scenery, or stopping to take photographs. Still the locals retained their friendly Nepali demeanor and I spent much of the day returning countless greetings. Apparently someone had told the kids that "Bye-Bye" was what you said to foreigners and that was mostly what I heard all day.

After a break at Chandchauta the road turned north and climbed to a low pass over a ridge. As sun bounced off the pavement and bashed into my pulsating face I prayed for cloud cover to obscure the sun as I climbed. Fortunately clouds came with the topography.

I rolled down the other side of the 625 meter (2,050 foot) pass and crossed the Rapti River. The last 25 kilometers (15 miles) to Lamahi was fast and straight with a mild tailwind and slight decline. The concrete and brick homes had been replaced with quaint mud and thatch homes, the foothills were closer and more visible, I even summoned the energy to stop and take photos. In Lamahi, dazed by heat and exhaustion, it took me a while to find the least seedy of the hotels. In the evening a stream of locals came to the restaurant for the daily dal baht meal.

I spent most of the next day following the broad gentle Rapti River valley in a constant undulation, dropping and climbing through a series of side streams draining out of the hills visible to the north, flowing to the river invisible to the south. It may have been the monsoon but most of the streams were just expanses of hot grey rocks with little or no stream flow. Unlike the population of the day before, I cycled through mostly forest, the road was correspondingly quiet and I spent most of the day cycling down the middle of the road. But the apparent lack of habitation didn't stop locals from appearing out of nowhere, in the middle of nowhere, and I wondered where they all came from. Folks herded their goats and buffalo through the forest. Occasionally the road would near the Rapti and there would be homes and fields of corn that grew high and thick over the flood plain of the river. It seemed a poorer and simpler lifestyle to those folks in the hills, more like the simple homes of jungle people. For the morning at least I had cloud cover which kept the heat under control. In the afternoon the sun appeared, turning up the heat as I left the side streams behind. The road ran in long straights cut as a canyon through the trees.

I stopped in Kohalpur, an improvement over Lamahi. Later, at a tea stall, a young kid started to talk to me. He was 12 and had been going to school since the age of 3, his parents paying for his education from the rent they charged shopkeepers in their road-fronted building. He spoke good English with an almost British accent, probably from watching the BBC. He talked of Albert Einstein, the French Revolution and the Nepali Revolution, the transfer of power from the king to the government. He anticipated going to Kathmandu to study mathematics.

I left Kohalpur against a stream of hundreds of cyclists, guys in groups, kids, women, all heading the other way at a sedate pace. Further on there as a tidal flow of kids, walking or cycling, in three different uniforms heading to, or from, school. Two cycle rickshaws went by, each with a covered wagon full of perhaps 8 to 10 tiny kids in uniform who waved and yelled as I went by.

For a good section of the ride I followed a huge raised irrigation canal. Further on I passed a weir that diverted water into the canal. Fish, over a foot long, were trying to jump up the spillway. I saw monkeys and a group of seven spotted deer. The road climbed and converged with the Karnali River which originates not far from Mt Kailash and drains most of western Nepal. Just before the bridge I cycled through a large police checkpoint. Guidebooks had warned against Maoist activity in western Nepal and had advised against travel along the road I had been cycling since Butwal.

Scattered along all the roads of Nepal there had been checkpoints where oil drums, rocks, tires, traffic cones, and sundry other obstacles had been placed on the road to slow, or stop, traffic. Sometimes there were boom gates that were almost always up, and sentries beside the road. The posts were small bunkers made from sand bags, with a roof, and a guy inside with a big gun. Indeed, around anything of importance in Nepal, police stations, army barracks, bridges, and intersections, were bunkers and barbed wire. In Kathmandu there had been patrols of uniformed men in single file who, between them, carried a big stick, a big gun, a radio, and sometimes nothing at all. They seemed woefully unequipped for the attack they were supposed to prevent. It was all for the purpose of capturing or reducing the activities of the Maoists. With the Maoist insurgency largely over, all this police and army activity seemed largely unwarranted. It was all completely peaceful as I cycled along the highway. I cruised through all the checkpoints without stopping.

With no accommodation options for another 70 kilometers (40 miles) I opted for a short day, stopping in Chisapani. I found a simple and basic guesthouse with covered porch view over the Karnali River. The afternoon heat was much easier to deal with, hanging out in the shade not cycling. The evening entertainment for myself, and the locals, was the bridge over the river. With the sun low, folks ventured out onto the bridge to enjoy the late afternoon air, and the fresh breeze that came down the Karnali. Immediately to the north the Karnali left the forested hills after its long journey from the Tibetan plateau. To the south the river fanned out into several channels onto the plains, dropping its sediment load. A brief rain shower sent everyone scurrying, emptying the bridge.

My last full day in Nepal was a long flat ride to the border town of Mahendranagar. As so often happened on this flat Terai section of the journey, I rode against a flow of cyclists in the morning. Considering the small size of Chisapani it was surprising that so many folks wanted to go there.

It wasn't hard for me to move faster than the folks going in my direction. I had a load, but I also had modern technology and they had old rusty clunkers that barely held together. Periodically I would pass a young guy and then would later hear the approaching rattling sound of fast pedaling coming up behind me. It was a scenario that had happened to me all over the non-western world. It was the same guy I had just passed taking up the challenge of overtaking a white guy on a bike, the competitive male ego getting the better of him. They would most often overtake me without recognition, some would immediately turn off, mission accomplished, others would cycle ahead of me for a few kilometers, others would hang just behind my shoulder. I would just keep cycling at my same speed. Sometimes they would pull up along side and want to chat, bombarding me with questions with the little English they knew; "What country?", "Where are you going?", "What is your job?". While the competitive issue was comical, the talking while cycling I found to be dangerous, given everything else usually going on on the road. Down in this heat cycling and talking was just too much at once. I did the best to discourage it.

I had my most expensive night's accommodation in Nepal six kilometers (4 miles) down the road from India. I braced.

6

INDIA

I cycled up to the edge of one seventh of the world's population with significant trepidation. I had been to India before, and been on its roads, albeit in the relative comfort and safety of buses and trucks. It was no place for a lone white guy on a bike. Size was the only rule on Indian roads, the horn only slightly less valuable than the wheels, steel hard nerves standard equipment. I would be cycling through Uttarkhand, one of India's more populated states, in the world's second most populated country, in the middle of the hottest months. I couldn't wait.

I had crossed into the no-mans land between Nepal and India without even knowing it. When I realized my error I backtracked to the small, very-easy-to-miss immigration building with an open office and nobody there. After a while a man showed up. He was only the assistant and couldn't punch me out of Nepal. He called the officer in charge, who was at home in Mahendranagar. It took him an hour to get to work, an hour of cool morning going to waste. When he did show up he was so nice and apologetic I could hardly get angry at him.

I ran off the end of the pavement in the no-mans land and I wound over to the Indian immigration office. It took three men to sign me in; one to write me in the book, one to tear the immigration card, and the boss to date and sign my passport. Indian bureaucracy was alive and well.

I cycled over the weir across the Mahakali River, and followed a large irrigation canal into the chaos of

Banbassa. A sign indicted 297 kilometers (185 miles) to Haridwar, my next destination three days away.

Initially the cycling was smooth and fast but in Katima it was bedlam, the dirty dusty road choked with crowds of people that even the passing trucks had to horn their way through. There were no signs and I overshot a turn by a kilometer before a local sent me back.

Out in the countryside the scene had changed little from Nepal, vast expenses of rice fields, with the addition of sugar cane, and mountains barely discernible in the hazy distance. The roads were reasonably smooth, the traffic manageable, the homes the standard concrete and brick structures, the general scene green, often peaceful, and verging on nice. The road, though, required constant vigilance. There were oxcarts, dogs, cows, people walking or cycling all over the road. There were motorcycles that carried mum, dad and as many kids as they had, all on one bike. There were men pushing old heavy wooden carts loaded with fruit and vegetables. There were three wheeled taxis that carried upwards of a dozen people that produced clouds of exhaust that were so thick the taxis almost disappeared behind them when they passed. There were lines of uniformed school kids walking down the side of the road who didn't dress nearly as well as their Nepalese counterparts. There were vehicles in a variety of sizes and decibels, all overtaking each other with little regard for others or what was coming down the road in the opposite direction. It wasn't unusual to see a bus overtaking a car, that was overtaking a bicycle, that was overtaking an ox cart, all at the same place, and time, and in the same direction.

But it was the towns that created the Indian impact. At the slightest hint of a town, even a village, the quality of environment and life deteriorated instantly. They were staggeringly frenetic, ugly and chaotic. The roads were filthy, potholed, unsigned, lined with unattractive stalls and buildings, and full of humans, bicycles, rickshaws and vehicles. It was a whole slew of legs and wheels going every which way. It was intense just making it through, winding through the melee, finding the right way out to the other side. I had no desire to stop.

Then, out in the middle of the countryside, I came upon four white ladies, between the ages of 42 and 53, cycling the other way. They had started four months previously in London and had ridden to Istanbul. They flew to Delhi, got a ride 200 kilometers (125 miles) out from the city and started riding. It was their second day on the Indian roads. In the following 15 months they would ride the exact route I had just done, in the opposite direction, to Kunming, then ride south through South-East Asia and across Australia to Sydney. I was completely impressed and I could've talked to them for hours. But we were on the side of the road in the middle of nowhere. In spite of the contact information and my later efforts I never heard how their journey had progressed.

Just as the day's heat was peaking I came into Kichha, another unappealing town that was all about trucks, truck repair, and assorted industry. I found the hotel the women had spoke of and got in. I spent the afternoon under the ceiling fan. After dinner in the hotel restaurant I walked up the street a little to a tea shop. As I sipped my two teas a local fellow bought me a packet of biscuits and, as I would find out later, the teas as well. We had a conversation of sorts, without a common word, with lots of hand waving and head wobbling. From what I could understand, he owned the tea stall. Considering our relative wealth I was shocked and touched by his magnanimous gesture. But it was India, in among the chaos and dirt and noise and stink and crowds was a passionate heart, a deep conviction, great delights in the most unexpected places, and memories that wouldn't leave you alone.

I started a habit of waking at 5 AM and being on the road at 5:45 AM, the first light of day. At that hour the cycling was really quite pleasant, there was little traffic, the road peaceful and the temperature was just on the warm side of comfortable. The only problem was that the day deteriorated considerably from there. I continued west on highway 74. After 43 kilometers (27 Miles) I started another habit, stopping at a little roadside stall, buying a two liter bottle of soda and drinking almost the entire thing on the spot. It made for some entertainment for the locals. The cold wet sugar was just the ticket. I continued, feeling reasonable peppy.

The people I passed were a religiously diverse bunch. I saw Sikhs, the men with their tall stature and curled beards, with hair tucked up into their tightly bound turbans. I saw their places of worship, the gurdwaras, usually the nicest house in the street. I passed Muslims, the men with caps and beards, and in Dhampur, the occasional woman covered in a tent-like black burkha. I saw what I could only describe as flat panel mosques. The classic mosque was a four walled structure around an open courtyard, or a large roofed room, where men gathered to pray. Along this road mosques had only one wall, with small towers, little minarets, at each end. The wall faced Mecca, which the devotees faced to pray. The majority of the folks were Hindu, less distinguishable than Sikhs or Muslims, but their temples dotted the landscape.

As the day progressed the heat soared, the traffic swelled, and the experience moved firmly into the unpleasant. Getting it over with became top priority. Driven by the need for accommodation I rode the second longest day of the journey, 135 kilometers (84 miles), to the grotty town of Dhanpur. I wandered the streets in search of a hotel and it was looking like there might not be one. I spent the afternoon in the less unpleasant of the only two options.

Later, I took a stroll down the narrow commercial street of town. Unlike the horrible scene on the highway, the maze of narrow alleys of the town center was a nice mix of commerce and peace. It was clean, the only motors were motorcycles, and men sat in their stores waiting for business. The stores opened onto the street and sold the whole plethora of goods from Indian sweets, to fabrics, clothing, hardware, and basic electronics. Treading where white folks rarely go I created a minor wave of interest with turned heads, chitty-chat behind my back, and eyes following my every move. I brought back fruit and cookies for dinner and the day ahead.

My 5:40 AM start was not early enough to beat the traffic as the road was already full of folks on wheels. The day's ride was a speedy deterioration at the hands of heat as the road turned north and converged with the low foothills of the Himalayas. The temperature escalated, the traffic verged on suicidal, my energy dwindled, and even the two-liter soda struggled to revive me.

Eventually a temple on a far hill appeared, and then Haridwar came into view on the opposite side of the Ganges. I crossed the river on the long bridge, barely cognizant that I was traversing one of the great rivers of the world. Dazed, I wound through the choked streets and found a room.

Haridwar, located at the place where the holy river Ganges passes through the last and lowest of the Himalayan foothills, is considered to be one of the seven holiest places for Hindus. According to legend, Haridwar is one of four places where drops of Amrit, the elixir of mortality, accidentally spilled from the pitcher carried by the celestial bird Garuda. Every three years, at one of the four locations, the Kumbha Mela is celebrated. Up to 70 million (thats seventy, 7-0, million) pilgrims come from all over India, and the world, to bathe in the Ganges, to wash away sins to attain Moksha, the end of the suffering of the cycle of death and rebirth. Pilgrimage to Haridwar is not restricted to the Kumbha Mela and Hindus flock to Haridwar year round to bathe in the Ganges and to join the evening prayer (Aarti) on the river's banks. The river is lined with ghats, steps that lead down to the river, of which the holiest is Har Ki Pauri.

Resuscitated from the ride, I walked up the main tourist street of Haridwar. The fleets of tourists and pilgrims that came to Haridwar by the million, and the local merchants that serviced them, gave the town more a feeling of a beachside resort than of its inherent holiness. The road was lined with gift shops, restaurants and hotels. Touts called out over the masses promoting their wares. A constant moving throng of visitors moved down the street in a scene of semi-permanent chaos.

The ghats gave the river a man-made feel and the river ripped down the channel with purpose. Folks by the hundred gathered along the ghats by the river, standing, sitting, dipping their feet in, or swimming in the river. Most of the swimmers were male, stripped to their underwear, with a few women who were fully clothed. Fortunately the river was shallow, otherwise the current would have taken most of them out onto the plains. Beside the river were temples, the towers painted in white and orange, the walls all painted pink, the predominant color of much of the town. In the middle of the river was a level man-made island with steps leading down to the water on all sides and linked to the mainland by three bridges. This, and the ghats across the channel, was Har Ki Pauri.

I was quite happy to take the next day off. I set off to visit one of the many temples that dotted the landscape around the holy city. I opted to make the climb up to Mansa Devi Temple set on a hill several hundred feet directly above the town. I would get a religious experience and a view. I could've taken the gondola up the hill but I thought I would get more merit from the effort of hiking. I joined a line of devotees for the short sweaty climb past stalls selling little bags of food offerings for the temple.

The temple, housing several small shrines, was an unattractive concrete structure painted pink. The most important of the shrines had a maze leading up to it to help manage the crowds. But by the time the devotees made it to the shrine itself it was a mad scene of pushing and shoving as people madly gave their offerings to the temple attendants who simply threw the stuff onto the ground. While there was no shortage of devotion, the mad crush of people seemed like an odd way to express it.

This wasn't an unusual situation and I had often been to Hindu temples where it felt more like an agitated football crowd than a reverent pilgrimage. It was in contrast to most of the other mainstream religions where folks entered churches, mosques or Buddhist temples with considerable decorum, respect and silence, to the point of reserved stiffness. While people pushed each other around at the Mansa Devi temple, I was hassled for carrying my shoes, not wanting to leave them sitting around with everyone else's at the temple entrance, and given some grief for not pushing hard enough.

I walked away from the crowds and enjoyed the view out over the town and river. To the south the hazy plains wandered off into the distance and the teeming millions that was India. To the north the steep forested hills lead eventually to the high peaks of the Himalaya.

Back in the hotel I spent some quality time with my bike. I had remembered that I had heard the familiar ping of a breaking spoke a few days before when I had neither the time, energy, or frame of mind to deal with it. It was an easy replacement.

Later I ventured out, walking the tourist strip, to Har Ki Pauri ghat for the sunset Aarti ceremony.

As the sun sank below the nearby hill, pilgrims began to gather, covering the steps on either side of the channel of the Ganges. All over the ghat men in blue shirts were taking donations and giving receipts. The recipient of the donations remained a mystery, but they did a ripping business working the swelling crowd.

Vendors around the ghat sold little boats, diyas, made from big green leaves which carried small piles of pink and white flower petals. While most of the diyas were 15 to 30 centimeters (6 to 12 inches) long, some were as large as 30 centimeters (two feet) long and contained a huge mound of petals. Folks bought the boats, took them down to the river, and lit a small candle in the middle of the petals. They then cast the diyas out onto the river as a way of commemorating their dead ancestors. It was a beautiful scene, the stalls with their rows of diyas for sale, the pilgrims in their ritual, and the flickering light of the diyas floating down the river in the darkness.

By the time the Aarti ceremony began it was almost dark and the crowds were at least ten deep on all sides of the river and ghats. The ceremony of Aarti is sung or performed to develop the highest love for god. The devotional song was broadcast over the crowd. Three men standing by the river lit small flaming vases, which they then waved around themselves at arms length. This was supposed to acquire the power of the deity. Then as many as 15 similar flaming vases were circulated through the crowds. Kids walked through the crowds carrying a tray with a burning flame. People waved their hands through, or over the flames then rubbed their hands over their faces and heads. The purifying blessing had been transferred from the deity, to the flame, and on to the devotees.

The whole ceremony lasted about ten minutes. The music stopped, the flames extinguished, the crowds returned to the streets. It had been as beautiful, symbolic and rich as it had been short. It was India, the unsavory towns were the sour, the strength of the faith was the sweet.

I took another early 5:40 start in the morning but India was way faster than me and the road was already full of wheels, people, horns and exhaust. Fortunately it was only 28 kilometers (17 miles) to the next stop, Rishikesh. Installed in a guesthouse before most of the inhabitants had risen I set off to do a loop walk linking the two long pedestrian bridges across the river.

I walked down to the upper bridge near Lakshman Jhula, with its view across the Ganges to two large 13 story concrete temples with towers that made up for lack of style with impressive size. The large swing bridge was packed with people. It wasn't till later that I learnt that Indian Independence Day was the next day and Indians were out in force. Busy, jovial holiday-makers swarmed over the bridge and along the surrounding lanes. The crowd was full of well dressed, well off, and largely overweight Indians. The obesity epidemic had hit India.

A sadhu, Hindu holy man, begs for alms in Rishikesh

Indians have a different relationship with size than folks in the west. In the west, models and actors are thin and fit looking. Across these societies excess weight is considered unattractive and unhealthy. While this hasn't stopped huge numbers of people from becoming drastically overweight, the idolized form is trim, and thin is used to sell clothing, goods, movies, cars, and ironically, food.

In India, thinness is associated with hunger, deprivation, poverty and low income. Huge, colorful, hand painted movie billboards show actors with solid hips and guts and round, well-fed faces. Being big is a symbol of wealth, having plenty, and a sign of financial prosperity. The health of being oversize was never an issue. In Rishkesh any woman old enough to be a mother had substantial rolls of fat barely hidden in the bright colorful folds of fabric of her sari. Any man old enough to be a father sported a significant gut pushing out his western attire.

A week later I picked up an 'India Today' magazine off a coffee table at the hotel I was staying. The cover story titled, 'Girth of a Nation', concerned the growing obesity rates in India, a product of increased numbers of desk jobs, western fast foods, and the cultural aspect of large size being a declaration of wealth. Apparently it was getting to be a problem for India too.

From Lakshman Jhula I followed peaceful paths parallel to the Ganges proceeding downstream, past an assortment of ashrams that made Rishikesh the self-proclaimed yoga capital of the world. I wandered down to the ghats alongside the river. I crossed the lower bridge, Ram Jhula, and wandered back upstream to the guesthouse.

I took a day off and took a leisurely stroll around the same bridge-to-bridge loop I had done the day before, talking to travelers along the way. There was a Romanian teacher who had married a German friend solely to get out of Romania, and an Italian woman who had travelled to India just to spend 20 days in one of the local ashrams. I walked down to a beach on the river where two Indians were deep in some kind of puja. While one read aloud at speed from a prayer book, the other poured water through a curving brass funnel into the sand. Curious.

Riding out of Rishikesh the next morning I came upon a curious sight in an area of forest beyond the edge of town. Indians were out exercising on the quiet smooth pavement. Most walked, a few ran, some did stretching exercises. Perhaps they had read the 'India Today' article.

India was not a country where people did willful exercise. Exercise was something you did because you had to, to plant the fields, to transport goods, to make a living. Indians, along with a lot of people of non-western countries, thought it a bit strange when westerners came to their country and went out exercising out of choice, for fun. The attitude towards exercise fit in nicely with the obesity issues in India. Exercise was something you did to stay alive. Not exercising was a symbol of financial security, one could afford not to exercise. This societal attitude towards exercise was reflected in their worldwide sporting performance. On a per capita basis at the Olympics, they were close to the bottom of the medal tally, collecting fewer medals than countries a tiny fraction of its size. To be out exercising for enjoyment, or health, was as much about the changing attitude of middle and upper class Indians in response to becoming more western.

The road continued as the most pleasant so far in India, peaceful, enjoyable and climbed gradually towards Dehra Dun. I had anticipated staying a night in Dehra Dun, to check the place out. By the time I made it into the railway station I voted against it and opted to continue on. It just wasn't that appealing. I followed the main road away from the center but came to a sign giving the distance to New Delhi. Oops, wrong way. I got directions, backtracked to the right road, and left town.

Dehra Dun had been on a low imperceptible hill and the afternoon's ride was largely downhill to the holy Yumuna River. Being holy though, didn't prevent the river from being dammed, sent along canals, and routed through a huge hydro power station. I crossed the river into the state of Himachal Pradesh and into the town of Paonta Sahib, home of a significant Sikh Gurdwara beside the river.

I had always had good interactions with the Sikhs. They were an organized and dedicated people who were well educated and held better than average positions in society. They spoke good English, were friendly and welcoming, and had a good sense of humor. They were usually taller than most Indians, possibly a result of their better standard of living and diet, which together with their turbans made them very easy to spot. Looking for directions I asked a Sikh whenever I could.

Sikhism is a monotheistic religion founded in the 15th century in the Punjab, a region currently on the border of India and Pakistan. There are about 30 million Sikhs worldwide, the majority still in the Punjab, making it the world's fifth largest organized religion. While it has one omnipresent, infinite, all powerful god, it has no priests. From the 15th to 18th centuries Sikhism had a progression of ten non-reincarnated gurus, the last of which did not have a human form, and instead lives on as the holy scripture.

The Sikhs were a fierce warrior class and they had their own empire that covered much of present day Afghanistan, Pakistan and northern India from the beginning of the 18th century. The Sikh empire was the only group in India the British were unable to beat in battle and they settled on a truce. The Sikh religion has about 11 prohibitions including adultery, intoxication and material obsession. The most noticeable prohibits hair cutting. Sikh men thus have long hair which they curl up into a distinctive, usually colorful, turban, one altogether quite different to any turban worn by a Muslim.

I walked into the gurdwara, the Sikh temple, in Paonta Sahib. Women sat around singing and playing music, an impressive Sikh guarded the holy scripture housed under a golden cloth that lay under an arch in the main hall. A part of the Sikh custom is Langar, the community meal. All gurdwaras are open to the public, of any faith, for a free meal. A team of servers dished out rice, dal, chapatti, and chai, and a few of them approached me and we chatted for a while. Even though they were just visiting the area they had come to the gurdwara to help prepare and serve the meal.

The pleasant riding continued the next morning, but was short lived. About 40 kilometers (25 miles) into the day the road began to climb through forest to Nahan, perched on a ridge. Fortunately the road took a turn before climbing all the way to the town and I rolled down a bumpy road to the unpleasant truck stop town of Kala Amb. The rest of the day was a series of roads with heavy traffic, extreme heat, and my fading physical and emotional state. I came into Panchkula and took a turn that had me climbing the last 10 kilometers (6 miles) to the end of the day. My breaks became more frequent, my progress slower. I stopped in Pinjore, site of 17th century Mughal gardens. I got a room in the hotel adjoining the gardens. Later, after I had recovered, I took a stroll through the peaceful green gardens.

The road deteriorated as I continued west. I lost much of early morning truck traffic at an industrial area, and most of the width of the road halfway into the day. I was on a collision course with the hills to the north and I began to climb. Fortunately traffic decreased and road quality increased, but it was still a 12 kilometer (8 mile) climb winding back and forth across the hillsides. I rose above the plains and the band of pollution and haze that hovered above it. The plains dissolved into the haze as I climbed. I wound up to Swarghat, a small village located in the saddle on the first ridge. I rolled down the other side of the ridge a few kilometers and found a simple guesthouse with a great view over the valley and lake far below, and ridges in the distance. It was only noon but this was plenty far enough. At 1050 meters (3500 feet) I was finally done with the plains after 13 baking days. I was also done with cycling north-west.

From Butwal, Nepal, I had followed the plains west-north-west parallel to the Himalayas. As I continued through India my route had gradually veered north-west, as the mountain range also bent northwards. In starting the day's climb to Swarghat I had turned fully north. My route for the next two or three weeks would wind up into the Himalaya, aiming for Ladakh, the high altitude desert located on the dry rain-shadow north side of the range. I would cross over a succession of parallel ranges, the Pir Panjal, the Zanskar and the Ladakh ranges, crossing ever higher passes, cycling evermore north and deeper into the mountains. I would then turn west once again for the last week to the end of the journey. I had made the trade once again. Heat, humidity and chaos for gravity, and plenty of it.

 I sat on the porch in the morning in the slightest morning light. The air was still and as thick as mud, the view a soggy grayness, lightning flashed through the ethos that had no up or down. With a little more light, a band of fog rose up out of the valley and obscured even the nearest hillside. Now the traffic wouldn't be able to see me at all. By the time I got onto the road the fog had lifted and I could see, but the trucks were already in full swing. After a couple of weeks of having to pedal for every meter, the sensation of coasting in effortless speed was fun, slinging the bike through tight steep bends. It was also nerve wracking as each bend held the threat of upcoming trucks and their maniac overtaking moves.

 It began to rain with increasing intensity. I put on my jacket, which worked well until the road bottomed out and I had to climb. The effort of cycling uphill created a sauna inside the jacket. I stopped at a tea stall for breakfast and watched the trucks, hundreds an hour, pass by. They were all the ubiquitous Indian Tata trucks, THE truck of India. Simple, basic trucks, they were the workhorses of the Indian roads, frequently overloaded, often sitting by the road being worked on by driver and crew, rarely comfortable, often colorfully decorated and painted. They billowed exhaust, were terribly loud and, with help, lasted forever. On the back of the trucks were usually painted words: "BLOW HORN", "USE DIPPER AT NIGHT", "GOOD LUCK". "WAIT FOR SIGNAL", "OH GOD SAVE ME", or "NO LIFE WITHOUT WIFE". All particularly pertinent. And while most of the trucks looked like they were straight from neolithic times there was nothing backward about the Tata

Group that made them. The Tata Group was a huge Indian based multinational company that had over 100 operating companies in 80 countries in a spectrum of business sectors.

The rain eased and I continued. The road contoured, then undulated steeply to Bilaspur. Further, the road rose and fell through a thickly green hilly landscape of forest, cornfields, and homes, that all blended together in the hazy grayness. I had wondered where the monsoon had gone.

Initially my first preoccupation with cycling through India in the summer had been not so much the heat but the rain. It was supposed to be the monsoon, but I had made it two weeks across the plains with barely a drop. While no fan of cycling in the rain, the rain would have been welcome relief from the debilitating heat that had been my nemesis. In retrospect though, it surely would've been one evil or the other. Rain may have been some comfort from the heat but it would've turned all those dirty dusty roads into mud. I would've been perpetually coated in muck.

Back in the hills the monsoon had returned.

I passed through a town that was a truck service depot lined with mechanic's stalls and partly disassembled Tatas. Up the road was a massive traffic jam. Trucks were parked along the road for hundreds of meters. Just beyond was an enormous cement plant and a much larger scar on the side of the valley that explained the truck traffic. Passing that I was instantly returned to a traffic flow that was somewhat more normal, the cycling way more enjoyable.

The road crossed a major river where there was a dam, power station and huge power lines. It then climbed all the way up to Sundernagar. The rain stopped, the landscape dried, the sun even made an appearance. Sundernagar was sprawled out over a broad saddle in a ridge. Folks seemed to be in celebration mode with pine bough covered arches over the road and lots of Indian flags. Perhaps Independence Day was still raging in the hills. It was a long gentle decent through a more open landscape to Mandi. Part way down there was an elephant beside the road, one leg tied to a tree.

A lady from a nearby house came by to feed it corn stalks. I watched it for a while only to have it spit at me when I went to leave. I followed a river into Mandi and it rained as I pulled into town.

    I got a room in a delightful hotel that had once been the palace of the local maharaja. It was all comfort and cleanliness, with wood panelling, poofy lounge chairs, and staff dressed as though they were serving the prince himself.

    Later I took a stroll around town. Mandi sat on the junction of the Beas and a tributary river, below steep forested slopes. The town was centered around an unusual, attractive, sunken marketplace. The market was essentially a large square with a garden and surrounding covered walkways and stores on the lower level. Below the town, along the rivers, were eight temples, some in natural carved stone, many painted in a palate of bold bright colors. An old suspension bridge carried vehicles, pedestrians, and animals across the river. It was peaceful and attractive in the moist late light. I found my way back into town and along a street that was the fabric store section of town. A couple of dozen brightly lit stores held hundreds of bolts of fabric in a range of colors. The vendors, men and families, mostly Sikhs, whiled away the time inside the stores. The town had the sense to erect cables as barriers across the streets which restricted traffic, including motorcycles, and gave the inner town a peace rare in Indian towns.

    I took a side excursion the next day, catching a bus 24 kilometers (15 miles) to Rewalsar Lake. The lake, set on the side of a forested hill, is sacred to Hindus, Buddhists and Sikhs. There were three temples, two monasteries and a gurdwara gathered around the shallow unremarkable lake, along with modern concrete buildings, trinket stalls, and restaurants. For all its spiritual significance the place left me cold. There was neither natural beauty, nor apparent spiritual energy or activity, so I set off to walk the gentle descent back along the road towards Mandi.

For a while, at least, it made for a quiet peaceful hike across verdant hills of pine and broadleaf forest, terraces of corn and rice, past homes of the concrete and brick variety, but also traditional homes of stone or mud brick with slate roofs that nestled nicely in the foliage. It was hazy, gray and rain threatened, but I welcomed the casual wander, peering off the edge of the embankment, far from the madding crowds and roads of the last couple of weeks. First came the thunder, then rain began and continued for most of the 11 kilometers (7 miles) I walked. It took ages for a bus to materialize going towards Mandi and predictably it was packed, a large tin can of solid humanity, and the Indians saw the humor in the situation and dealt with it.

I was reminded about the difference in the personal space between westerners and non-westerners. When conditions in buses became crowded and parents with kids couldn't get to a seat, it wasn't unusual for the parents to pass their kids over to total strangers who had the space and comfort of a seat. Those seated had no problems letting some unfamiliar kid rest in their lap, and the child was perfectly content being held by a stranger. When space opened up, or someone got off the bus, the kid was handed back. It was all so practical, a sense of common humanity in trying situations. Try doing that in the west.

As I walked back through Mandi's streets I heard music floating over the buildings. I took a B-line and intercepted the source of the sound. I found a procession of about 30 men moving slowly down the street. In the front were two men carrying silver colored trumpets, each trumpet was about 1.7 meters (5 feet) long and 40 centimeters (15 inches) wide at the open end. They would move along the street, alternating walking short segments with raising their horns to head height and giving them a blast. Behind them were five drummers who kept up a consistent, uninterrupted beat, changing tempo or gusto periodically. In with the drummers was a lone clarinet player who kept up a shrill, piercing, quite unmelodic sound. Forming a second group behind the musicians were men that carried, palanquin style, sculpted images of deities with silver faces and wrapped in blue embroidered fabric. The procession slowly worked its way past the market, along fabric street, and down to the river, crossing the bridge, and following a road downstream.

The procession then descended between two unremarkable buildings. In a tiny courtyard a live goat was then thrown over the front of the palanquin carrying the deity images. A huge knife was produced and one of the men did a particularly lousy job of hacking off the goat's head, needing several whacks and some sawing to get it done. The headless body was then dragged around the palanquin leaving a circle of blood. The goat's head was then taken to the drummers who dipped the end of their drumsticks into the wet end of the head and touched it to their drums as if blessing the instruments. The palanquin poles were then removed from the deity images and the images put away until next time. It was over. I could only guess that it was some celebration for Kali.

I walked away impressed and moved by the minor spectacle of culture and faith I had just stumbled upon quite by accident. I also laughed as this was India, and it was why India had such a magnetic attraction and repulsion. In among the noise and dirt and chaos and heat and teeming humanity were scenes of magic beauty, touching devotion, unexplainable activity and ancient ritual. So much of it was mysterious and incomprehensible and sometimes the sweet and sour happened all at once. I had taken the excursion to Rewalsar for a magic moment and it turned out to be parading through the streets of Mandi.

My ride continued at 5:30 the next morning and I followed the Beas River upstream. The road rose and fell gently as it wound up the valley under thickly gray skies. Fog hung suspended above the water of the river, cloud patches clung to the steep hillsides. Above Pandoh I crossed the river on a dam and was whistled at by the guards to keep moving. The road climbed above the still gray waters of the dam's reservoir into a narrowing gorge. The road cut a narrow ledge into the near vertical gorge sides that rose into clouds above. As steep as it was the cliffs were covered in moss, bushes, even trees. There was little to stop a vehicle, or a bicycle, from a quick dramatic drop into the waters below.

On the opposite wall of the gorge was a temple perched on the cliff face with a narrow path winding up to it from the river. Further along a cable dropped about 300 meters (1,000 feet) from the lip of the opposite valley side and men unloaded bags of cauliflowers from the small cargo cable car. I passed the mouths of large tunnels that lead to hydro electric projects buried inside the mountain. The road took a righthand bend it too disappeared into the mountain. Without signs I would've expected that the tunnel would be a short little thing, say about 100 meters (100 yards), but it went on for several kilometers. Had I known its length I would've taken the old road around it rather than deal with the exhaust trapped inside.

Beyond the tunnel the valley opened out, traffic picked up, and the road continued the climb to Kullu. I left the main road, crossed the Beas and followed a quiet narrow lane on the opposite side. I was soon wandering through groves of apple trees in which the locals were out, busy harvesting. Beside the road, in among the trees, under yellow tarpaulin tents, locals were packing apples in cardboard boxes, plastic crates, and wooden boxes they had made themselves using straw as packing material.

While most homes were variations on concrete and brick, sprinkled about the orchards were beautiful large dark stained timber homes with cantilevered upper levels. I climbed steeply to Naggar Castle built by Sikh Rajas in the 15th century. Recently renovated in wood and stone, it was now a beautiful hotel and I moved in. It was perched 300 meters (1000 feet) above the river with a commanding view over orchards and terraced fields below, and steep mountainsides of forest rising into the clouds above.

In the morning I continued up-valley on the road, through orchards, past locals busy packing apples among the trees, and men walking down the narrow road carrying heavy conical baskets of apples.

I came into Manali, a tourist town for Indian and foreigner alike. It was something of a mountain getaway for Indian families and honeymoon couples who travelled here to catch some cool mountain air and their first sight of snow on Rohtang La, on the road to Ladakh. I continued through the busy new town to Old Manali, an international backpacker's ghetto area. The one narrow road was lined with the usual assortment of internet cafes, restaurants, travel agents, guesthouses, and gift shops that springs up anywhere in the non-western world where foreigners visit in quantity. Likes attract, people immigrated overseas and formed enclave communities of like heritage in their new home country. They travelled overseas as tourists and gravitated to services and folks that were as similar to their home as possible. A curious, social bunch those humans. I joined them.

I had a few days to spend in Manali. A friend, Monika, was to join me for my final ride through the mountains to Ladakh. By the time I had arrived in Manali she had flown into Delhi from Europe, but the airline had lost her luggage. She was in Delhi waiting for it to arrive, I was in Manali waiting for her to arrive. Meanwhile I went through my familiar routine of organizing, cleaning, bike maintenance, recovery from the last weeks and preparing for the next. After resting I set off to have a look around the neighborhood.

Just up the road was the real Old Manali, a collection of wonderful homes with lower floors of thick stone walls and upper floors of dark carved timber, homes that seemed a world away from the two other variations on Manali just down the track. The village clustered around the Manu Maharishi Temple. In a curious parallel with Noah's Ark, legend has it that the sage Manu stepped off his boat in

Manali to recreate humanity after a terrible flood had deluged the world.

I continued past the village following an assortment of trails used by the local herders with the intention of following the main Beas valley upstream. Having climbed way too high on the valley sides, asked for directions from a local cow herder who sent me contouring through a mix of meadows and forest. Part way along I was attacked by a small swarm of large and determined bees, and I was sent running back, arms flailing around my head. I returned forward, giving the bees a wide birth, and descended down into the valley to join a valley vehicle track. After two hours of hiking I had barely made any headway up-valley.

I made better time up the track through orchards and the yellow-tarp-apple-packing operations of the locals. Across the valley was the main highway that I would follow to Ladakh, as it wound up the valley sides in long switchbacks. I converged with the highway only to leave it soon after to continue up a road to Solang Nullah.

Solang was home to one of India's few ski areas. There was a rope tow strung up one grass slope and a line of chair lift towers, with no cable or chairs, up another. It seemed fairly small scale. Just the thought of a ski area in India seemed a bit incongruous, a certain miss-match between the hot confusion of the Indian street scene and the cold, overdressed, western skill-set of downhill skiing. But the scene was peaceful and green, with subalpine meadows, steep forested slopes, and tilled fields surrounding the village of Solang, across the valley. I walked back to the highway and caught a bus back to Manali. I arrived just in time for the all the day's clouds to amount to something and it let loose. It took me several sprints between dry spots to get back to the room.

Monika had found her luggage and caught the overnight bus up to Manali. I walked down to the open dirt field that was the bus station, to meet her at the supposed arrival time. Three hours later I gave up waiting and went back up the hill. She would finally arrive several hours later still, it was India after all, and we met at the room. A familiar face after months of relative solitude was rather delightful.

Monika had a backpack, not a bicycle, and we devised a mutually beneficial plan of forward progress. I would cycle and she would ride the bus. We agreed on meeting place, usually a guesthouse, in a town, one, two, three, or four days up the road, at an approximate time based on how long I thought it would take me to get there. She would, of course, get there first, find the place, or another if that was full or unsuitable, and leave a note. It gave both of us time to do our own thing, in our own time, but we had the added spice of knowing that in a day, or more, we would meet up and spend some time together before repeating the process. It was simple and logical and just one resolution for those who lacked the creativity and resource to make differences work.

It helped that Monika was well accustomed to travel. She had taken any opportunity she could to leave her Swiss homeland and disappear to a far land, or a European island, to find solitude or a different cultural or environmental experience. She also had a strong reclusive element to her nature, as I had, and was perfectly content holing up in some isolated location for days, or weeks, at a time. Coming to India had been the start of a whole new chapter in her life. Weeks before she had tossed in the towel on her nursing career, her nice small apartment in Switzerland, and a somewhat traditional lifestyle to find something that brought more contentment, that she felt sure to find in some exotic Asian locale.

It was on one of those islands that we had met two years before, in the Canaries, a part of Spain. Our meeting was enough that we had met a year later in Canada, for a month of hiking and camping in the Rockies. She had impressed me with her physical strength, capability, resilience, her desire for wild isolated places, and her cooking ability over a single burner backpacking stove.

There was a strong measure of coincidence in our meeting in Manali, but also heavy doses of planning and mutual attraction.

Our first destination was Keylong in Lahaul, just over the main spine of the Himalayas and Rohtang La, about a day and a half away.

Monika went to find her bus and I set off uphill. The first dozen kilometers (8 miles) up the Beas valley were familiar after my excursion a few days before. The road then turned and climbed out of the valley and wound up into a higher side valley. A bus went by and I saw a white hand waving out a window. The road alternated between good pavement and thankfully short-lived sections of rock. It wound up through forest and open grass into the clouds which were hanging low on the surrounding peaks. I rode though a grey gloom, with lonely isolated trees my only visual connection with the landscape. Higher up the clouds parted briefly to reveal an instantly dramatic landscape. The road cut across very steep grass slopes littered with huge boulders. Nearly vertical slopes lined a deep basin and climbed to more clouds above.

The road wound up through the boulders, with areas of pavement washed out by streams and over use. The clouds closed in. The grade of the landscape eased and I climbed up a ridge to a motley collection of restaurants at Marhi, two-thirds of the way up to the pass from Manali. It started raining just as I arrived and I made a dash for one of the restaurants.

Rohtang La was an Indian tourist destination and I had been passed by cars and 4WDs packed with Indians heading up for a day trip to their mountain experience. I received a variety of responses from the tourists as I climbed. Some waves, some clear signs of encouragement and agreement, a lot of ignoring, or just watching, some chorus of voices and laughter. But one was special. A small Suzuki car pulled up slowly beside me without horn or noise. A mid-aged Indian woman said peacefully out the window,

"Well done, well done." The vehicle continued on without fanfare. I was left wishing that a few more folks could be as sincere and as quiet as she had been.

All along the lower sections of the road leading to the pass there had been stores renting out clothing and boots to the Indian tourists who rarely experienced cold. Higher up, the Indians were dressed in long fluffy jackets and boots which were still hopelessly inadequate in the rain. Some of them took horseback rides, which in the wetness seemed like a bit of a miserable experience.

As I got up to leave the restaurant the clouds parted and the rain temporarily eased. I could see the bank of switchbacks climbing the steep grass slopes leading up to the clouds. Local shepherds herded large groups of goats across the deeply green hillsides. The clouds sank, the rain returned, with more vigor than it had been before, and it kept going for my remaining 8 to 10 kilometers (5 to 6 miles) to the summit. Even with the effort of climbing I was getting cold. About two kilometers from the summit there was a little plastic covered stall in the soaking wet gloom and I stopped to put on two layers of fleece. I was frozen, my legs shivering, I'd been going uphill for 7 hours and my food intake had not kept pace with the effort. The boys in the stall invited me in to huddle by their kerosene stove. I did tea and biscuits. Slightly revived I returned outside into the pelting rain and rode to the summit where a big yellow concrete sign announced the pass.

The Border Roads Organization is an arm of the Indian government that was responsible for building and maintaining all the roads around the borders of India, from the high passes of the Himalayas, to the deserts of Rajasthan, to the swamps of West Bengal. It also was responsible for all the catchy yellow signs along their roads written with pearls of wisdom and advice to slow down and drive carefully. Big handy signs on pass summits gave altitudes. On Rohtang La I was on the spine of the Pir Panjal Range, at 3,978 meters

(13,051 feet), 51 kilometers (30 miles) of constant uphill riding from Manali.

I started down the other side. The road curled around a broad high basin, then into the deep valley of the Chandra River that flowed west across the northern route I had been taking. Visibility improved enough that I could see the 600 meters (2,000 feet) into the abyss, and over the valley to the gloomy mountain forms on the other side. The road deteriorated considerably, with about 5 kilometers (3 miles) of rocks, mud, water and occasional pavement. The rain tapered, visibility continued to improve, the pavement returned and I began to enjoy the long winding descent into the huge, wildly beautiful landscape of the valley. I had lost all the cars and 4WDs of the Indian tourists but I gained the petrol tankers that were returning from resupplying Ladakh.

The Manali-Leh highway was open for about 4 months a year from the spring, when snow moving equipment dug their way through the high mountain snows, to the fall when the snows returned for the winter and closed the passes. Ladakh, with its numerous towns and military bases, had to be totally supplied during these summer months. There were only two roads into Ladakh (and to Leh, its capital) from India. The route via Kashmir had been restricted for years due to the ongoing conflict as Pakistan, India, and Kashmir fought over who should control Kashmir. Everything in Ladakh, save what they grew themselves, had been coming in from Manali.

With dry pavement and more agreeable conditions I began to think about camping. As I neared the river there were planted fields and rock walls. I found a cozy little spot by the river. With the day's weather and roads, the clean bike and panniers I had started with in the morning were coated with mud by the afternoon.

I returned to the road the next morning expecting an easy down valley ride following the Chandra River as it flowed west. I passed through Koksar and my first passport check on the highway to Leh. There would be several passport checks along the highway to Leh, all formalities. Unlike Tibet, it was totally legal for me to be cycling to Leh, but the entire northern Indian region was politically and militarily sensitive and the Indians weren't shy about putting officials in the middle of nowhere to check passports. Each check post involved getting off the bike and presenting my passport to officials behind desks in small buildings. They copied, at length, all the vital information into huge ledgers. It was highly unlikely that human eyes would ever see that information again, the ledgers would join the huge piles of previous ledgers piled up against the walls in an age-old rite of Indian bureaucracy inherited from the British. One set of police told me the checkposts were for the safety of travelers just in case they were to go missing. If nothing else it was a nice chance to stop, rest and chat with the bored officials, who occasionally, saw the comedy in the situation.

The road crossed the river and began climbing. The road wound through a series of villages that clung to valley sides looking across at the massive mountain wall that rose up into the clouds. Occasionally the cloud was high enough that I could see up to dirty white glacial toes. Cascading creeks tumbled out of the glaciers and clouds, dropping over impressive falls, down into the Chandra. Below the clouds were patches of forest which enjoyed the cooler wetter aspect of the valley. Meanwhile the homes and surrounding fields I passed enjoyed the warmth and longer growing season of the south facing slopes.

While there was forest and fields it was all significantly drier than the south side of the Pir Panjal. I had crossed to the drier rain-shadow side of the range, and it would only get drier the further north I went.

I had dropped off Rohtang La into the small region of Lahaul that was limited to the drainages of the Chandra and Bhaga rivers. Most Lahaulis follow a combination of Hinduism and Tibetan Buddhism. The homes were large two story concrete block structures that lacked the beauty or aesthetics of a traditional mountain community. Many of the women wore a traditional flowing dress in maroon or burgundy that extended from wrists to ankles and trimmed in gold along the fabric edges. They wore a scarf over their head. The men wore totally western clothes.

This is often the case in many non-western cultures that bordered on the brink of cultural dilution. Men tended to quickly adopt new customs, dress and lifestyle, while women more consistently retained time honored ways and traditional dress. Men quickly abandoned the past as they sought for a better tomorrow. Women saw the value of tradition and past ways developed over centuries. Women, therefore, were the carriers of culture into the future.

By the time I topped out I was about 450 meters (1,500 feet) above the river. The road wound back to the river and curled around to the junction with the Bhaga. Together the Chandra and the Bhaga formed the Chenab, which continued west, flowed out onto the plains and joined the Indus in Pakistan. From the junction I turned back north, after my brief jog west, and the climb to the next pass, Baralacha La, began. Seven kilometers up the road I came to Keylong, the capital of Lahaul. The town, perched 300 meters (1,000 feet) above the river, was little more than a typical small Indian town, a cluster of narrow parallel streets, albeit with a spectacular location. I found the hotel, and Monika, as arranged.

We took a stroll after lunch, following a path down the valley side to a bridge over a narrow gorge in the river. We climbed up the other side to a contouring road. There were fields of potatoes and vegetables, ladies bringing home produce for dinner, a clump of 2.5 meter (8 foot) high marijuana plants, groves of willows which surrounded the road and path, and a bucolic sense of peace in the late afternoon light. By the time we returned to town it was dark and we spent some time organizing for the next leg though the mountains.

Our next leg was all the way to Leh, five days of cycling ahead, there were no other opportunities for Monika to stop and stay in between. Monika left at 5 AM to catch her bus, I took a more leisurely start. My next climb was 75 kilometers (47 miles), and 2,000 meters (6,600 feet) of climbing to the summit of Baralacha La.

The highway continued up the valley, circumventing a gorge of the river below by climbing high, cutting across steep cliff faces. The landscape was impressively vertical. On a terrace, about 300 meters (1,000 feet) below, a village clustered, surrounded by green fields, and backed by a solid rock wall that climbed thousands of feet to a glaciated peak swirling with clouds. The road wound down into the valley as the grade of the valley sides relaxed. The cycling became more gentle and straightforward as it wound up the valley through villages and fields, all rather calm after the initial gorge. I passed several mule trains walking along the road.

Further up, the highway curved around into a huge four-way intersection of river valleys that left a large expense of gravel, interlaced with river channels, and a huge tongue shaped boulder field extending into it from one mountain side. I presumed that the tongue was the result of a huge mountain side collapse, a landslide on a grand scale, but the material was all in a brown weathered tarnish that bore no resemblance to anything anywhere else in the landscape. The road swung around the intersection and climbed through switchbacks on the slopes above into an upper valley where folks tended fields of potatoes. It seemed that there were proportionally far more fields in Lahaul for the number of homes, and thus people to work them. For many it must've been a long walk from the nearest homes to the fields.

I passed small villages, a road workers' depot, an abandoned army barracks, and climbed through another bank of switchbacks across an enormous rock pile. The promise of sun had never materialized, the clouds still hung low, and at the high elevation it was getting cold and my body temperature dropped. It was getting to feel inhospitable in the late day light. I found a field, put up the tent, and got in.

It was joyously clear in the morning. The first 11 kilometers (7 miles) up the pass was brand new pavement, a thin ribbon of black though a landscape of rocks covered in a new dusting of snow that glistened bright in the early morning light. With distance from Keylong the landscape had progressively dried, there was little left of natural vegetation, it was all rock, sand and dirt, the mountainsides just huge flanks of geology rising to permanent snowfields and glaciers. The road wound up to what looked like the pass summit but it turned out to be just an inflection in the valley. Beyond, the pavement ended, the road curved around a lake caught in the crook of the valley, its blue waters looking chilly but inviting. Above the lake was a long ragged high ridge, completely white with new snow, that extended off into the distance. I was back to rough slow going.

Above the lake, crews of dark-faced lowland Indians worked on the roads. Some were in sizable groups, others in teams of two or three. They created road from rock by hand at geologic speeds, their efforts minute against the forces opposing them, the road crumbling under the weight of gravity and overloaded trucks faster than they could put it back together. They seemed so hopelessly out of place, used as they were to the conditions under which I had sweated and labored on the plains. They wore heavy jackets and pants and scarves wrapped around their heads. They sucked dust and the fumes of the bitumen they heated up in beat-up metal drums with fires lit below. They lived in grotty workers camps beside the road and were shuttled around by the blue BRO trucks. They stood and watched me go by, some blank, some with beaming smiles, others buried deep within the cloth wrapped around their faces. It must have been a miserable way to make a living.

I climbed through yet another bank of switchbacks to an understated sign that said Baralacha La, elevation exactly 5,000 meters (16,500 feet).

It was a broad open crossroads of a pass on the crest of the Zanskar Range, with several valleys extending off into the distance that provided access to a variety of adjoining mountain regions; Spiti, Zanskar, Ladakh, and Lahaul. I wanted to continue north along the road but I also just wanted to head off across the smooth slopes to the south-east and see where I could end up. I stayed an hour on the pass in the sun, soaking up views, and weather, and geographic position.

The road got worse, if anything, on the way down the other side, as Indian laborers moved rocks and earth, trying their best to make it better. I came to a cyclist coming up the hill. He was Swiss, on an apparently poor quality Indian mountain bike with one large white bag of stuff on the back and nothing else. At least he wore a helmet.

I had a curious relationship with cycling helmets. I had only once worn a helmet on a long distance cycling journey. It was in New Zealand and it was because it was the law. Otherwise I avoided them as being cumbersome, uncomfortable to wear for long days, day after day, and just another piece of junk to carry around, deal with, and probably lose, or destroy (while not even on my head). On these cycle journeys I rode a huge heavy bike that moved slowly, I rode deliberately and cautiously, the nature of the beast was thoughtful and methodical. Alternatively, its weight meant that its braking time was long, my adventures took me on abysmal roads, through frenzied environments, full of obstacles that could impede me at any nanosecond. Vehicles, people, and bicycles pulled out in front of me without hesitation, on a regular basis. Dogs made sport of chasing me. The next whizzing descent held unexpected hazards. But I weighed my options, took my risks, and left my helmet at home.

When I was at home, though, I took my helmet with me. On rides around the neighborhood, or about the local roads, I always wore a helmet. The ride would be short, the speed may be fast, it remained on my head the entire time so it never became an obstructive piece of luggage, and I may not do it again the next day. On a journey a helmet was pain in the neck. On a day ride I felt naked without it.

I continued down the road from the Swiss cyclist and met his brother, in the process of hitching a ride on a truck, his bicycle no longer operational. The pair was a good story in the making.

The road improved slowly with the descent. It followed a wide gravel bed of a stream that ran below craggy and colorful peaks of naked geology, straight and curving strata, talus and scree slopes dragging a palate of earthtones down from cliff-lines to the grey of the stream gravel. I passed a workers camp happily called Killing Sarai, then wound between massive piles of boulders deposited on the valley floor, and dropped into a lower valley. The pavement improved, the road straightened, the grade continued downhill, a tailwind picked from the rear and I was soon rocketing along. I traversed a widening and smooth terrace plain that dropped to the milky Lingti Chu river in steep mobile scree slopes punctuated by regularly spaced hoodoos, towers of solidified terrace material.

I came into Sarchu, went through my third check post, and stopped at one of the many dhabas, small simple restaurants, to eat. Sarchu was the official southern limit of Ladakh and the dhaba owner had a typically Tibetan face as if to emphasize the geography. Dhabas were a regular feature of the Manali-Leh highway. They sprung up along the road whereever there was a village, a river crossing, or a road junction, and they made life so much more comfortable with cheap easy food to fuel by. I really would've appreciated dhabas in eastern Tibet.

The wonderful cycling continued down the Lingti Chu, even with an 8 kilometer (5 mile) diversion away from the river to cross a tributary. The milky blue braided stream contrasted against the tall terrace walls and the sheer mountain sides of rock, the road making easy going across the terrace. The day came to an end at the base of the Gator loops, a series of 21 switchbacks, the road's exit out of the

Lingti Chu valley to the next pass. It was too late in the day to embark on another stiff climb. I camped with a grand panorama.

The Gator loops made short work of the climb out of the valley in the morning. The road wound back and forth across the same piece of mountainside 22 times to ever more spectacular views out over the landscape of rocky mountains, river, and sky. By the top of the loops I was 450 meters (1,500 feet) directly above my camp, but the end of the loops was not the end of the climbing. The road curled around into a side valley and kept on at it, rising up to highpoints, or a bend in the valley. With each segment of the climbing done, another was revealed with another exasperated expletive. What I anticipated to be a relatively easy climb, after the previous two giants, turned into a long tiring monster. The road topped out at Nakee La, which was not a pass at all but rather merely a highpoint where the road climbed above a gorge below and did not cross into another drainage. The next 10 kilometers (6 miles) to Lachulung La, the real pass, was visible ahead, winding down into the valley and climbing up the other side. But it seemed that all the day's trucks and 4WDs going along the highway were along that 10 kilometers. I was beat, the vehicles were wreckless and obnoxious, and for fear of life and limb I had to get off the road for everyone of them. It had also become overcast, the scene far less inspiring and dramatic. I ate cookies on the pass and watched as road workers asked for food from anyone who stopped.

Dropping down the other side of the pass the valley was initially wide and smooth. After five kilometers, the valley became a narrow defile, the Gorge of Pang, barely wide enough at the base for the stream. The road cut into the rock and scree alongside the stream, and orange brown walls of rock extended thousands of feet to pointy ragged peaks. Much of the overcast had cleared leaving a mosaic of clouds that created sunspots that roamed across the rockwork. Further down, the gorge widened just a little and the road cut across ledges cut into cliffs, then switchbacked down past hoodoo towers and a huge boulder field to a stream junction and a one lane bridge. Beyond, the valley became smoother, tamer. Smooth scree slopes in orange, brown, gray and white lined the valley. Hoodoos protruded through the scree and stood guard over the landscape. The valley coalesced with other side valleys and came to Pang.

Pang was nothing more than a checkpost and a line of restaurants, large round white tents with chairs and tables out the front. I was at the base of the next ascent which was 70 kilometers (43 miles) and 1,000 meters (3,300 feet) of climbing to the highest cycling pass of the journey thus far. Although early, I opted to camp and leave the climb to the next day. But with the restaurants and road workers depot nearby, finding a camp was a challenge and I had to push my bike up a steep trail onto a terrace to a peaceful, beautiful spot away from humanity.

I walked back to the road in the morning, passing the local guys who were hiking up onto the terrace for their morning ablutions, and then cycled out past the workers camp where men squatted, scattered across the rocks, cleaning their teeth and nasal passages.

The road climbed through a bank of switchbacks. Part way up the road workers were already at work lighting fires under their drums of black bitumen. The fires produced horrible black toxic clouds that billowed across the road, the workers, and me. It was periodically tough going, cycling uphill at 4,400 meters (14,400 feet), holding my breath.

The road curled into a wide flat valley, the Morey Plains, and the next 40 kilometers (25 miles) to the base of the final climb to the pass was excellent cycling. Almost immediately the road forked. I chose the paved option which sent me across several culverts under construction, that sent all the traffic down the other side of the valley. The valley was level, the pavement smooth, the wind behind me, the cycling fun and fast. High, remote, with a smooth valley, it felt very much like Tibet. Local Ladakhis had homes tucked into side valleys and took their animals out into the main valley to graze. Scattered across the grass of the valley were huge groups of goats and yak tended by locals on foot or horse.

I crossed the valley and began the climb to Taglang La which I could see 18 kilometers (11 miles) ahead, at the end of a long even grade up a side valley. While it was the highest pass on the journey, it was the easiest of the Manali Leh road passes. The grade was mild, the traffic slight, even with the rejoining of the road, and the altitude gain the shortest. But with the altitude, the temperature dropped dramatically, the wind picked up, and along with the ugly buildings and construction trash of the summit it was not a place to linger. So much effort, so little reward.

I wound down the switchbacks on the north side of the pass. In a typical style for this highway the road surface alternated between good pavement, and rough rocks and gravel. The road eventually joined the thin ribbon of natural green along a stream, pavement became consistent and the cycling improved. After a meal at a cluster of dhabas I pushed my bike up a side valley to a camp on real green grass beside the stream. It was cold and windy, but it was peaceful and I had views down the valley to colorful rock ridges across the main valley.

Clouds hung low and cold in the morning. I wore just about everything I had as I continued down the valley towards the Indus River. I passed through Rumtse, the first real Ladakhi village since entering the region, and the first of a string of villages along the road. The village was decorated with old large chortens, long mani walls, and surrounded by fields of brown barley being harvested by the locals. The homes were the typical solid packed mud wall homes similar to those in Tibet. I had once again entered the Tibetan lands.

The humanity came to an end lower down as the valley entered a dramatic gorge. The road and river cut through vertical geologic strata colored purple and green. Some of the strata was hard and formed ribs of solid rock, other strata were soft and formed loose gravelly ramps between the ribs. The gorge temporarily opened out and I passed through Minu where I met a cute boy on his way to school, carrying a football and a packet of crackers for lunch.

Along the road the Border Roads Organization had been particularly active with their priceless wordy gems providing hilarity along the way. The BRO loved to build yellow solid concrete signs along their roads with poignant quips that urged drivers to drive slowly or carefully. But the verbage ultimately provided as much distraction from driving safely as they provided humor. Somewhere in an office, somewhere in India, somebody made a living thinking up these one liners:

Mountains and pleasure but only when driving with leisure.
Danger creeps when safety sleeps.
Heaven, hell or mother earth, the choice is yours.
After whiskey, driving risky.
Reach for the stars even if you have to stand on a cactus.
A dead end is just a good place to turn around.
Mind your brakes or break your mind.
If you want to donate blood, do not do it on the road, do it at the blood bank.
When you go home tell them about us, for their tomorrow, we gave out today.
Peep peep, don't sleep.
I like you darling but not so fast.
When going gets tough, tough get going.
Love your neighbor, but not while driving.
Alert to life, rough to death.
It is not ralley, enjoy the valley.
Life without vision, courage, and depth is a blind existence.
To be good to others is to be best to yourself.
God made Ladakh and we connect it to the rest of the world.
The smallest of deed is greater than the best intention.
You may be American or African but all is one.

The road left the gorge and came out into the Indus valley. I crossed the river that was another of the great rivers of Asia. Starting near the flanks of the holy Mt. Kailash it flowed west, on the north side of the Himalaya, across some of the most remote areas of the Tibetan plateau. It crossed into northern India, flowed across Ladakh, then into Pakistan. It curled around Nanga Parbat, the westernmost of the Himalayan 8,000 meter (26,200 feet) peaks, forming the official western end of the range. The river flowed south, spilling out onto the plains, and flowing across most of Pakistan to the Arabian Sea.

I hit a T-intersection amid a cluster of dhabas. I could have turned right and cycled up the Indus to Mt Kailash, if that would've been remotely possible and legal. But it required crossing the India-China border and these two countries didn't exactly get along.

The invasion of Tibet in the fifties by the Maoist Chinese government didn't go down well with the Indians. It was the unannounced expansion by the Chinese into the Aksai Chin and other parts of Indian held Tibetan Plateau, in the north near Ladakh and the east near Assam, that caused the greatest friction. This led to protests by India, with border clashes and ultimately a short war in 1962, in which the Indians lost more ground. Relations suffered further with the alignment between China and India's arch rival Pakistan. Indeed China backed Pakistan in the 1965 India-Pakistan war. China kept up an active propaganda campaign against India and supplied ideological and financial assistance to north-east Indian dissident tribes. There were skirmishes in Sikkim in 1967 between soldiers of the Chinese and Indian militaries, and another India-Pakistan war the same year. A flourishing wool, spice, and fur trade across the Tibetan-Indian border was severed. The Chinese built a road across territory claimed by India, linking the Chinese Xinjiang province with Pakistan, in a move India was helpless to do anything about. After all that, relations between the two countries began to improve in 1979 and an undulating course of hot and cold relations ran into the 21st century.

The border regions between the two countries had thus been off limits to foreigners during the whole ordeal. Neither government wanted people strolling around at will, unwittingly getting involved in military maneuvers, and crossing borders the countries couldn't come to peace over. China still didn't need another route for foreigners to enter Tibet, regardless of the relationship with India. China wanted Tibet and its visitors on a very short leash and that included as few entry and exit points as possible.

Indeed, I could have just missed the whole sultry Indian plains experience by staying on the north side of the Himalayas, continuing up the Yarlung Tsangpo from Xigatse, past Mt. Kailash, and cycling down the Indus, a dreamy, heady ride of isolation and grandeur if ever there was one. All I had to do was to convince two arch rivals, two global powers, to kiss and make up, and get China to take a valium.

I anticipated, or hoped for, an easy level down-valley ride for a quick 50 kilometers along the Indus to Leh. There was a strong similarity with my last day's ride into Lhasa. I was coming down off a chilly wet pass, to a main valley and an easy down-valley ride, to a fabled capital starting with 'L'. But instead the road undulated quite steeply, rising over large colluvial fans that spread out into the Indus from side valleys and hillsides, and climbed to a small pass. Recent rains had washed dirt and rocks over the road and there was a good up-valley wind adding to the labor intensity.

I came down off the pass to ride through an enormous military camp spread out along 5 kilometers (3 miles) or so of road. Curiously, the fancy new buildings of the facility were decorated with Chinese style dragons. And in an interesting throw back to Tibet there were billboards announcing how the army was benefiting the progress of Ladakh. It was military installations like this, and their resupply, that accounted for much of the truck traffic I had encountered along the road from Manali.

Following the village of Karu the wind eased, the road quality improved and became more level, and my speed increased. I passed gompas perched on rocky hills at Stakna, Tiksey, Shey, and across the valley at Matho and Stok. I rode down pleasant avenues lined with poplar trees and tall walls that hid solid blocky Ladakhi homes that resembled their Tibetan cousins. Fields and man-planted groves of trees stretched out over the broad level valley floor bounded by arid mountainsides of rock that rose into the clouds.

Looking down-valley I could see a nasty wall of rain and cloud moving up-valley to greet me. Sure enough, as I made the long uphill climb towards Leh, through yet another military camp, it began to rain and kept it up for the last 8 kilometers into the town. The Indus valley had grown to a huge expanse dozens of kilometers across and Leh sat high and far from the Indus at the top end of long straight slopes. I could barely make out the old palace that perched on the craggy hill above the town. Directly below it was the town center, and sprawling down towards the Indus was the bulk of the town that was so prolonged and dreary in the rain. It was an altogether different entrance to that coming into Lhasa. So much for comparisons.

Close into the town center I went straight to a bakery to appease my soggy spirits but the line was so long I gave up and went off in search of Monika. I found the agreed guesthouse and a note from Monika saying that she was staying in a different place. Back on the street, as I was attempting to get directions, she materialized out of the ethos. She took me back to a cozy room, a hot shower and food.

We spent a couple of days around Leh, relaxing and going on very short forays into the surrounds. We climbed to the palace and gompa above the old town to expansive views across the broad Indus valley to the south and up to Kardung La, my road ahead, to the north. We wandered through the town and out into a system of lovely rock wall lined lanes that traversed the side valley leading up to Kardung La, linking homes, fields and stupas. We walked up to Tisseru Stupa. It wasn't exactly clear by looking at it whether this brown 11th century ruin was half built, half falling apart or under renovation. It had elements that appeared to be new while most of it appeared to be crumbling. We walked down the street to the bright white, and relatively new, Shanti Stupa, that sat prominently on a low hill west of Leh and made a great spot for some good views and idle contemplation.

We took a bus down the road, past the airport, to Spituk Gompa, that clung improbably to a hill that protruded out of the plain beside the Indus. We wandered slowly through the maze of alleys, paths and buildings around the gompa complex and sat listening to the deep guteral sounds of six monks performing puja (prayer) in the main hall. Up on the roof the view was half wonderful, half deplorable. To the north-west and extending westwards was a mess of the airport and military facilities, with long fences, ugly buildings, piles of construction materials and roads. Coming down the middle of the valley from the east wound the Indus, and the broad plain of green irrigated land, fields, trees, and grass alongside it. Long straight slopes of the valley sides led to barren ranges, the Zanskar to the south, and the Ladakh to the north. A dusting of snow highlighted the Ladakh Range white. We walked down the Indus along quiet paths alongside rock walls that surrounded green fields, in a bucolic scene far removed from the crap on the other side of the hill. The sun was low, a warm glow bathed the river, the trees alongside it, and the gompa and range that rose beyond.

Leh had changed. I had been here in 1986 and my traveling companion and I had been two of the 10 foreigners in the town. There were only a couple of restaurants that catered to westerners and a couple of guesthouses that housed them. The old town was primarily the domain of the

Ladakhi. It was their town, with their stores, and the place still had the feeling of being a lonely outpost buried deep in the mountains. It took half a day at the bank to change money. By the time I had returned 20 years later, the main bazaar and some of the radiating streets had become lined with the same tourist businesses, as in Manali, Kathmandu, and Pokhara, that seemed to follow tourists where ever they went. Restaurants, guesthouses, gift shops, internet cafes, and travel agents were standard fare.

    I guessed that there were upwards of 300 foreigners in Leh while I was there, and this was just the shoulder season. Indeed the tourist business in any of these places displaced the very things the tourists had come to experience, the culture of the people. Yet the tourists also demanded these things, they wanted food that was either familiar or a blend of familiar and local. They wanted to be able to send messages to folks back home, to have comfortable beds in comfortable rooms, and to have day trips and tours organized for them. Ultimately what they got was a homogenization of culture, where one place was barely any different from the other. And the situation worked for everyone, the tourists got their services, the locals got an income and lifestyle previously unimagined. For the first time tourist they didn't notice the change, the deterioration in the local culture, they had nothing to compare it to. The local people thought they were advancing with the rest of the world and a loss of culture was a small price to pay for the financial wealth and more westernized standard of living.

    We had arrived in Leh just in time for a local festival organized by the local tourist organization in order to promote tourist visitation at the tail end of the season. There was a parade that was supposed to be a caravan serai from the days of the Silk Road. There was about two dozen half interested, half hearted locals, dressed as Central Asians on the Silk Road who were outnumbered by camera-toting tourists. There was a horse polo game attended by locals and tourists alike. Nothing about the festival seemed too genuine.

Monks blow horns from Spituk gompa in the Indus Valley

The other change was in the locals themselves and what they wore. In 1986 Leh was full of Ladakhis that wore traditional maroon robes, the standard attire of the land. Twenty years later Ladakhis shared their town with Kashmiris, plains Indians, and foreigners, and few Ladakhis wore maroon. Most wore a form of western clothes or the shalwar kameez, the typical attire of plains Indians, Nepalis and Kashmiris.

The whole scene reminded me of why I try not to visit the same place more than once. It was indeed, never as good as the first time, the world was changing and as far as I was concerned it wasn't for the better. I travelled to visit beautiful places, to find exotic traditional cultures, and experience a place as it is, not as I would want it to be, nor to be comfortable, nor to have the services I needed. Through my travels it had become clear that cultures across the world were disappearing, along with their traditional ways, clothing, habits, homes, rituals, religions and languages. Driven by visions of wealth and modernity people were only to happy to sacrifice tradition for progress and a western-style homogeneity where folks bore little difference from one region to another. There would be a point in the not so distant future when all of humanity would wear jeans and a t-shirt, work nine to five jobs, do their shopping in malls and supermarkets, and come home to watch TV at night. While loss of biodiversity received all sorts of press, the loss of cultural diversity went by in silence, partly because there was no doubt in the minds of all involved that progress was all for the good, that everyone was complicit in the process, and everyone was too busy getting rich to consider what they had lost. But loss it was indeed and the world would be all the worse for it.

I felt that coming back to a place a second time was recipe for disappointment. The first visit created a vision, a memory of what a particular place was like and created an expectation of what it would be like the second time. We all know how dangerous expectations can be. Considering progress, there was little chance a foreign land and its people could survive intact and live up to the original experience of the first visit. It was better for me to go somewhere new, a place that was expectation free, a place that was certain to have been a victim of progress, but at least I didn't have anything to compare it to.

I had come back to Leh a second time, but it was a part of a bigger plan, to ride through Tibet and along the

Himalaya. It was one of three places that I had been a second time, along with Kathmandu and Pokhara, all had changed and grown and all had been relatively disappointing. And all had been largely unavoidable given the route I had chosen.

My route would continue north from Leh. Monika caught the 5 am bus, I worked on the bike and set off at 6:30 am. The way ahead was a dead end, a round trip, I would be coming back to Leh. I had whittled my luggage down to the barest minimum and left most of it in Leh. Monika carried some and I was left with one front pannier on the rear rack. I had good reason, I was going to cycle over the highest vehicular road in the world. Or so the sign said.

Instantly free of the burden of my usual weight the climb up towards Khardung La was smooth and relatively fast. I cycled up beside the tongue of green of the irrigated fields above Leh, then started in on a long series of switchbacks that wound up the side of the Ladakh range. The views became ever more expansive, out over Leh, down across the Indus, and up to the snow capped Zanskar Range with 6,151 meter (20,182 foot) Stok Kangri standing impressively above the range in a cloudless sky. With less weight I moved faster, and with less effort. I greeted the interminable switchbacks more with delight than dread. I passed through a checkpost and ran off the end of the pavement. The rocky road that followed was so much easier to negotiate without the load. The pass itself was little more than a cleft in the narrow range, it housed a host of ugly military buildings, and no less than ten signs that boasted it being the highest motorable road in the world. All of them were clearly wrong.

While the signs claimed the altitude of the pass to be 5,602 meters (18,379 feet), modern technology had clearly reported the height at around 5,359 meters (17,582 feet). The BRO had chosen notoriety over accuracy and left the historical, but inaccurate, information in place. There are higher motorable passes in western Tibet: Suge La at 5,430 meters (17,815 feet), and Sumo La at 5,565 meters (18,258 feet). There is also Marsimik La at 5,582 meters (18,313 feet) in the Ladakh range, north-east of Khardung La, although whether this one is motorable is debatable. Regardless, Khardung La would be my highest cycled pass. Not quite happy with that I tried to hike higher up the ridge but was prevented from going far by poor, crusty, breakable snow.

The road down the other side was terrible, very much a 4WD road as it cut across the steep snow covered slopes. About three kilometers down I came upon a familiar sight, Monika, standing in the middle of the road. Her bus had lost its brakes, fortunately without coming to grief, and the driver and his helper had been working on it for the past four hours with little chance of success. With virtually zero traffic the options for her forward progress were not looking good for Monika. Eventually a few vehicles did materialize and Monika hopped a ride in the back of a pickup and I continued my descent.

The descent into the Shyok valley, a major river that drained the Ladakh and Karakoram ranges, was spectacular. With good pavement, the road swooped down into a vertical world of rocks and earth tone pastels to a series of villages that made terraces and green from the less steep of the slopes. The road curled around into the huge valley of the Shyok. Huge mountainsides rose above wide level gravel plains and the multiple channels of the braided river. Triangular shaped villages of green covered alluvial fans that spread from the mouths of narrow canyons into the valley. The road dropped down to the river and followed it downstream into an Indus like up-valley wind. But as the valley widened, approaching the vast gravel flats at the Nubra River junction, the wind calmed. Low, late-day light cast over the landscape and rays of sun moved across the mountainsides. I cycled up the gentle slopes away from the river to Diskit, a village surviving from a side-valley's meltwater, and found Monika at the prearranged guesthouse. She had arrived barely 20 minutes before me.

The survival of Diskit, like so many of the villages on the dry side of the Himalaya, and like so many I had passed on this journey, depended on the meltwater coming down side valleys from glaciers and snow fields far above the valley floors. Winter snows were stored in bodies of ice high on the mountains and were released slowly and conveniently during the growing season when the villagers needed the water most. Judging by the barren mountainsides, there just wasn't enough summer precipitation for vegetation and crops to grow from rainfall alone. With the continued prominence of climate change and global warming the prospects of continued survival of these villages was not looking good. As the planet heated up those glaciers and snowfields would melt out of existence, leaving the feeding streams dry for most of the growing season. Without crops to sustain them, the people who lived in these environments would be forced out of their homes of centuries, forced into towns, or to the southern wet side of the Himalayas, and an alien environment, an altogether different lifestyle and an already crowded landscape. These cultures and their home landscapes would cease to exist.

We took a wander up the hill above Diskit the next morning, past a line of large white chortens, and a school for little monks that was closed and quiet. We climbed past a gompa to a perch on a narrow ridge between the narrow side valley gorge and the main Shyok valley. The landscape here was immense. The valley floor was at 3,000 meters (10,000 feet) altitude and was several miles of gravel and irrigated fields across. Mountainsides rose another 3,000 meters (10,000 feet) of naked geology in one dramatic step to glaciated peaks. We returned to the gompa and found an old smiley bent over monk who opened the temples for us to have a look.

Back at the guesthouse we decided to continue down valley to the next village, Hunder. I rode and Monika walked, we would meet there. It was an easy and short 7 kilometers past a collection of sand dunes to the village. But the village had no center, I rode past the entire village before realizing it. I came to the next checkpost, and a man with a gun, as far as any foreigner could go on this road. From there the road continued down the Shyok valley and slid into northern Pakistan, to join the Indus that then flowed past Skardu, the principle town in Baltistan, wound around Nanga Parbat and dropped through the foothills to the plains. It was another great ride spoiled by the idiocy of man's eternal squabbles. I would've happily lugged all my panniers over Khardung La to continue down this road, to wander at will far into the mountains of northern Pakistan, though Baltistan, Gilgit, Hunza and Chitral, to come out of the mountains in some place like Peshawar, at the base of the Khyber Pass and the Afghanistan border. Instead I returned along the road and turned into the greenery of Hunder and wandered around in circles for 45 aggravating minutes before finally locating the guesthouse where I met Monika.

What had made for a trial of destination orientated cycling made for a delightful, directionless afternoon's amble. We followed our noses for several hours around a lovely maze of paths, irrigation canals, and rough roads that wound through fields and past solid Ladakhi homes that sat amid colorful displays of flower and vegetable gardens. It was unusual to see floral gardens in these environments. So much of what was grown had a utilitarian purpose; food, wood, feed for animals, that flowers seemed almost frivolous. There was so much variety in the gardens and yards of these folks that we couldn't help but peek over the fences to see what they had around their homes. Part way along we were chased down by a young lady who invited us into have tea in her home. We joined a large group of people and were given tea with a large dob of butter floating on the top. That was followed by some extremely weak black tea that was more sugar than tea. It was a very social occasion, people chatted away and came and went on a regular basis. With many refills of tea consumed we excused ourselves and continued on our stroll.

We spent the day in Hunder, climbing up the valley side 400 meters (1,300 feet) to a spectacular high point with views to snowy pinnacles to the south and the Shyok valley to the north. In the afternoon we continued our stroll of the previous afternoon into another area of the village that was not nearly as developed or well established. The homes were newer, the gardens nonexistent. We came out onto a grass field, young boys played cricket, three young girls squatted nearby, watching us watch them. Later the town's goats wandered back up the trail from the day's grazing on the wide valley floor. The goats had clearly done this all before and they split up and all headed off to their respective houses without being herded.

The next morning we leap-frogged our way back up the Shyok, and then up the Nubra valley, to Sumur. I left Monika on the side of the road to catch a bus, or whatever else happened to be coming down the road. I wound past Diskit, was passed by Monika in a tiny Suzuki car, returning to the intersection I had passed three days before, to find Monika sitting by the road. Monika soon had a ride in a military vehicle and I continued, crossing the Shyok, and winding around into the Nubra, to Sumur. I found Monika sitting outside a deserted guesthouse. There were apparently no laws in India about using the name of another guesthouse for one's own. Pirated restaurant, hotel and guesthouse names were a ubiquitous part of Indian travel, sometimes the names varied by the addition of 'New' or '1'. Monika was sitting at the wrong guesthouse. The one we wanted, with the same name, was just around the corner.

The next day we continued up the Nubra Valley as an out-and-back day trip. Again I rode, leaving Monika to find a motor. It was a lovely ride along good pavement with little traffic past a line up of dry mountainsides, green villages, alluvial fans and rocky pinnacles. Monika's bus pulled into Panamik just I arrived. We continued along the road north together, Monika walking and I cycling very slowly. We were going to see how far we could get. We initially thought the check post would be just on the edge of Panamik. Instead it was 5 kilometers (3 miles) up the road. Indeed we walked right past it before a local man called out to us and we returned to find the policeman, fresh from his midday nap. This was the furthest north we could go in India. From there the Nubra valley continued north to the Siachen Glacier, scene of the world's highest battleground.

At 70 kilometers (43 miles) long, the Siachen Glacier is the second longest glacier outside of the polar regions. It drains a remote corner of the Karakoram Mountains where the Indian, Pakistani and Chinese borders meet. It is far too high and isolated for anyone to live there yet India and Pakistan have been waging a protracted war over the region since 1984. During the conflict, from 1984 to 2003, when a cease fire was reached, about 2,000 men died mostly from weather extremes, altitude sickness, avalanches and the other natural hazards of mountain warfare, rather than the war itself. Each country had camps with thousands of men, each country spent hundreds of millions of dollars on the conflict, and poured thousands of tons of trash into the crevasses of the glacier. The conflict was instigated by the Indians in response to intrusions by the Pakistanis into Indian held territory. India came out of the conflict ahead, adding about 1,000 square miles to its land area. While there is a cease fire, there is still an armed presence and still deaths. Men continue to be killed by avalanches.

This whole absurd conflict was a just a chapter in the long running dispute between India and Pakistan over its common border. The partition of British India into Muslim dominated Pakistan and Hindu dominated India in 1947 set into motion a series of wars and an arms race, which has turned nuclear, that centers largely on the control of Kashmir, the mountainous region in the north. The first war, still in 1947, pushed the border into Indian territory, with India losing much of the Islamic dominated mountains to Pakistan. The resulting cease fire line, a.k.a. the border, though still leaves the prized, and Muslim dominated, Vale of Kashmir in the hands of the Indians. In 1989 an armed insurgency started in Kashmir fueled by Kashmiri separatists, Pakistani and Afghani militants, and Pakistani government influences, against the ruling Indian government. Again, after years of conflict Kashmir remains in the control of the Indians. In an echo of the Palestine-Israeli conflict it would be an interminable dispute. Kashmiris would always want their own state, Pakistan would always want Kashmir, and the Indians would never give it up willingly. Humanity was such a bull-headed state of existence.

The ride further up the Nubra valley was another great ride gone to waste at the hands of man's incessant bickering.

We turned around and walked down-valley until Monika hitched a ride. I was left to have a superlative ride back to Sumur. Back in the village I went out for a stroll in the late afternoon light. It was a gorgeous walk with sun casting long shadows, highlighting golden fields of grain and vibrant green trees, white glacial peaks standing proudly across the valley. There were quaint walled paths winding by fields and chortens, and prayer wheels at surprising and strategic locations. Local folks were finishing their field work for the day, bringing in animals or hanging out in their rustic home yards.

It was a beautiful dramatic place the Shyok. Tranquil subsistence activity took place below grand and spectacular mountains, the contrast as deep as between the village oases and the barren mountainsides. Dark intimidating afternoon thunderstorms glided across the valleys, leaving glistening rocks, rainbows and solitary sunbeams casting into the valleys in their path. Peaceful paved roads wound between isolated villages that were havens of life and culture in a landscape that dwarfed and humbled. Thick, yellow flowering seabuckhorn thornbush partially covered gravel plains where two humped bactrian camels roamed. Life rambled on peacefully, growing and sustaining, working in collusion with elements that dominated so dramatically.

The summer was a busy time for the couple that owned the guesthouse. They ran the guesthouse but were also a teacher and a student assistant. At the end of the summer season they turned off the water into the house and carried it in from a nearby well. They shut up most of the house and lived in the central room with the stove. The winter was slow but there were many festivals to keep them active. The war at the head of the valley had had little effect on them other than the military vehicles that plied the roads and occasional booms that echoed through the night.

Forward progress meant back tracking to Leh. I wasn't really up for the 1,800 meter (6,000 foot) climb back over a pass I had already climbed, so I joined Monika for a hitch in whatever motor we could find coming down the road. After the death of Monika's bus over Khardung La, on the way out, and the absence of a bus arriving from Leh the previous day, there probably wasn't going to be a bus back to Leh. Our transport turned out to be a jeep. With 11 people and belongings on board it wasn't bound to be comfortable. Fortunately it took enough breaks to offset the cramped conditions. The views certainly weren't the same as riding over Khardung La. As is often the case I was reminded why I chose the bicycle over cramped, confined tin cans with limited views and little freedom.

We spent a couple of days in Leh getting organized for the journey ahead, The end of the cycling was not that far down the road, but our journey together would continue through the mountains. There was sure to be a shortage of supplies in the villages so we loaded up, unsure of where the next sustenance would be. That done we set off on some small excursions into the surrounds.

The seasons were progressing. We wound through the maze of fields, paths, walls and canals behind Leh, trees in dull yellow stood among green ones, folks were out harvesting grain in the late afternoon light, and fallen leaves covered paths and grass. It was a reminder that we needed to keep moving if we were to be out of the mountains by the time the snow flew and the passes closed. In this desert, floods had hit the local area hard, roads and bridges had been carried away, fields were covered in mud washed down from overflowing banks.

We took the bus up the Indus valley to an old palace and gompa in Shey, then walked through the fields to the gompa at Tiksey. The main attraction at Tiksey gompa was the massive two story high golden Buddha housed inside one of the main buildings.

Ladakh was known by some non-Ladakhis as Little Tibet. It had that high dry mountainous environment hidden beyond the ranges, and the strong Tibetan Buddhist culture. Indeed Ladakh's culture and religion had survived the last century unscathed by invading armies and outside regimes bent on destruction and assimilation. Its gompas had not been destroyed, its monks and lay people had not been killed, tortured or forced to commit acts against their will. Even the invasion of military bases had left the culture and religion intact. Tibetan culture in Ladakh was considered to be more genuine and stronger than in Tibet itself.

We returned to our leap-frogging form of duel transport for a series of four one-day hops, to continue down the Indus toward the Pakistan border and Kargil, the end of my ride. Monika set off for the bus and I rolled down a quiet side road out of Leh. Joining the main road brought 8 kilometers (5 miles) of ugly traffic-marred cycling as I rode past the airport, and the series of military camps, with trucks, convoys, and buses. Beyond the bases I was returned to relative peace and a road width that shrunk to one lane. The road climbed away from the Indus to a small pass. Approaching the summit, the surrounding smooth gentle slopes were covered in purple flowers, possibly erupting in response to the recent rains.

Although parallel and not that far away, the Indus had a very different geomorphology to the Shyok to the north. The Shyok valley had vast wide gravel flats and ridge-lines that rose in one enormous steep pitch to its summits.

The valley of the Indus, downstream of Leh, was much narrower, the river flowing through a clearly defined V-shaped gorge. The slopes rose away from it more gently with intervening hills, broader side valleys, angled smooth terrace areas, and a more complex landform that was far less open and visible.

I came down from the pass to a viewpoint over the junction of the light gray Zanskar River, and the darker green-grey Indus River. A little further on there was a turnoff for the road that wound up the Zanskar. There was a sign that had a listing of villages and locales; Chilling, Padum, Shingo La and Darcha, and the distances to each up that road. The sign was more a vision of the future than current actuality as the road hadn't yet been built to many of the places listed. But it was a sign of the time when the whole of Zanskar, a mountain locked region of the Himalaya, would be criss-crossed by a system of roads that would make travel through the mountains infinitely easier and irrevocably change the lives of the people who lived there.

I had come down the Zanskar twenty years before. I had been on a trek with two others. We had started in Lamayuru, crossed over two passes, and came out on the Zanskar at the village of Chilling, an isolated village where locals made metal pots. The sound of repeated metallic hammering echoed over the village. The trek down the Zanskar had been exciting and eye opening. A rough, narrow trail, that was as much guess-work as actuality, clung to valley sides of loose rock and cliffs. Periodically it was built from rough bits of wood that precariously traversed cliff-faces. The muddy Zanskar River flowed by unconcerned directly below. It was the main route to Chilling for the locals, but they preferred the winter, when the river froze over, and they could just simply walk up the ice. We had eventually hit the road that was being advanced up the valley by a hard working dusty road crew with picks and the most rudimentary of mechanical drills. The road's progress was painfully slow and twenty years later it only extended up the gorge just past Chilling, still far from the wider valley of Zanskar beyond. This road and all the others in the mountains brought change, development, western ways, and cultural dilution, inherent in progress. While I was about to have benefit from the recently built Zanskar River road I wasn't too happy about its nasty side effects. Progress was a bitter sweet pill.

With a short day to Alchi, my day's destination, I decided to take the side trip up the Zanskar for a look-see and a little wander up memory lane. Dead end and paved, it was one of the nicest rides of the journey. There were constant river views, almost no traffic, a slight tailwind going up and a downhill advantage returning, easy gentle riding, and the scenery a dramatic blaze of geology in a variety of colors, forms, and angles. I gazed up at the valley sides and wondered how I had managed to negotiate the cliffs and rock ribs on foot before the road made it into an easy roll. I made it 21 kilometers (13 miles) up the valley, stopped at a tea stall to resupply, and returned back to the Indus.

I continued west and down-valley, through Nimmu, which was largely under construction, through another military base, and then up through Basgo. The road began to climb again to a small unexpected pass, which didn't seem so small now that the day was getting long. My side trip up the Zanskar was beginning to take its toll. Adding to my decline, road signs indicated that it was much further to Alchi than I had planned. I sat at the top of the pass eating. A van pulled up and six clearly drunk guys jumped out and danced to loud music thumping from the vehicle. I left them to their revelry and rolled down off the pass.

The road wound back down to the Indus through Saspul and crossed the river. I took a side road up to Alchi. It had been a whole lot more day than I had anticipated and there was little of it left by the time I got there. I found the guesthouse and Monika, just as we had arranged. With steep valley sides behind it to the south and west, a cool northern exposure, and with all the fields harvested, lifeless and dry, Alchi seemed cold and dark, quite unlike the verdant green of the Shyok, or fields surrounding Leh.

The next morning Monika took a bus for our next destination, Lamayuru. I continued down the Indus, deep in its spectacular gorge, the road gentle rising and falling above the river, below huge cliffs and colorful mountainsides. Just down valley from Khalsi the road forked, right continued down the Indus to prohibited lands, left took the up and over route to Kargil. There was a police check post at the junction and as usual the police were asleep. I rolled slowly by, testing them, and was called back after I was about 100 meters down the road.

The road dropped, crossed the Indus, curled into a side stream, and began its 13 kilometer (8 mile) climb to Lamayuru. The road wound into a steepening gorge, passing a junction, and began to ascend with more vigor. The road cut cross near vertical sides with a straight plunge off the side hundreds of feet to the creek below. The gorge opened out and passed by the lowest fields of Lamayuru. It wound up through the fields, and the village, and I found Monika standing by the side of the road. She had seen me laboring uphill from the guesthouse roof terrace and came out to greet me.

After food and tea we set off to walk the village. We climbed up onto the ridge above the village to a chorten and view out over the gompa, homes and the surrounding landscape. Lamayuru had been traditionally dominated by its fine old gompa that sat improbably on a spur on the valley side. The monks, wanting to capitalize on the passing travelers, built a hotel above the gompa. While it was built in a Ladakhi style, its new angularity, conformity of windows, its four stories and its dominating ridgetop location above the gompa stole dramatically from the sanctity of the view and the presence of the gompa.

In a courtyard of the gompa monks were practicing chams dance, ritual masked dancing with social and spiritual messages, performed by monks decorated with huge colorful masks and cloaks, to traditional music, most often during festivals. They practiced their routines in just their usual maroon robes.

We wound down past the gompa into a small labyrinth of alleys of the old town of Lamayuru. It was a very medieval place with narrow twisty alleys, tiny wooden doors to homes, dark passages, goods piled on flat roofs, with a smell and atmosphere of centuries past. Many buildings were half fallen down, homes crumbling beside those still occupied. It seemed a bit miraculous that they were still able to cling to the steep slopes below the gompa at all.

It was my turn to set off first in the morning and I made the slow climb to the first of the day's two passes, Fotu La. After climbing ever higher passes as I headed north into Ladakh, the passes were now shrinking and I was able to crank two into a day.. Fotu La was 4,108 meters (13,478 feet), and Namika la, was a mere 3,760 meters (12,336 feet).

It was a straightforward and relatively short climb to the summit of Fotu la. The ride down the other side was superlative, good pavement, few vehicles, and views to a spectacular ridge on the south side of the valley cut with deep vertical sided canyons, walls of strata, spires, and ragged ridge-tops. I followed a valley past a yet another military base and several small villages. The road left the main valley for a even shorter climb, 8 kilometers (5 miles), to the summit of Namika La. On the way up a bus went by with a white hand waving out the window, Monika. On the summit a brisk strong wind made for a short stay. It was too risky to take out my camera and put it on a tripod to take a photo of myself and the scenery on the last pass of the journey.

The descent was another wonderful speedy smooth ride down alongside the same spectacular ridge line as on the previous descent. Part way down I passed several men slapping white wash paint on concrete barrels and posts that lined the edge of the road. There was also a man sweeping the road, pushing a thin line of gravel, that ran down the middle of the road, all over the road. The tasks seemed lonely, labor intensive, and pointless. It reminded me of lone road workers I had seen in China sweeping the road with long brooms out in the middle of nowhere, miles from anyone. It was probably the best of a poor range of other income options for these folks.

I hit the bottom of the valley and rolled down to find Monika, who had just arrived at our accommodation, a basic government run tourist bungalow that we had to ourselves. Later we set off for our daily afternoon walk around the village of Mulbekh. The valley was a curious boundary between the massive 1,500 meter (5,000 foot) high wall of rock, reminiscent of the Grand Canyon, on one side, and the smooth mellow slopes on the north side. It was tranquil green fields and smooth round hills, or intimidating verticality. We wandered through the fields, and along the green/arid interface of an irrigation canal, to the center of the village. Cut into a rock face on a roadside pinnacle was an 8 meter (13 feet) high image of a standing Buddha enveloped by a small gompa. We climbed to the top of another pinnacle to catch the last light of day, ate dinner in one of the small simple restaurants by the road, and walked back to the bungalow in the dark.

Mulbekh was a religious and cultural border town. We returned to the road in the morning and Monika soon caught a bus. Cycling down the valley I rode into the thick of Islamic culture. Kids walked to school wearing shalwar kameez and the girls wore head scarves. Mosques stood proudly and distinctly amid villages.

It was an easy ride down the widening valley and up onto a broad terrace, which the road crossed, to a view out over the sprawling town of Kargil. It was immediately an unappealing, unpleasant place, with ugly brown and grey mud and rock architecture, corrugated iron roofs, and military camps. The road cut long switchbacks off the terrace to a bridge, into the frenetic, male dominated, main street bazaar. I found Monika. Since there was no obvious accommodation, this time our meeting place had been a restaurant. It no longer existed, nor was there any other suitable. She had been waiting beside the road, becoming the center of attention for a bunch of local men. It was the only leap-frog that hadn't worked out well for both of us.

We found a hotel, but it was unsuitable. I put on long pants, in deference to local culture, left Monika at the hotel and went off in search of something better. I found a good hotel on the hill above town, with a porch and a view, above the madding crowd of the bazaar.

I had decided long ago that Kargil would be the end of my bicycle journey. And honestly I couldn't think of anywhere better. Even though I had tried. And tried. I had wanted to cycle to the western end of the Himalaya, essentially having cycled its length, even though I had not always been in the mountains themselves. Looking out over the motley collection of buildings, and the unfriendly male dominated bazaar, in the middle of the mountains, I had to wonder again why I chose to stop here.

So many of my journeys ended at places where large bodies of water halted further progress; Ushuaia (Argentina), Singapore, Nordkapp (Norway), Cape Matapan (Greece), Cape Point (South Africa), Slope Point (New Zealand). I had gazed out over the water at these places knowing for a fact, that I could not go any further and I could feel secure and conclusive having definitively come to the end. But in Kargil, I was surrounded by mountains, mountains that weren't all that dissimilar to those I had been going through for months, that continued on across Pakistan, and into Afghanistan. There was nothing conclusive about it.

Given the choice, though, I would've happily continued. Right past Nanga Parbat, the 8,000 meter peak (26,200 feet) that was the western end, and anchor of the Himalaya, and clear into Afghanistan. But the mountains ahead were contentious places with long standing border disputes and recurring wars that forbid forward movement, especially by some foreigner.

Journey's end in Kargil. Note the mosque bottom left.

In Kargil I was as close as I could get to the Pakistan-India ceasefire line, it was about 5 kilometers (3 miles) down the street. To progress further west through these mountains, to get to Nanga Parbat, I would have to cross over Zoji La into Kashmir, turn south, cross the Pir Panjal Range, drop onto the plains of India, go to Delhi to get a Pakistan visa (if the embassy would be willing to part with one), cross the border between Amritsar and Lahore, and cycle back north, through Ralwalpindi and Islamabad, back into the mountains, up the Karakoram highway. This lousy, frenetically busy, circuitous, multi-thousand kilometer detour, would get me the straight line 160 kilometers (100 miles) from Kargil to Nanga Parbat. Getting to Afghanistan would also require leaving the mountains, even if it wouldn't be nearly as far, but crossing the border into Afghanistan would be idiocy in time of war. Kargil would just have to do.

Kargil, though, was more than just an unattractive town in the middle of the mountains. It was the start of the Islamic world that stretched uninterrupted from there to the Atlantic Ocean. I had spent four months traversing the world of the Tibetan Buddhists, and the related Hindus, from the once communists of China, to the Muslims by the Pakistan border. My journey had been across a large chunk of Tibet, and along the Himalayas, through the Indian plains, but its unifying force had been the culture, the people, and their religion. The male dominated bazaar and the domes and minarets that protruded above the town of Kargil were clear signs that my journey, my traverse of the Tibetan lands was complete. The journey had clearly been a very physical one, but it had also been an exploration of a people, a faith, and the environment that had molded them, and that they had molded.

In the 132 days of the journey I had cycled 5,908 kilometers (3,671 miles), climbed a vertical 63,490 meters (208,300 feet) over 38 passes, and spent 423 hours on the go. Adding in the hiking made the distance 6,749 kilometers (4,194 miles), the vertical 84,125 meters (276,000 feet), the passes 42. Of those passes, 18 were over 5,000 meters (16,500 feet).

Indeed it had been a physical journey, but even that side had its internal, spiritual manifestation. Like so many adventures my journeys were never easy cups of tea. More often than I care to think about there had been times when traffic, topography, weather, road surface, or my health had made progress tedious, difficult, unenjoyable, or just a trial. I took plenty of opportunities to curse the foes to my enjoyment and travel, expletives that dispelled pointlessly into the wind. These largely uncontrollable difficulties though were elemental parts of the experience, inherent to the landscape, the road, the time that I was there. I could not control them but I could control myself. And the one unifying factor of all of these difficulties was that they would all eventually come to an end. And I would continue on. The road would smoothen, the road would go down, the weather would clear, I would find a quiet road and hopefully, I would get well. There would be a delight around some bend, a grand sight, a great human experience, a smile from a local, a thrilling decent, a beautiful place to stop, rest or camp. And I never knew where or when it would happen. It was the trial and the joy of the unknown, that made it all worthwhile, and continuing on was the only way to find it. By unconsciously eliminating the concept of failure from the possible outcomes I had made success the only possibility. Appreciating and overcoming the difficulties was as elemental to the experience as enjoying the beauties and savoring the rewards. The bicycle was just a tool.

And this tool allows for perspective of scale. It is easy for those in motorized conveyances and the comfort of a lounge chairs and modern communications to feel the shrinking size of the planet. But bound by muscular capability, distance and verticality retains its individual-dwarfing dominance. From the vantage point of my bicycle seat there was no mistaking the space between points, the altitude of the mountains, and the effort to get there. It was easy to respect the planet, its size, and the elements that had such control over my time and experience. It was a lot more difficult to reconcile oneself to these natural factors, to achieve one's desired ends given one's own physical limitations. Adjusting human capability to planetary scale was all a part of the process of the journey.

By setting a journey, and overcoming the obstacles that I had unwittingly set before me, I had explored my earth-bound nirvana of internal exploration and superlative environment. A nirvana that was as much a process as an end state. For I was little more enlightened, no more deeply tranquil than when I started. It was a nirvana of doing and achieving what felt like my life's purpose; exploring the world, finding its peoples, its beauties, treasures and delights along with its trials, and usually man-made ugliness. It was overcoming difficulties, realizing goals, sacrificing comforts, physically, mentally, and emotionally, for greater returns down the road. It was finding an internal peace through accomplishment, and reaching the end, wherever that would be, through one's own efforts. It was perhaps, what the Tibetan Buddhist pilgrimage was all about.

Of course I was not done, the process would continue, there would be other red lines for me to draw across maps of the world, other obstacles that I would plant before myself and hopefully learn to live with. It was my life's purpose after all. I would eventually return to some place more comfortable and stable and enjoy it for a while until the yearning for exploration itched again and I cast my eyes about for another direction to drive myself.

For now though, I just had to get out of Kargil.

7

THE JOURNEY OUT

Getting out of Kargil quickly turned into be a pain in the neck. It wasn't the kind of place to linger enjoying local ambiance. The town had a overlying dusty dirty seediness, with a main street packed with semi-idle males, with unappealing, pokey and rudimentary restaurants that served stinky meat stews. There was not a female in sight.

Without backtracking we had a choice of two directions to make our way out of the mountains. We could go forward, continuing on the Leh to Srinagar road over Zoji La, dropping into Kashmir and a green landscape. The second option was to bounce off the Islamic world and turn south, returning into Buddhist society, venturing into Zanskar, a mountainous region between Ladakh and the Pir Panjal Range, a route that would eventually bring us back to Manali. I had been to Kashmir before the decade long insurgency. The conflict had certainly not left the Vale any better off and I was happy with my memory of bucolic lakes, tree-lined canals, and a friendly welcoming Islamic folk who lived on the water. I did not have to muddy these fine waters with a country that was surely tainted by conflict. After only a few hours in Kargil Monika was of no mind to further her Islamic experience. Neither of us had been to Zanskar and the region held all the mystic of a lost mountain Shangri la. It was no competition.

Kargil, though, was not representative of the whole. I had travelled to other Islamic states; Pakistan, Kashmir, Kashgar, Zanzibar, Malaysia. In Chitral, in northern

Pakistan, I couldn't go out the door of the guesthouse without being approached or called over by someone, somewhere along the way, as I walked, to join them for tea, food, or conversation. In Zanzibar there were women aplenty in markets, in the streets, often wearing head scarves, but visible, full members of the community. There were attractive colorful markets and the wonderful maze of streets of Old Town that lured one to wander. In Malaysia the women were the main attraction of the scene as they drove cars, rode motorcycles, walked the streets, and did business in the market, wearing brilliantly colorful flowing robes and head scarves. There were large interior markets, attractive homes, and mosques. In Kashgar there had been an enormous market, narrow lanes, the colorful Uyghur people, and dirt tracks that wandered along irrigation canals out into the green oasis made from the desert. I had enjoyed Islamic societies, the people were often friendly, the faith was strong, the culture mingled with varying states of westernization. Every country, culture, and people had its grungy element. In Tibet the people had been beautiful, the towns were often unattractive. And the Islamic Indian mountains had Kargil.

The afternoon stroll ritual we had developed as we traveled had lost its appeal in Kargil, but we set off on foot anyway to research transport to Zanskar. We did the rounds of the public and private bus stands, little more than tracts of dirt, and from what we could gather, there would be a bus in two days. Yippee, a day in Kargil.

Yet when we arrived at the bus stand the next morning to buy tickets, as we had been instructed, we could get neither clear answers to our questions about the next bus, nor could we get tickets. There was either no bus tomorrow, or maybe there would be a bus tomorrow. Nobody really seemed to know. It seemed to hinge on whether a bus would arrive from Leh bound for Zanskar. And nobody would know that until it arrived. We returned to the bus stand in the afternoon. Still no bus or news. But there was a German with a private jeep, and far as he was concerned we could hitch a ride on his jeep the next day. But when we arrived at the prearranged spot the next morning, loaded up and ready to go, the driver vetoed the idea, claiming we had too much gear. Admittedly we were now hauling around a bicycle, a backpack and six panniers, but he had the room, he just didn't want us on board.

With no bus, no jeep, and in fear of spending another day in Kargil, we scurried. We had met a couple of Russians the day before who wanted to get a private jeep towards Zanskar. We roused them out of bed and had a quorum to hire a jeep, albeit at many times the price of the bus that didn't exist. We found a jeep and a driver to take us to Rangdum, about halfway to Padum, the main town at the center of Zanskar.

We motored slowly out of the town and up the Suru valley, stopping for diesel and air, to say hello to the driver's friends, and to stop at his home, to say goodbye to his family. The road was almost immediately a rough potholed mess as it wound through a succession of small villages clustered around mosques along the valley.

It was a different sensation, movement without effort, sitting in the comparative luxury of a jeep watching the world go by. But I had strong twinges of regret that I was also missing something in this tin can being unable to stop, or see the entire view, my schedule in the hands of someone else. Indeed the whole transport issue in Kargil would've been different if I had been by myself. Hell, no bus? I would've just loaded up on food and cycled up the Suru.

Approaching the village of Pannikar, the great glaciated mass of Nun Kun came into view rising above a smooth low level ridge. Nun and Kun are a pair of peaks rising to just over 7,000 meters (23,000 feet), their twin summits startling and brilliant in the clear blue sky, arresting after so much rock. The valley narrowed and curled around the end of the low ridge, with massive peaks above, and villages below. We crossed the river at a slot canyon where a mass of rock and debris had fallen into the canyon so that the river was effectively going underground.

After climbing steeply, we came out onto the relatively level treeless green of Parkachik. Both Monika and I had noticed the drooping eyelids of the sleepy driver but failed to do anything about it. Then all of a sudden Monika sprung forward from our rear seat, yelling and turning the steering wheel as the jeep veered toward the roadside ditch, the driver having nodded off. With the noise, the driver slammed on the brakes and the vehicle came to rest about 3 inches from a 1 meter (3 foot) drop into the ditch. Monika's lightning fast reactions had definitely saved us from a nasty tumble off the road, a tumble that would've been nothing compared to many of the drop-offs we had been driving by since Kargil. We all unloaded from the jeep. The vehicle was perched with one front wheel sagging off the road, in a position the driver could not drive out of. I took my bike off the roof just in case the jeep should roll. The driver enlisted a local man's help. After twenty minutes of shoveling, followed by a fast acceleration, the jeep was back in the middle of the road. The relatively benign ride had gained an edge.

We continued up the valley below huge walls that rose 3000 meters (10,000 feet) up to the summits of Nun and Kun, and down which flowed dirty glaciers that came almost to the river. The valley gradually opened out into a broad level plain. We came into Rangdum, the end of our ride, a small village that spread out over the thin grassland. We took a stroll around the village and down to the river in the late daylight. It was a magnificent place, with the huge back-lit block of Nun and Kun down the valley, the broad plain of the valley surrounded by mighty geologic forms, great sweeps of strata curling down the valley sides. We cooked dinner outside so as to spend as little time as possible in the grotty room of the bungalow, the only accommodation choice in the village. It was a brilliant starry night.

We were far up the Suru valley, beyond the reach of any reasonable transport options. We optimistically anticipated we had a three day, 100 kilometer (62 mile), walk along the 4WD track to get to Padum. We loaded all our gear, save Monika's daypack, onto the bike, which made for one very heavy bike, and set off walking.

Rangdum gompa sits atop a hill below massive geology in the Suru Valley

The valley made a long broad curve 180 degrees. Part way round was Rangdum gompa, magnificently perched on an isolated hill in the middle of the wide plain of the valley floor. Clearly we had returned to the Buddhist lands. At the base of the hill was a small school and the kids were lined up outside the buildings, saying prayers before heading into class.

We continued around the valley's curve and up the valley, past Tashizonglay, and a military camp of about two dozen tents, and a dozen guys, that appeared to have no particular purpose. The road began a long steady climb up to Pensi La, the pass that marked the official border of Zanskar. The road cut in one long diagonal up the side of the valley. To the south there were views up side valleys to peaks and glaciers of the main range of the Himalaya. A bank of cloud moved in. With a headwind the land became cool, grey, and unfriendly.

Used to the heavy work of cycling and unrestrained pace of the solo existence I had been setting a cracking pace, pushing the ridiculously heavy bike along the track. Early in the day Monika had been able to keep up with my speed, even though she certainly hadn't the fitness training I had been giving myself for the last four months. As the day progressed she had faded, the gaps between us grew, and I was waiting longer periods for her to catch up. Once we had begun climbing the pass, camp spots totally disappeared into the steep sides of the valley. With the day coming to a close we had an imperative to get to the summit, an urgency that only exacerbated the growing tension between us. The deteriorating weather reflected, and contributed to, a declining mood. Alone, at 4,300 meters (14,000 feet), on the edge of the pass plateau, amid Himalayan scale elements, personal interaction issues had to be resolved.

We wound over the undulating pass plateau for two kilometers, past a sign welcoming us to the Zanskar Valley, and past a couple of men who collected yak dung to be burnt later as cooking and heating fuel. Right on the summit of the pass was a conveniently located lake. We camped in a nice spot on the lee of a small hill. It was good to be camping once again, alone and away from dubious hotel rooms, even if we were exhausted from the long hike.

We woke in the morning to a dusting of snow on the tent, pots with a layer of ice on the water within them, and a grand view over the Drang Drung glacier. The 23 kilometer (14 mile) long glacier swept off the range to the south, curving around glaciated Doda Peak (6,550meters, 21,490 feet) and down into the valley, to be the headwaters of the Stod River, which we were would follow for the next two days. The first hour's walk, dropping off the pass into the Stod, was spectacular with peak and glaciers views. Once in the valley though, the initial pep to the walk faded as the magnificence mellowed and we were left with a rather dull trudge along long straights in the road through a deep, but unremarkable, valley. After the previous day's bicycle pushing handicap I now had a downhill advantage. I rode slow enough not to get too far ahead of Monika, slow enough to be merciful to my ridiculously overloaded bicycle and I stopped regularly to allow Monika to catch up.

Our lunch was the best Kargil had to offer, coconut cookies with seabuckthorn jam. We found seabuckthorn bushes scattered across the riverine gravels in Nubra and the Ladakhis made a jam from the orange berries that are extremely high in Vitamin C. Considering the intensely thorny nature of the seabuckthorn bushes, harvesting the small berries must've been a challenge.

What Kargil lacked in quality of food it made up for in quantity of coconut cookies. There had been little else in the town that could do as a lunch snack, so we bought a pile of the small packets that would get us to Padum and beyond.

The scenery and interest improved after lunch, with valleys from the south opening up to reveal views to more peaks and glaciers. The track climbed high above the river onto a hilly terrace. Storm after storm floated off the range towards us only to dissipate into the dry air. They brought dark skies but no rain. By late afternoon the sky looked even more threatening, the wind picked up, our pace was slowing and there was no water in the environment for us to camp. Scouting above the track I found a herders camp where rock walls had been built to make corrals for goats and sheep around a huge overhanging boulder. Nearby there was a slow seeping spring that provided just enough water for a camp. We pitched the tent on a smooth surface of dried goat poop and enjoyed a protected spot overlooking what had grown into a grand mountain scene.

We woke to hear folks herding animals on the other side of the valley, 2 or 3 kilometers (1 or 2 miles) away. Outside grasshoppers were everywhere. We would learn later that Zanskar was experiencing a plague of the insects which had eaten most of the grass and crops in the region. Nobody knew where they had come from, or why, and western scientists had come and gone without resolving the issue. It did not look good for the region's animals during the winter.

We rejoined the track and continued towards Padum. The novelty of walking down the road had worn off and we were more concerned about hitching a ride and getting to Padum than soaking in more scenery at walking pace. Still, with not one vehicle going our way in two days of walking the prospects were not too promising. We kept walking just in case it happened to be the only way we were going to get there. We immediately ran into scattered homes on both sides of the valley which gave us some diversion and folks to greet. The scenery, though, had returned to dull and uninteresting, with the road making long straight lines down a gently undulating valley, stretches of road 8 to 10 kilometers (5 to 6 miles) long visible ahead. Part way along, some kids ran up to us and gave us some roasted barley as a snack. It was a wonderful gesture, it buoyed our spirits and we felt better about our predicament. While it was frustrating to be walking when we wanted to progress faster I tried to console myself, realizing that it could be worse. That walking down a big valley in the Himalaya, past occasional glaciated peaks and slopes of raw naked geology, past simple folk and traditional lifestyle, with my partner, was a whole lot better than being stuck in traffic.

For all the trials that I had been through, and this journey wasn't short of them, my lot could've easily been worse. Indeed, part of the whole point of travel was to see how other people were living life.

Across the world I had seen people in relatively torrid states of existence. Scouring piles of garbage for food and recyclable materials, enveloped in toxic clouds of exhaust and smoke, hauling ridiculously heavy loads on their backs, living in slums and shanties, or doing horrible work, in appalling conditions, for a pittance of pay. For the most part their choices were all but non-existent. They were the victims of circumstance, society, upbringing, caste, birth, and a situation that made education, advancement, and alternatives near impossible. For the most part they continued resolutely, doing the best they could to survive, feed their family, and make a life from very little. Sometimes they still bore a pride, cheer, and a feeling of self worth in spite of the overwhelming odds. It was the case throughout the non-western world and even in the poorer sections of the west, where the capitalistic dream was not what it seemed.

One step higher up the economic ladder there were folks that had sufficient to eat, their children were able to go to school, they had simple but comfortable homes, but their lives were basic, elemental, full of hard labor and work, extremely low on material and financial wealth and they gained enjoyment from simple pleasures, family, faith, and community. They had elements of choice but were still tightly bound by their geography, environment, family circumstance, and their meager resources.

Meanwhile I rode through these lands at will. At any time, when the going became too tough, I could stop, get a room, catch a bus, and make my life easier, cushioned as I was by financial resources far beyond the scale of the vast majority in the land through which I was traveling. On many occasions, when the going was getting hard, or the locals were being unruly or difficult, or I was in cultural situations that I found extremely trying, I reassured myself that I was the one who had the last laugh because I could leave and they had no choice but to stay. While I chose cycling for the sheer joy of self propelled movement, and the sights and experiences that it produced, it was inherently prone to labors and difficulties. I had the choice and the resources to stop and leave, and all of these people did not. It was the vast gap that separated us.

I took strength and resolution from these people through which I travelled. They gave me perspective on the scale of my own life and endeavors. For my daily trials of the road and trail were fleeting against the lifetime of many of the folks I travelled by. Regardless of the difficulties I encountered, they always came to an end, the next bend could always bring a change to the circumstance, my day could always instantly improve, life could become better, and I almost always had the choice to change it of my own accord. The rewards of continuing on always out classed the feelings of copping out, giving up, or choosing the easy way out that was not part of my original plan. Difficulties, trials and hardships could always be improved with a change of focus, with a realignment of priorities, with the perspective of relativity. Life could be so much better, so much more enjoyable, if I could just look at it from the right angle.

Halfway into the afternoon a jeep finally came by and we managed to convince them to take Monika, her pack, and some of my panniers. Free of much of my weight and the need to be traveling at walking pace I was able to accelerate from 3 to 5 kilometers per hour (2 to 3 miles per hour) up to a mighty 12 kilometers per hour (8 miles per hour). There were more villages, kids that ran up to the road yelling as I went by, and even trees in clumps beside homes. The valley widened as it neared the great bend of the valley, as it joined with the Tsarap River, and turned north. After a lot of rough rocky road I hit pavement for the last few kilometers into Padum and I found Monika in the middle of the street.

The scruffy little settlement of Padum sits on the side of a vast smooth valley, scattered with homes, surrounded by huge valley sides in geologic earthtones. In a way it was reminiscent of the Nubra/Shyok river junction, but in Zanskar there were no oases, no clusters of verdant greenery, fields, and trees being fed by a system of irrigation canals. In Zanskar there was just enough rainfall creeping over the Himalayas to allow natural grasslands, if not trees, to grow and for homes to be located anywhere. The grass allowed for an animal based agriculture, if the grasshoppers didn't get to it first.

Padum was roughly halfway in our journey from Kargil to Manali. If we thought getting out of Kargil was difficult then we were about to embark on trying to get out of Padum. For Padum it was the shoulder tourist season, many of the stores along the rough main street were closed and boarded up, and supplies in the stores that remained were limited. The next leg of our journey was the 150 kilometer (94 mile) trek over the 5,096 meter (16,720 feet) high Shingo La back into Lahaul, the region I had passed through between Manali and Leh. While a road was being built at a snail's pace from each end over the pass, the vast majority of the distance was trekking trail. With our small mountain of gear we needed horses and a man to go with them.

While Monika had been waiting for me to arrive by bike she had inquired around Padum about horses. The horseman she had been talking to arrived at our door the next morning. While he was a Zanskari, he brought along a suspect looking Muslim man who was trying to get back to his home near Manali after a summer in Zanskar, and was clearly hoping that he could make some money along the way. He quickly made demands about advance payment and making a decision NOW about whether we would hire him. We recoiled and passed.

Later we found Jimmy, a Zanskari who had worked for foreign tour companies for 26 years, who knew a local man who would take us. But by late afternoon, that horseman had not arrived and we were back to hunting down our original Muslim fellow for lack of anything else. We cracked a deal and agreed to meet the next morning. We scoured the few remaining stores in Padum for food and were happy that we had lugged food from Kargil. With that, and what we could find in Padum, we had enough for the 7 day trek to Lahaul, including 14 packets of coconut cookies, the staple of Ladakhi cuisine.

The horseman arrived at 8:30 in the morning and proceeded to divide our gear among his five horses. The wheels and pedals came off the bike, the seat dropped, and the handlebars turned. The frame and one wheel went on one horse, the other wheel on another, and our panniers and packs were distributed into equally weighted loads and strapped onto the sides of horses. We set off, walking through the streets of Padum, to the amusement of locals looking at our bicycle laden horses. We followed the dirt road heading up the Tsarap Valley. The road would eventually link Padum with Darcha, a village I had cycled through north of Keylong, on the Manali Leh road. It was also the same road that would go down the Zanskar River and come out on the Indus where I had been on the Leh Kargil road. This was the road that would, when completed, thoroughly change life and society in Zanskar.

From Padum the road soon entered a gorge. Part way up we encountered about a hundred Indian road workers taking a lunch break. They were a friendly enough bunch, especially considering they spent all day bashing rocks and laying down dirt to make a smooth road. Yes, my periodic trials sometimes paled by comparison.

Further up we passed through the tiny village of Barden that had a gompa perched on a rock bluff 100 meters (300 feet) vertically above the river. Further still, we took a short cut to avoid a wide bend in the road. It hardly seemed worth it, for the trail became rocky and indistinct and the horses scattered. It was everything the horseman could do to get them back on course. Indeed the horses seemed reluctant about the whole exercise. They had to be pushed, yelled at, and pressured the entire way, the horseman in constant attention in an effort that was almost as much as carrying the load. Fortunately it was not our effort. By the time we were back on the main trail we had passed the limit of the road. Thankfully for those who saw the road as a detriment to Zanskar, its progress was comically slow. In the previous 5 years the road had been pushed three kilometers (2 miles) up the valley.

We crossed a side stream and began a long climb to Itchar, our day's destination. The first visible signs of the village were the cell phone towers and satellite dishes standing on the hill above it. We camped on a grassy terrace by the river several hundred feet below the village with barely enough light to set up camp, let alone explore the village.

We had not been the only ones to set off for Darcha in the morning. There had been two young friendly local guys who were going to make the trek on horse in four days, a bit too fast for us. And there were the Russians we had shared the jeep to Rangdum with.

The Russians had sat in Rangdum long enough for a jeep to materialize. They got a ride to Padum, then got horses and a horseman for a 10 day trek to Darcha. They had set off from Padum carrying nothing but a camera, with no water and no food, leaving the horses to carry everything. They had paid for the complete service, horses, man, food, cooking and camping equipment (we did our own food and cooking and had our own gear). But the horseman worked on Zanskari principles, and clearly had faster horses than ours, and left them behind, going all the way to camp without stopping. The Russians were left thirsty and hungry and doing mileage far beyond their experience and fitness. One was clearly overweight, and slow, and had been left behind, even by his own comrade. The last we saw of him he was wilted, red faced and overheating, taking frequent stops, still with kilometers to go. There was little we could do to help him. He was having his own brush with mortality, a scary tale of doing everything wrong.

We spent the next day rising and falling along the sides of the Tsarap gorge. Below us was the brilliant milky turquoise of the river, above clear blue skies, around us the imposing slopes of rocks, cliffs and scree. The trail was cut into the steep sides and built up by hand with rock retaining walls holding the trail to the loose gravely slopes. While it was often comfortably wide, it frequently narrowed, and I was left wondering about the capability of the horses and the security of our stuff perched on the sides of them. Our appreciation of the horses though soon wained.

In order to keep the horses moving the horseman had to keep up a constant barrage of harassment. I had to wonder if this was because they were just an recalcitrant group of horses or if the animals, after a tough summer of hauling, were just fed up, or too tired, to continue willingly. His noise, their slow speed and the dust the horses kicked up made for a lousy close-up experience. So we soon learnt to avoid them as much as possible, either by falling far behind, or scooting far ahead, to clean air, peace and unfettered spectacular scenery.

While most of the folks we met the day before had been road workers, this day it was mostly local Zanskaris going about their daily autumnal rituals. Anywhere in the landscape where the land was level enough and smooth enough for agriculture, there were homes, singularly, or in groups of three or four, in the typical white solid blocky Tibetan style. They were surrounded by dry, grey-brown harvested fields, dotted with trees and huge piles of straw. The grain stalk had been harvested, the grain separated, and the fields were covered in piles of stalk. Folks gathered the stalk and carried it home on their backs to make huge deep stacks of animal fodder on the flat roofs of the homes.

Women walked up into the hills and cut low bushes that were scattered through the mountains. They tied them into huge round bundles, many times their own body size, then carted them laboriously on their backs downhill to their homes. The bundles then joined the massive spongy piles of green, beige, and brown, of grain stalk, yak dung, and sticks that would keep their animals fed, the house warm, and the food cooked through the long cold winter.

It was beautiful and warming to see the progression of seasons. In eastern Tibet folks had been plowing and planting. In central Tibet, valleys were full of deep green fields of growth and grain that added life and contrast to the surrounding arid hills. In Ladakh folks had been harvesting the brown grain by hand. In Zanskar the grain had been harvested and was being processed, the stalk and local resources stockpiled. I was reassured that the timing of my journey had been perfect. I had experienced the cycle of the growing seasons, with the human activity, and the visual delight of the range of scenery it produced.

Coming down the trail were men with long trains of pack horses heading down valley to get supplies for homes upstream. Late in the day we were passed by about 70 horses in several groups tended by men covered in dust kicked up by the horses.

The slow speed of our horses made the relatively short daily distance into an all day affair and we pulled in to camp at Pune in the last light yet again.

The next day was blessedly free of horses. We let the horseman take the horses up to the next village, Tetha, while we took a side trip, continuing up the Tsarap River, to Phugtal Gompa. A short day for the horses, and a good day for us.

Free of the slow speed of the horses, we made short work of the six kilometers (4 miles) up the Tsarap Valley. Rounding a corner in the valley the gompa came into view. Supposedly 2,500 years old, the gompa clung tentatively, yet tenaciously, to the side of a vertical cliff, as if smeared into place. A line of chortens and mani walls lead along the trail up to the gompa. We climbed to the ancient warren of monk cells and temples with tiny doors, steps, passages, and balconies that all hung on the side of the cliff with a medieval air. We arrived just as lunch was being served and monks in a variety of ages appeared from their cells and disappeared into the assembly hall to eat, and later do puja. A group of little kids from the school below the gompa came up for lunch and provided most of the entertainment while we were there.

We returned down the Tsarap to Pune, then followed the Kargyak River upstream. The valley opened out becoming broad and smooth, offering plenty of room for spacious villages and wide fields. We found our horseman and gear just outside of Tetha.

We were soon inundated with a flood of about 15 cute little kids in a variety of sizes with snotty noses and dirty ragged clothes. Several of the older kids, perhaps only 8 years old, carried their younger brothers and sisters, each only two to four years old, on their backs with sheets of fabric. At first it was fun playing with the kids and watching the kids watch us. But when the late afternoon cool sent us to putting up the tent and starting the stove it became a little more tiresome. At one point I had two heads between me and the stove I was struggling to light. I finally had to get Monika out of the tent to distract the kids. With the stove going and Monika lining the kids up in a neat row, things calmed considerably. When a local passing mama came by I encouraged her to take them all. She laughed and took three. The cold and approaching darkness eventually sent them all wandering back home leaving us in peace. Like kids anywhere, they were adorable, but exhausting.

The wide gentle valley continued as we walked upstream the next morning. Fields, chortens, and mani walls continued uninterrupted all the way to the next village, Karu. The valley made a great curve to the south, and then another back to the east. We stopped for the day on a lovely grass terrace by the river below the village of Kargyak, the highest village in Zanskar, and the last settlement before the pass. We were far enough away from the village that we were left in relative peace, almost as though we were camping out in the middle of the mountains by ourselves.

We received a visit from a Czech man who had spent the summer in Kargyak. He and his partner had the intention of equipping the village for the onslaught of the coming road by building a school. They hoped to have the local people build it to maximize local involvement and commitment, but had few financial resources, and nothing yet had actually been done. There were schools in the valley but many of the teachers collected the state government salary yet spent little more than a month actually teaching, instead working as horsemen for tourists or tending their own fields. Considering the Czech's progress it remained something of a mystery what the couple did for the two summers they had been living in the village.

The route upstream went through Kargyak and followed a long striking line of chortens and mani walls, both parallel and perpendicular to the trail, in an impressive display of labor and devotion. As we continued up the valley we approached the imposing flanks of Gumbarajan, a granitic monolith of a peak that rose thousands of feet in one great tower on the side of the valley. The huge smooth pale walls contrasted with the darker angular contorted and colorful sedimentary and metamorphic shapes typical of most of the mountains of the Himalayan ranges. We passed beneath the walls and stopped to camp beyond it at a herder's camp at the base of the final pitch up to Shingo La.

The next morning was frigid. The water in my mug had a 15 mm (5/8 ths inch) thick cap of ice, and the creek nearby, which had been entirely liquid the previous afternoon, was covered in ice. We climbed into a world of dark grey talus and scree, of rock and more rock. In just over 2 hours we were on the pass, the 19th time I had been above 5,000 meters (16,500 feet) since the start of the journey in

Dali. We sat on the pass surrounded by prayer flags and glaciated peaks that were only moderately grand by Himalayan standards. We let the horses get an hour head start and then followed them down. Disappointingly we soon caught up to them where the horseman had let them rest and graze. Our peaceful walk in the mountains then came to a crashing end.

As far as we were concerned we only needed the horses up until the end of the road that was inching its way up the Darcha River valley from Darcha towards Shingo La. Once on the road the bike would again be functional, we could load it up and continue by ourselves unaided. From what we were told in Padum the road had been built as far as Sumdo. We had then agreed with the horseman in Padum that it was to Sumdo that we would require his services, and that it would be a six day trek to get there. Below Shingo La the horseman was hoping for another day's pay by slowing the pace, claiming the horses needed rest and food, something that they had never needed before during the day. He wanted to stop for the night at Rumjak, a locality 6 kilometers before Sumdo, necessitating another day's walk, and pay, to get to Sumdo. After some tense discussion we forced the point and we continued down the valley. The pace though was miserably slow. The horseman deliberately slowed the speed of the horses and we stayed behind, acting as a sheep dog for the horseman, so that he didn't stop altogether. We continually had to stop to allow the horses to get ahead, so that we didn't get smothered in the dust and the farts of the horses.

After the colorful rock landscape of Ladakh and Zanskar, the endless scree and cliffs coming down the valley was a landscape in dull, uninspiring grey. The long distance of the descent, aggravated by the tedious speed and underlying tension with the horseman, made for a long afternoon. We made the final drop out of the side valley, into the Darcha valley, to the walled grass field of Sumdo, arriving with little light to spare. It was clear was that there was no road.

I had never liked guided trips. I never liked traveling to someone else's tune. It always seemed that, although I was a paying customer, the guide always had some kind of agenda that was contrary to mine. Having a guide, or be it just a porter or a horseman, for me was because there was no other choice, or that some government agency mandated it. And occasionally I needed one because I didn't know where the hell I was going. Almost always there seemed to be some clash along the way where the guide wanted to do something else, or on some other timetable, or at some other fee schedule than had been already agreed upon. Sometimes it felt better just to experience the feeling of being lost than have to deal with some icky interpersonal business relationship that was costing me money.

Road or no road we were done with our horseman. We paid him off and let him go. I was happy to see the end of the dust, slow speed, and the camping schedule that put us at camp too late to enjoy the place. So much for his so-called need-for-rest-for-the-horses story, he was gone at 7:30 in the morning, an hour before he normally got going with us.

We loaded up the bike, unsure of what the trail would bring, and made it all of 200 meters (200 yards) before coming to a dismal halt. Fanning out from a high glacial tributary was an enormous alluvial fan that formed a massive boulder field with rocks up to the size of small bathrooms. It was without a doubt the most difficult part of the trek and we had unwittingly chosen to do it without the aid of horses. I began muscling the bike over rocks and boulders, swearing mercilessly into the air, falling over in the process, all within sight of camp. I took more and more gear off the bike and onto my back. We finally distributed the gear between the two of us while I wheeled the bike. We lugged the lot over boulders, through gullies, around ridges. It was ridiculously and painfully slow herculean work and it sucked. The next piece of grass, Palamo, 8 kilometers (5 miles) down the valley, seemed very far away.

From a vantage point we could see a small plume of dust and smoke rising up from the boulders about 1.5 kilometers (1 mile) down valley. Bulldozers. The size of the boulders shrunk and the going became marginally less horrific. Further down we could hear the groaning motors of the machines. Further still I came over a rise and there were the dozers, cutting and inching their way across a steep slope of boulders. Never have I been so happy to see a bulldozer. We dropped down to the newly made road and celebrated our dramatic change in speed, work load, prospects and attitude. I took a photo of the bulldozer. Road workers chiseled away at a boulder with a jack hammer. It had taken us two and a half hours to go 3 kilometers (2 miles).

I was one of those who deplored the invasion and advancement of the road into Zanskar, but for the first few kilometers down the Darcha valley it was a beautiful thing. For a road it was a rough rocky thing, but pure silk after what we had been through that morning. As we made our way down the valley towards Darcha we resumed our familiar routine of Monika walking while I mixed slow cycling with regular breaks. With distance down-valley, life increased. From lifeless boulder fields to grass, brush, fields, homes, and naturally occurring trees. With more relief we hit the pavement of the Manali Leh road and had enough time in the dhabas of Darcha for tea before a local bus came along and carried us to Keylong. The bus rattled and bumped, the road worse than I remembered, but the views were familiar and incredible. The landscape had changed in the month since my last passing. Fields that were once green with potato plants were bare, brown, and being harvested, the fields dotted with sacks of spuds. Some of the trees were now yellow and the skies were clear and cloudless. We enjoyed civilization, as simple as it was, in Keylong.

We squeezed tight into an early morning bus for the ride to Manali. The peaks that had been buried in clouds a month before stood regal and white against a clear blue sky. The smooth grassy expanse of Rohtang La seemed a miraculously easy route through the great wall of the Himalayas. The bus wound down the road I had so laboriously climbed, the entire scene visible, through rocks, grass, forest, to the apple orchards of the valley, with cliffs, gorges and waterfalls. The road wound interminably down, returning it seemed to India, to the lush luxuriance south of the range, to a world altogether different to the dry mountains hiding north of the Himalaya.

****

I had completed my bicycle journey, we had trekked back to the south side of the Himalaya, but alas we were still not done. We had time, desire and lands still untouched. There were Tibetan cultural lands still to be explored and the Tibetan exile community near Dharamsala. We left the bicycle and a pile of unnecessary gear in Manali and set off as bus-based backpackers. I would be joining Monika on what she had been doing all along. We would go off in search of more of the Tibetan lands and its peoples.

We crossed Rohtang La for the third time, but on the other side we turned right, following the Chandra River upstream, climbing Kumzum La, and dropping into the Spiti valley, to the town of Kaza. Spiti, the Middle Land that is between India and Tibet, was a return to the dry Tibetan Buddhist landscape of arid mountain grandeur.

We spent a week traveling slowly down the Spiti Valley, stopping for spectacular hikes up the sides of the valley to lofty viewpoints over the villages, gompas, river, and the surrounding peaks. We took a jeep to Kibber, a village located 20 kilometers up-valley from Kaza, and took an over-the-top route across the hills, and along the top of huge cliffs that lined the main valley, to a spectacular vantage point 300 meters (1,000 feet) above Ki gompa. We found a rough steep trail, built-up against the cliff face by the locals, that switchbacked down through the cliffs, dropping directly to the gompa. The gompa was an improbable, arresting cluster of white buildings coating the top and sides of a small hill on the side of the valley.

We continued down the Spiti valley by bus, past groves of bright yellow trees in full autumnal glory, to Tabo. Unlike the gompa at Ki, and most gompas in general, Tabo Gompa sat on the level valley floor amid the village, as hidden as Ki was commanding. The gompa was apparently 1,000 years old and had a quite different look to most gompas, with a light brown stucco-like finish that gave it more of a Saharan or south-west USA pueblo appearance. We hiked to a small hermitage up a side valley and hiked straight up the valley sides to grand views up and down the Spiti valley.

The Spiti River valley drained east towards the Tibetan border. Travel along the road required a permit that was more bureaucratic formality and hassle than anything else. At one point we were only 5 to 10 kilometers (3 to 6 miles) from Tibet, and about 100 kilometers (60 miles) in a straight line from Guge, the remote lost kingdom of far western Tibet. Like Kargil's relationship with the mountains to its west, it would be one very long roundabout journey of a couple of thousand kilometers through plains India, Nepal, and western Tibet, to get to Guge, to a landscape and people that were so similar and so close.

The road and valley turned south and paralleled the border. The road climbed out of the valley climbing in a series of long switchbacks. The road had deteriorated considerably, becoming absurdly narrow, rough and dusty, its grip on the valley sides extremely tenuous, the drop off the side growing to 600 meters (2,000 feet), the bus grinding slowly uphill in first gear.

We stopped at Nako. The village clustered around the improbable, a lake sitting in a cup in the arid land, far above the valley below, with grand views to the surrounding mountains. The old village was a maze of narrow alleys, stone buildings, chortens, mani walls, animal pens, and centuries of use. While Monika lay in the room immobilized by diarrhea, I wandered through the village, around the lake, through beautifully made stone-walled terraced fields laced with water channels, and dotted with idle cows and golden trees. I climbed to a ridgetop vantage point with views over lake, village, and glaciated peaks in four directions. I dropped past the lake and followed the terraces downslope, and surprisingly found green grass, apple trees, and growing vegetables only 150 meters (500 feet) below the village that was long since past its growing season.

With Monika slowly recovering the next day we rejoined the bus and continued down-valley. The road wound back down to the river but retained its eye-popping danger element. We were rarely more than a half a foot, or a half a second, from a nasty plunge off the side, into the gorge and river.

I had to wonder about the bus drivers who spent their days so continually close to death. For hours every working day they lived a few feet, or a few inches, away from a long terrible tumble off the edge. A momentary lapse in concentration, a slight misjudgment, or bad luck with road geology or moisture content, could easily mean the end of them and a packed busload of humanity. How must it be to live and work perpetually so close to one's end, so close to fear, always having to be alert against such dire consequences? While this road was one of the scariest I had been on, it wasn't an unfamiliar situation and there were plenty of drivers in non-western mountain lands living that life. At one point we had about 80 people packed into the bus, the aisle a solid mass of condensed life and clothing. I had to deepen my faith in driver and machine.

I felt that on the bicycle there was a wider margin of error. Of all the elements I had to deal with, gravity, road surface, weather, it was always traffic that bothered me the most. Partly because it stole so much from the peace and aesthetics of a ride or landscape, but mostly because of its potential inherent ability to do me harm. Without traffic I was responsible for my own end, I didn't have to put my continued health in the hands of anyone else, I just had to pay attention. In cycling the rider had to have faith in the traffic that went by. In catching the bus the faith was in the driver, and to some extent also the other drivers on the road with which the bus driver would have to contend. Getting on the bus, any bus, but particularly on buses that drove such dangerous roads, a passenger was effectively making a pact of faith with the driver, that the driver would get the passengers to their destination unharmed, regardless of the conditions. The only choice the passenger had was whether to get on the bus in the first place, or to stay on the bus once the danger of the situation revealed itself. Getting on the bus, and staying on the bus, was an act of surrender.

At the lower end of the valley, the Spiti River flowed into the Sutlej River which flowed west, curling around to the south side of the Himalaya. As the river wound down into what becomes the Kinnaur Valley, the landscape became increasingly moist, green, and life returned. Small patches of forest appeared. The groves gained in size and density with distance down the valley, while the beauty and danger of the gorge continued. We passed out of the strategically sensitive Inner Line area, the area close to the Tibetan border that required a permit. At an old bridge over the river the entire contents of the bus had to get off the bus and walk across to minimize the chances of bridge colapse. Even with the bus empty the bridge sagged under the weight.

Further down the valley the road began to climb out of the gorge, away from the river, to Rekong Peo. There was continuous forest, apple orchards, terraced fields, and the 6,000 meter (20,000 feet) high Kinnaur Kailash, a line of glaciated peaks rising in one huge flank, on the opposite side of the river.

We took day hikes up the valley side above Rekong Peo and Kalpa, the village in which we stayed. The human landscape was expanding up the valley sides into the forest. Men cut trees and hauled logs downhill to small sawmills to build furniture and beams for houses. They cut into the hillside and built retaining walls from rocks to make terraces for orchards and grazing grass. There were newly built concrete irrigation canals that criss-crossed the hillsides and metal water pipes that laced the terraces. They were slowly cutting down the forest and planting apple trees.

We continued down the Kinnaur valley. In the upper sections of the valley the people were Buddhist. With distance down the valley, the Buddhist people phased out, to be replaced by Hindus. The style of dress changed. The women all wore loose fitting shalwar kameez, in a variety of colors, with brightly colored sweaters or vests. The men wore western clothing, many with a wool jacket or vest in a grey or brown color. They all wore a unique flat-topped, vertical-sided, felt hat, a thepang, that was more decorative than utilitarian, but set the Kinnaur people apart from visitors or any other Indians. With medium dark skin, an almost European face, and long black hair the women were very attractive, more so than any other group I had seen in India. Kinnaur had been traditionally very inaccessible and the people had been elevated to almost godlike status as a result. The region remained closed to outsiders until 1989.

The ruggedness of the gorge continued, the road cutting across cliffs and through tunnels above the river. We passed by a massive construction project. It seemed that a river was in the process of being dammed. The place was a mess with heavy machinery, blasting, work camps and wholesale destruction. Clearly, judging by the tunnels that disappeared into the mountainsides, and the gushing torrents of water that spewed from cliff faces, there was, or would be, a hydro-electric plant buried inside the mountain.

If there was anywhere that embodied contrast it was India. A contrast that perpetually left me shaking my head and laughing. India was a country that had nuclear bombs, jet fighters, I-T workers by the thousands that were sought after the world over, and here it was building a power plant inside a mountain. Yet its roads were a rough suicidal mess, folks still traveled by ox cart and human powered rickshaws, beggars were an elemental part of the urban experience, buses and trucks looked like they had been on the road for centuries, the most simplest of procedures often became long protracted bureaucratic nightmares, the electricity gave out on a regular basis, human power was still the primary form of construction technique, and it was often hard to tell if a building was half built or half falling apart. There was barely any water pressure in the pipes but just down the street they were building a power plant inside a mountain. The contrast between what one saw on the street, the every day human and technological experience, was so dramatically different to what the country as a whole was capable of. Looking around in the west, with its fancy cars, high-speed rail, modern buildings, and computer technology everywhere it was imaginable that that society could launch rockets, look at distant stars, and develop nuclear warheads. In India it was completely unfathomable.

We took a side trip to Sangla, a village up a side valley of the Sutlej. The road topped out on the fear and danger meter. It cut across a tall vertical cliff, the road little more than a ledge 150 meters (500 feet) above the creek with nothing to stop the bus taking a quick plunge to the rocks vertically below. There was no road visible from the window, just the creek far below.

The town of Sangla was an altogether unappealing place, an unattractive collection of concrete and brick buildings that housed stores and restaurants strung out along the main street. But its streets were a constant parade of local Kinnauris in their traditional clothes and caps. We took strolls around the town, up to Kumar, the quaint traditional village that Sangla was not. We wandered around the small maze of alleys, past old homes of stone and dark wood, with carved wood balconies, doors and walls. The slate roofs were works of art in of themselves, Each slate piece had been neatly cut and shaped into a V, then arranged neatly on the roof to form a curving parabolic shape that rose to a sharp ridgeline. Above the village was a lovely old wooden temple with several buildings and a wooden tower arranged around a stone courtyard.

We hiked up the quiet road up the valley to Chitkul, through apple orchards, dry harvested fields, scattered homes, evergreen and deciduous forests, rocks walls that were testament to the proliferation of rocks in the area, and massive boulder fields, chunks of mountainside that had fallen from the slopes above. Chitkul was another traditional village of stone and wood.

We continued by bus down the Sutlej River, along more arresting cliff-cutting roads, past a string of construction projects that seemed hell bent in destroying the river and its remarkable gorge. The traffic increased, the vegetation became thicker and greener, the population density thickened. We stopped in Sarahan, to admire its fine Hindu temple and stroll out into the countryside. The road climbed out of the gorge and wound out across the hills. When our bus broke down we lost our relatively comfortable seats and joined the crowds on a following bus. Two busloads crammed into one left us standing, jammed in the stairwell. Further down the road, when we did secure a seat, I ended up in the aisle seat with a cute young local lady squeezed up against me, my shoulder wedged in between her butt cheeks, which didn't seem to bother her at all. I was only thankful that the person was indeed a cute young woman.

We eventually came to Shimla, once the country's summer capital, a so-called hill station, where the British Raj government came to live, socialize, and do business, escaping the torrid summer heat of the plains. It sat improbably on a long sharp ridge, buildings seeming to cascade down the steep slopes from the crest in a temporarily arrested landslide of motley architecture. Along the ridgetop was the mall, an open pedestrian street and social center of the town, where government employees and their families, and now wealthy Indian tourists and school kids in uniform, came to stroll, chat, see and be seen. Like anywhere where tourists congregated the streets were wall-to-wall tourist shops selling gifts and goods at inflated prices. The leftover colonialism, the upscale tourist community, and the government influence has given Shimla, at least along its ridgetop, a remarkably quiet, civilized, and organized feel, relative to the dirty maelstroms of many Indian towns. Narrow fence lined roads wound along the ridge away from the town itself, interconnected by stairs and ramps. Grand old colonial buildings gave the place character and history. It was a nice place to stroll, to gaze out over the foothills of the Himalaya, to the peaks that lay concealed behind a floating layer of thick air pollution. It was really about the only thing to do there.

After our demanding bus ride to Shimla, our 10 hour bus to Dharamsala seemed rather effortless and relaxed. The bus did not break down, it was not crowded, and it took forty minutes less than advertised. Shiva was finally smiling upon us. It wound through steep foothills of forest, scrub, fields and brown grass. Later in the day the topography calmed and we seemed to wander aimlessly through a calm, but hilly, landscape that was much greener and dotted with cute homes with peaked slate roofs.

For most of the morning the driver had been having a nice time driving at a good clip, careening around corners and having numerous very close encounters with oncoming vehicles, including a few that were quickly followed by the stench of burning rubber. Then all of a sudden he drove at a slow and sedate speed for a while. After a stop at the next town he was back to ripping down the road.

There was only one thing scarier than driving on Indian roads and that was doing so at night. We made the final climb up into Dharamsala, and towards the mountains, after sunset against a flow of motorcycles coming downhill. Most were coasting, engines off, many with no headlights. One motorcyclist was coasting, no lights, one handed, while talking on his cell phone in the other hand. We took another bus further up the hill to Mcleod Ganj, the home of the Dalai Lama, the government of Tibet, and the large Tibetan community in exile.

It only seemed appropriate that a journey through the Tibetan lands include the home of its spiritual leader, its government, and the people that had fled the Chinese rule of Tibet over the last half century.

Ever since the 5th Dalai Lama in the 17th century, Tibet had been ruled from the Potala in the summer, and Norbulingka in the winter, both in Lhasa. With the invasion of the Chinese government in 1950, and the failed Tibetan uprising in 1959, the Tibetan administration feared for the safety of the 14th Dalai Lama. Under the cover of darkness and disguise, the Dalai Lama fled Tibet over the Himalayas into India. The then Indian Prime Minister, Jawaharlal Nehru, allowed the Dalai Lama and Tibetan government officials to live in exile in McLeod Ganj, known better as Dharamsala, for the larger town just down the street, located at 2,000 meters (6,600 feet) in the hills of Himachal Pradesh state.

Upon arrival, the Dalai Lama soon established the Central Tibetan Administration, better known as the Tibetan Government in Exile, with the goal of rehabilitating Tibetan refugees and restoring freedom and happiness in Tibet. It has been working for political advocacy and administers a network of schools, health services, cultural activities and economic development projects for Tibetans in India. It claims to represent not only the Tibetans in India but also throughout the Tibetan lands currently under control of the People's Republic of China, in the Tibet Autonomous Region, and the Chinese provinces of Gansu, Qinghai, Yunnan and Sichuan. Since then, thousands of Tibetans have followed suit, fleeing the imposed, oppressive regime of the

Chinese, to not just Dharamsala, but to many areas of India and the world.

The McLeod Ganj Tibetan community has steadily grown to a population of about 100,000 with a further 1,000 added each year. Over the decades there has been a gradual authority transition from the Dalai Lama to a democratically elected cabinet. The CTA is not recognized by any government but survives through financial aid from other governments and international organizations for its welfare work. It was a founding member of the Unrepresented Nations and Peoples Organization. Meanwhile the Dalai Lama has used his home there as a base to travel the world with his messages of Buddhism, peace, non-violence and freedom for the Tibetan people.

McLeod Ganj sits on the side of the Dhaula Dar range, an impressive wall that rises from the 500 meters elevation of the plains to 5,000 meter (16,500 feet) peaks in one continuous climb. It was a perfect mechanism to create rain and clouds, which the place had in abundance while we were there. The center of the town was much like Manali, a densely compacted area of restaurants, gift shops, guesthouses, internet cafes and travel agents that attested to the steady flow of western tourists. The foreign tourists clearly outnumbered the Tibetans. For the long haul traveler it was a place to relax and enjoy more peaceful and comfortable surrounds, a time out from the frenetic plains below. For many though, it was the destination in of itself, folks who came solely to take classes in Tibetan culture or religion, to hear the Dalai Lama, or somehow get involved in Tibet without actually going there. But there didn't seem to be very much Tibetan about the place, at least on the surface.

With a glimpse to snow clad peaks I hiked up the side of the range through groves of conifers, forests of rhododendrons and fields of grass and rock to Triund, an alpine meadow, where dhaba owners made tea and food for passing hikers. The cloud had long since moved in and there was little to see beyond the edge of the meadow. I continued higher, through forest where cloud wafted through the limbs in moist peacefulness. I descended past herds of goats as thunder echoed through the clouds and bounced around the mountainsides.

The next day was, for us, the primary attraction of McLeod Ganj, celebrations commemorating the 46th anniversary of the Tibetan Children's Village, the primary school of the area's Tibetan people. We joined a solid stream of locals walking up the hill to the school and found a perch on the low hill surrounding the school's sports field. The Tibetans that were gathered ran the full range of modern Tibetan society from school kids in their grey and blue uniforms, to older ladies in their traditional chuba and apron, to most folks who wore some kind of western clothes. There were grandparents, infants, young adults in trendy cool wear, families with all the makings of a picnic, and monks dressed in maroon looking much the same as Tibetan Buddhist monks anywhere. Just watching them all pour into the arena was entertainment enough.

Then, with the arena jammed, a line of cars pulled into the field. The Dalai Lama, surrounded by his entourage of officials and guards, emptied out of the vehicles and walked down between two lines of traditionally dressed ladies and up the stairs of the grandstand, to take seat in front of the Tibetan flag. There was a parade of around 400 kids dressed in school uniform, with marching band and flag bearers. Then followed the usual round of speeches from a range of dignitaries, the last being the Dalai Lama. He spoke in Tibetan for about 15 minutes. Much of the crowd sat in rapt attention, some with palms pressed together. As the speech continued on though, folks became distracted and murmurings and chatter increased.

With the Dalai Lama's speech over the program moved into a series of dances. The first three were traditional style song and dance routines done by students and teachers in bright clean traditional outfits. Like most Tibetan traditional dance it involved a series of synchronized movements by individuals with no body contact. Then there was a dance routine by 350 little school kids. The last dance was performed by 640 older school kids that was more like a calisthenics routine. Initially they held a grid pattern but then they moved smoothly and efficiently through a series of figures using their bodies to make words or shapes in the field: "Long Live the Dalai Lama", the interdependence/interconnectedness symbol of Tibet, a thank you to the school's founder.

A monk pays respect at the Tibetan Children's Village

With that the formal celebrations were over and the crowd gradually got up and wandered off. But many stayed, continuing with their picnics on the spot or going outside to find some grass around the nearby Dal Lake to continue with the festivities with families and friends. Monks sat with each other or joined their families as partying continued through the afternoon.

Back over in the school grounds a Tibetan opera, Lhamo, was in full swing. Lhamo is a combination of dance, chants and song and relates stories from Buddhism and Tibetan history. The actors use large masks that carry symbolism along with identity. The operas can go on for many hours. The opera, "The Religious King Norsang", for example, can last up to seven hours and tells of how a Buddhist kingdom prevails and serves as a environmental cautionary tale and a revolutionary love story. A huge crowd had gathered and sat in rapt attention occasionally laughing at the performance.

Part way through the performance the Dalai Lama made an appearance from the nearby gompa where he had been since his speech. He slowly descended steps, walking through an adoring crowd, stopping to greet and shake hands, got in his car and was driven off.

Culminating in a near brush with his holiness, the Dalai Lama, our, and my, time in the mountains and Tibetan lands was complete. We could finally leave. We took a bus that wound through the foothills for twelve hours back to Manali. We spent the last couple of days in Manali taking hikes in great weather to spectacular vantage points high on the valley sides. Then we caught an overnight sleeper bus that wound down out of the mountains and out onto the plains in the darkness.

There was a certain sadness in finally leaving the mountains, with the journey and travels complete, such an epic of adventure and experience, so many connections with people, land and culture, now completely in the rear view mirror. But after five and a half months of daily challenges and demands I was quite happy to be leaving the mountains and India and making for somewhere peaceful and relaxing, like the west. In trading the bicycle for the bus I had gone from the joy and rigors of a solitary life on the road to the cramped confines of old debilitated buses that were crowded, slow, uncomfortable, prone to breakdowns and delays, but had up close and personal encounters with locals. Rewards of achievement, interactions, events and sights were countered by a plethora of demands and challenges that over the long haul left me wilted, impatient, tired, and weary. I was only too happy to be soon getting on a plane and leaving it all behind, to be moving on. It was very definitely time for a time out. I had to go home, rest, rejuvenate, let the whole vast experience sink in, to let the cycle of movement and stability take its course. I was happy to be going but I also knew that I would be starting the process anew as soon as I got back. I would be dreaming of the next grand adventure, mulling options and ways to do the whole process over, to be once again alone and at large on the planet, finding its beauties and demands, putting myself in the middle of some grand and wonderful experience, regardless of what it took to be there.

Printed in Germany
by Amazon Distribution
GmbH, Leipzig